E B Segel

Imperial Surge

Imperial Surge
The United States Abroad, The 1890s–Early 1900s

Edited by

Thomas G. Paterson
University of Connecticut

Stephen G. Rabe
University of Texas, Dallas

D. C. HEATH AND COMPANY
Lexington, Massachusetts   Toronto

Address editorial correspondence to:

D. C. Heath
125 Spring Street
Lexington, MA 02173

Cover: "A Bone in His Teeth," by C. R. Macauley as printed in *The World*, New York, December 18, 1907. Theodore Roosevelt Collection/Harvard College Library.

Published simultaneously in Canada.

Printed in the United States of America.

International Standard Book Number: 0-669-26915-8

Library of Congress Catalog Card Number: 91-70712

10 9 8 7 6 5 4 3 2 1

For Suzanne and Thomas Paterson, mother and father,
and Elizabeth Rose Rabe, daughter

The Editors

Thomas G. Paterson

Born in Oregon City, Oregon, and graduated from the University of New Hampshire (B.A., 1963) and the University of California, Berkeley (Ph.D., 1968), Thomas G. Paterson is now professor of history at the University of Connecticut. He has written *Meeting the Communist Threat* (1988), *On Every Front* (1979), *Soviet-American Confrontation* (1973), *American Foreign Policy* (3d edition, revised, 1991, with J. Garry Clifford and Kenneth J. Hagan), and *A People and a Nation* (3d edition, 1990, with Mary Beth Norton and others). Tom has edited and contributed to *Explaining the History of American Foreign Relations* (1991, with Michael J. Hogan), *The Origins of the Cold War* (1991, with Robert J. McMahon), *Kennedy's Quest for Victory* (1989), *Major Problems in American Foreign Policy* (3d edition, 1989), and *Cold War Critics* (1971). He also serves as the general editor for D. C. Heath's *Major Problems in American History* series. His many articles have appeared in such journals as the *American Historical Review, Journal of American History*, and *Diplomatic History*. He has sat on the editorial boards of the latter two journals. The National Endowment for the Humanities, Institute for the Study of World Politics, and the Guggenheim Foundation, among others, have assisted his research and writing. He has served as president of the Society for Historians of American Foreign Relations and has directed National Endowment for the Humanities Summer Seminars for College Teachers. Active in the profession, Tom has worked on committees of the Organization of American Historians and American Historical Association. He has lectured widely in the United States as well as in the Soviet Union, Puerto Rico, China, Canada, and New Zealand.

Stephen G. Rabe

Born in Hartford, Connecticut, and graduated from Hamilton College (B.A., 1970) and the University of Connecticut (Ph.D., 1977), Stephen G. Rabe is now professor of history at the University of Texas, Dallas. He has written two books: *Eisenhower and Latin America: The Foreign Policy of Anticommunism* (1988), which won the Stuart

L. Bernath Memorial Book Award of the Society for Historians of American Foreign Relations, and *The Road to OPEC: United States Relations with Venezuela, 1919–1976* (1982). With Richard D. Brown and Lawrence Goodheart he has edited *Slavery in American Society* (3d edition, forthcoming). Steve's articles have appeared in *Diplomatic History, Latin American Research Review, Peace and Change*, and *Mid-America*, among others. He has contributed chapters on U.S. relations with Latin America to Richard Immerman, ed., *John Foster Dulles and the Diplomacy of the Cold War* (1989) and Thomas G. Paterson, ed., *Kennedy's Quest for Victory* (1989). Steve's research and writing have been supported by the National Endowment for the Humanities, Rockefeller Archive Center, and the Lyndon Baines Johnson Foundation, among others. In 1988 the Society for Historians of American Foreign Relations honored him with its Stuart L. Bernath Lecture Prize, and in 1990–92 he served on the Executive Council of that organization. The winner of outstanding teaching awards, he was Mary Ball Washington Professor of American History at University College, Dublin, Ireland, for 1990–91.

Preface

Why and how the United States became a global power is a central question in modern international history. From an infant republic, newly independent from the British Empire in the 1770s, to a major actor on the international stage in the twentieth century, the United States has established a worldwide presence that few other nations have matched. This book explores a significant period in the expansion of U.S. power abroad—the 1890s and early 1900s, when U.S. imperialism dramatically surged through the international system and marked the United States as an active competitor with Great Britain, Germany, and Japan for influence in many parts of the globe.

The eighteen essays in this book represent different interpretations and approaches to the problem of turn-of-the-century U.S. imperialism. They address not only the sources of U.S. imperialism and the causes of the Spanish-American-Cuban-Filipino War but also the anti-imperialist critique, the international and domestic contexts for decision making, and the impact of U.S. policies on other peoples. We have included the scholarly work of both fresh and "classic" voices. The Introduction identifies the key questions and themes of this subject and relates the readings to them. The headnotes place the selections in broad, comparative perspective and provide sketches of the authors. The Chronology and the maps include important names and dates mentioned in the essays. The bibliography, organized by topic, can be consulted for additional reading.

We thank the authors and publishers of the works reprinted in this volume for their cooperation. *Imperial Surge* was improved by the constructive suggestions of Gerard Clarfield, University of Missouri, Columbia; Linda Papageorge, Kennesaw College; Michael Schaller, University of Arizona; and Charles Tull, Indiana University, South Bend.

The fine editors of D. C. Heath, as always, applied their high standards and expertise to this book. James Miller, history editor; Sylvia Mallory, developmental editor; Susan Brown, editorial assistant; Margaret Roll, permissions editor; Bryan Woodhouse (with the assistance of Cathy Brooks), production editor; Kenneth Hollman, book designer; and Martha Shethar, photo researcher, served this book well, and we thank them very much.

T. G. P.

S. G. R.

Contents

II. Anti-Imperialism: The Rejected Alternative

III. The Impact of U.S. Imperialism

Introduction

After competing with the European powers and Japan for international influence and colonies in the late nineteenth century, the United States entered the twentieth century as the overlord of societies in Asia and Latin America. Much of the U.S. empire formed in a burst of imperialist activity during the late 1890s and early 1900s. Seizing territories and subjugating other peoples, however, was nothing new for Americans, whose entire history was one of extending the frontier. Americans had already purchased Louisiana; annexed Florida, Oregon, and Texas; removed native Americans from the path of white migration westward; grabbed California and other western areas from Mexico; and acquired the Gadsden Purchase, the Midway Islands, and Alaska. Americans had already dramatically increased their influence in Hawaii, Samoa, Cuba, and Latin America in general; declared the Monroe Doctrine an important international principle restricting European involvement in hemispheric affairs; and articulated the principle of equal trade opportunity ("open door"). American products had already penetrated foreign markets, U.S. dollars had been invested in foreign enterprises, and American Christian missionaries had entered distant lands. A new steam-and-steel U.S. Navy had been launched to protect these overseas activities.

As in earlier periods, the imperial surge at the turn of the century did not come without controversy and violence. Protest erupted from anti-imperialists in the United States and from nationalists in areas that Americans came to dominate. Senator Henry Cabot Lodge of Massachusetts, an articulate imperialist, commented shortly after the Senate approved the treaty annexing the Philippines, Guam, and Puerto Rico that the treaty passed only after the "closest, most bitter, and most exciting struggle I have ever known, or ever expect to see in the Senate." When the Filipinos, among others, resisted American imperialism, they suffered war, military occupation, and political manipulation. Imperialists claimed that they were exporting the blessings of liberty, but critics charged that self-interest and national aggrandizement drove the United States into acts that violated cherished American principles. The debate continues among historians today.

American imperialism is a major question in U.S. history and in international history. This empire-building produced long-term consequences not only for American citizens but also for the peoples whom the United States dominated. The essays in this book reveal why American leaders at the turn of the century sought a larger empire, how they created it, and how their activities divided the American people and threw into question adherence to American ideals. The essays also explore the impact of imperialism—the enduring U.S. influence in the political, social, economic, and cultural development of the Chinese, Cubans, Filipinos, native Hawaiians, Panamanians, and Puerto Ricans. To this day, these peoples debate the aftermath of the U.S. presence in their countries. In other words, the legacy this wrenching experience bequeathed to succeeding generations is another important question in this book.

Different interpretations of imperialism stem in large part from varying definitions of the term. Some analysts mistakenly equate expansion—the outward movement of goods, dollars, ships, people, and ideas—with imperialism. Others define imperialism too narrowly as solely the annexation of colonies or territory. Many other scholars define the term more broadly, to account for the variety of ways in which imperial nations behave. For these analysts, imperialism is the imposition of control by a powerful nation over other peoples and regions to the point that they lose their freedom to determine their own lives. In short, they lose their sovereignty. The key to imperialism is power—the power to make others move as the imperial state dictates. As the British historian Tony Smith has noted, imperialism exists "when a weaker people cannot act with respect to what it regards as fundamental domestic or foreign concerns for fear of foreign reprisals." Imperialism can take several forms, both formal (annexation, colonialism, or military occupation) and informal (economic penetration, political subversion, or the threat of intervention).

The annexation of the Philippines and their retention until 1946 is clearly imperialism by any definition. The United States never annexed Cuba or Panama, to cite two different examples, but it occupied Cuba from 1898 to 1902 and forced the Cubans to accept the Platt Amendment (1901–33), which gave the United States the right to oversee Cuba's domestic and foreign affairs and granted the United States the naval base at Guantánamo Bay. U.S. investors dominated the island's economy, and U.S. merchants controlled Cuba's vital sugar trade. In Panama, the United States held complete judicial and police power and control over the new Canal Zone, although it did not claim full or titular sovereignty over the canal area. But as Secretary of War William Howard Taft observed in 1904, the absence of titular sovereignty "is of no real moment whatever," for the United States operated the Canal Zone as it pleased and from this base controlled Panama. Both formally and informally, Cuba and Panama became part of the U.S. empire.

Defining imperialism as the domination of one state over another does not eliminate all problems of interpretation. Scholars lack instruments to measure precisely the breadth and depth of domination. When effective domination is achieved through informal means such as trade and investment, moreover, the reality of imperialism can seem ambiguous. But, as Richard Graham, a scholar of Latin American history who has struggled with these methodological and conceptual problems, once remarked: "It may take a hydraulic engineer to measure the flow of water, but anyone can see it flows downhill." We may have imperfect measurements of power, but we can usually determine when it is applied and whether it dominates.

Historians differ widely in their interpretations of the history of U.S. imperialism. Six categories of questions, all addressed in Part I of this book, spotlight the differences.

The first problem is that of political process. Who made the decisions for empire, and who most influenced policymaking? Was U.S. power directed toward imperialist ventures by an elite that held decision-making authority or by an influential pressure group such as big business? Did the elite or interest groups shape public opinion? Or was imperialism spawned by an aroused popular will, perhaps stirred up by yellow journalism? Did imperialism spring from a mass movement of the American people eager for foreign adventure that compelled cautious—even reluctant—leaders toward war and empire?

The second category highlights the role of diplomacy. Could the war with Spain over Cuba have been avoided? Why did the diplomats fail to prevent war? Was acquisition of the Philippines the only course available to the United States at the Paris peace conference, after Spain's defeat?

The third question centers on the rationality and consciousness of U.S. imperialism. Was the exertion of U.S. power for imperial purposes rational, deliberate, planned, and derived from a careful assessment of the American national interest? Or was it irrational, emotional, unintentional, ill planned, and derived from a thoughtless, spur-of-the-moment response to explosive events and popular ideas? Did Uncle Sam stumble into empire, or did he design it?

The fourth problem is that of motivation. Which motive best explains the American drive for empire: nationalism, with its components of pride, duty, racial superiority, and prestige; humanitarianism; economic necessity and ambition; domestic unrest; social Darwinism; the restlessness of an adventuresome generation that had never before participated in war; international competition; or the perceived need for naval and strategic stations? If, as most observers agree, a number of these motives were at work simultaneously, which motives, or combination of motives, were most significant? More specifically, why did U.S. leaders pick the Philippines, Hawaii, Cuba, and other places in particular? What interests and opportunities pushed such areas to the top of the American list? And was the motivation for going to war with Spain the same as the motivation for annexing foreign real estate?

The fifth question focuses on a central preoccupation of historians—the problem of change and continuity. Was the imperial surge of the late 1890s and early 1900s the logical consequence of the nation's history, the extension or culmination of an American expansionist tradition? Or was it an aberration? Is the acquisition of noncontiguous territories a departure from the pattern of U.S. history? Where does this story of turn-of-the-century imperialism fit into the larger historical experience of the United States?

Historians also speak to a sixth problem—morality. Was U.S. imperialism right (good) or wrong (bad)? Do we agree with Emilio Aguinaldo, the leader of the Filipino independence movement, that Americans were "the true oppressors of nations and the tormentors of mankind"? Or do we accept the statement of President William McKinley, who prophesied that the Filipinos would "bless the American republic because it emancipated their fatherland, and set them in the pathway of the world's best civilization"?

The eight selections in Part I introduce these questions. Paul Kennedy, Michael H. Hunt, and Richard Hofstadter explore the background, motives, and domestic and international contexts of U.S. imperialism. Louis L. Gould and Walter LaFeber focus on the McKinley administration's decision for war against Spain in 1898. In the final three selections, Thomas J. McCormick, William Appleman

Williams, and David F. Healy examine the results of the war. They want to know why, in the process of defeating Spain, the United States annexed foreign territories and expounded bold policies—the Open Door and the Roosevelt Corollary—that lasted well into the twentieth century.

Part II examines the case brought against imperialism. The imposition of U.S. power upon Asians and Latin Americans did not go unchallenged, either at home or abroad. The anti-imperialist movement deserves study because a fair, balanced examination of any historical record must include analysis of those who lost, even though the "winners" have usually dominated the writing of history. But as the essays by Thomas J. Osborne, Robert L. Beisner, Allen F. Davis, and Richard E. Welch, Jr., reveal, influential and respected Americans from the political, business, academic, and literary worlds vigorously and passionately opposed imperialism. They lost, but by examining the views of notables like Jane Addams, William Jennings Bryan, Carl Schurz, William Graham Sumner, and Mark Twain, we remind ourselves that imperialists like William McKinley and Theodore Roosevelt did not have a proprietary right to define America's core interests and ideas.

An analysis of the anti-imperialist movement also reveals the lesson that history is neither inevitable nor inexorable. Through much of the literature on American imperialism and anti-imperialism in the 1890s, and especially after the beginning of the war in 1898, runs the theme that the United States could not have done otherwise—that for example, McKinley had no choice but to annex the Philippines. If we accept the inevitability of imperialism, do not the anti-imperialist alternatives and arguments seem irrelevant? Yet few scholars would dismiss the anti-imperialist critique as irrelevant. Indeed, to explain why the anti-imperialists, in the tug and pull of American politics, came up short, historians discuss the alternatives and options that the McKinley administration rejected.

Anti-imperialist movements also flourished in Cuba, Hawaii, Puerto Rico, and the Philippine Islands. Again we see, especially in the essay by Teodoro A. Agoncillo, that the study of the "losers" serves as a useful historical corrective. Historians have given considerable attention to the war against Spain. On the other hand, the bloody Philippine Insurrection, which began against Spain in 1896 and lasted until mid-1902 against the United States, has often been slighted. After reading Agoncillo, other Filipinos, and Cuban nationalists (who emphasize their revolution against Spain in the 1870s and 1895–1898), we can suggest that the Spanish-American War should be renamed the "Spanish-American-Cuban-Filipino War." That title accurately identifies the combatants, recognizes where the war was fought, and clarifies whose interests were primarily involved.

Part III of this book studies the nations that directly faced U.S. power. Historians not only analyze the policymaking process; they also ask how U.S. power and influence shaped institutions and cultural values in other lands. As the essays in Part III demonstrate, Washington's decisions had significant and lasting consequences for Puerto Ricans, Cubans, Panamanians, Filipinos, and Chinese.

By examining the impact of U.S. imperialism and expansionism on other societies, we also discover evidence to address the fundamental questions raised in Part I: Does the history of the postwar U.S. military occupation of Cuba reveal, as Louis A. Pérez, Jr., suggests in his essay, the initial intentions of the McKinley administration toward Cuba? Does the occupation help explain why the United States confronted Spain over the island in the first place? Can Arturo Morales Carrión's and Walter LaFeber's respective analyses of how the United States wielded power in Puerto Rico and Panama help us delineate the basic U.S. strategic-economic goals for the circum-Caribbean area? The essays by Stanley Karnow and Jane Hunter, which recount American encounters with Filipinos and Chinese, also help us to learn more about the racial prejudices and cultural chauvinism of white Americans.

The selections in Part III raise anew questions about definitions and interpretations of U.S. imperialism. The easily identifiable instruments of empire were colonial bureaucrats like Leonard Wood and William Howard Taft and military commanders like Admiral George Dewey. But what about the teachers, merchants, investors, missionaries, and philanthropists—often called nonstate actors—who ventured into Cuba, China, and the Philippines in the early twentieth century? Were they instruments of informal empire? However earnest and well intentioned, were these American men and women in essence attempting to shatter traditional cultures and recast them in the American mold? Did they succeed, and what were the consequences of their foreign ventures?

As the conflicting interpretations and different approaches in this book suggest, there is much to debate. We invite you to enter this important discussion, realizing that you are tackling questions that speak to the very meaning of the American experience and its intersection with international history over time.

Chronology

1893 *January:* Hawaiian Revolution; U.S. marines from the U.S.S. *Boston* helped dethrone Queen Liliuokalani. *March:* Cleveland withdrew Hawaiian annexation treaty. *May:* U.S. financial markets collapsed; economic depression began.

1894 *July:* Wilson-Gorman tariff hurt Cuban sugar exports to the United States and the Cuban economy. *August:* Sino-Japanese War over Korea.

1895 *February:* Opening of Cuban Revolution. *April:* China defeated by Japan. *July:* Olney's note to Britain on Venezuela.

1896 *February:* General Weyler established reconcentration camps in Cuba. *May:* Spain rejected U.S. offer to help end Cuban war. *August:* Beginning of rebellion in the Philippines. *November:* McKinley elected president; British agreed to arbitrate Venezuelan boundary dispute.

1897 *June:* McKinley sent new Hawaiian treaty of annexation to Senate. *November:* Spain recalled Weyler and reformed reconcentration policy.

1898 *February:* De Lôme letter and sinking of the U.S.S. *Maine*. *March:* Congress appropriated $50 million for defense; Senator Proctor reported on trip to Cuba; McKinley issued ultimatum to Spain; European powers established spheres of influence in China. *April:* Spain accepted temporary armistice and revoked reconcentration; McKinley asked Congress for authority to end Spain's war with Cuba; Congress declared Cuba independent and directed the president to use force; Spain declared war on the United States; Teller Amendment. *May:* Dewey defeated Spanish at Manila. *June:* U.S. troops departed for Cuba; Guam seized. *July:* Battle of San Juan Hill; Wake Island seized; Hawaii annexed (Newlands Resolution); Puerto Rico invaded; Spain asked for terms of peace. *August:*

Hostilities suspended; the United States captured Manila. *October:* American Peace Commission established. *November:* the United States demanded Philippines; Anti-Imperialist League organized. *December:* Treaty of Paris.

1899   *January:* U.S. military occupation of Cuba; Filipinos declared their independence. *February:* Philippine Insurrection against the United States began; U.S. Senate approved Treaty of Paris. *September:* Open Door Notes. *December:* The United States divided the Samoan archipelago with Germany.

1900   *April:* Foraker Act passed, making Puerto Rico a U.S. dependency. *June:* Boxer Rebellion in China. *July:* Open Door Notes. *August:* U.S. troops helped suppress Boxer Rebellion. *November:* McKinley reelected; the United States attempted to gain territorial concession in China (Samsah Bay).

1901   *March:* Aguinaldo captured by U.S. troops. *June:* Platt Amendment for Cuba. *September:* McKinley assassinated; Roosevelt became president. *December:* Senate approved Hay-Paunceforte Treaty, authorizing the United States to build and fortify a canal.

1902   *April:* Organized Filipino opposition collapsed. *May:* U.S. troops withdrawn from Cuba. *July:* Congress passed Philippine Government Act. *December:* Anglo-German naval blockade of Venezuela began; the United States requested arbitration of dispute.

1903   *February:* Anglo-German blockade lifted. *March:* Senate approved Hay-Herrán Treaty on canal. *May:* Platt Amendment formalized into treaty; the United States secured a naval base at Guantánamo. *August:* Colombian Senate unanimously rejected Hay-Herrán Treaty. *October:* Roosevelt met with Bunau-Varilla; U.S. warship sailed for Panama. *November:* Panamanian Revolution; the United States recognized Panamanian independence. *December:* Senate approved Cuban Reciprocity Treaty.

1904 *February:* Senate approved Hay-Bunau-Varilla Treaty. *November:* Roosevelt reelected president. *December:* Roosevelt announced Roosevelt Corollary to Monroe Doctrine.

Imperialism: The Spanish-American-Cuban-Filipino War and Empire

Paul Kennedy

THE RISE OF THE UNITED STATES
TO GREAT-POWER STATUS

The United States thrust itself upon the global stage at the end of the nineteenth century in an imperial surge that followed three decades of impressive post–Civil War economic growth. By the end of the 1890s, the United States had matched and even surpassed the leading European powers in agricultural and industrial productivity and technological prowess. Paul Kennedy discusses the causal connection between this economic growth and the rise of the United States to great-power status. Wealth usually underpins military power, and military power is usually needed to acquire and defend empire. Professor Kennedy, who teaches history at Yale University, has written extensively on the history of international relations. This essay is drawn from his sweeping, widely read study, *The Rise and Fall of the Great Powers*. Among his other books are *The Rise of Anglo-American Antagonism, 1860–1914* (1980), *The Rise and Fall of British Naval Mastery* (1976), and *The Samoan Tangle* (1974).

In the winter of 1884–1885, the Great Powers of the world, joined by a few smaller states, met in Berlin in an attempt to reach an agreement over trade, navigation, and boundaries in West Africa and the Congo and the principles of effective occupation in Africa more generally. In so many ways, the Berlin West Africa Conference can be seen, symbolically, as the zenith of Old Europe's period of predominance in global affairs. Japan was not a member of the conference; although modernizing swiftly, it was still regarded by the West as a quaint, backward state. The United States, by contrast, *was* at the Berlin Conference, since the issues of trade and navigation discussed there were seen by Washington as relevant to American interests abroad; but in most other respects the United States remained off the international scene, and it was not until 1892 that the European Great Powers upgraded the rank of their diplomatic representatives to Washington from minister to ambassador—the mark of a first-division nation. Russia, too, was at the conference; but while its interests in Asia were con-

From *The Rise and Fall of the Great Powers*, pp. 194–98, 242–48, by Paul Kennedy. Footnotes omitted. Copyright © 1987 by Paul Kennedy. Reprinted by permission of Random House, Inc.

siderable, in Africa it possessed little of note. It was, in fact, in the second list of states to be invited to the conference, and played no role other than generally giving support for France against Britain. The center of affairs was therefore the triangular relationship between London, Paris, and Berlin, with [Otto von] Bismarck in the all-important middle position. The fate of the planet still appeared to rest where it had seemed to rest for the preceding century or more: in the chancelleries of Europe. To be sure, if the conference had been deciding the future of the Ottoman Empire instead of the Congo basin, then countries such as Austria-Hungary and Russia would have played a larger role. But that still would not gainsay what was reckoned at the time to be an incontrovertible truth: that Europe was the center of the world. It was in this same period that the Russian general Dragimirov would declare that "Far Eastern affairs are decided in Europe."

Within another three decades—a short time indeed in the course of the Great Power system—that same continent of Europe would be tearing itself apart and several of its members would be close to collapse. Three decades further, and the end would be complete; much of the continent would be economically devastated, parts of it would be in ruins, and its very future would be in the hands of decision-makers in Washington and Moscow.

While it is obvious that no one in 1885 could accurately forecast the ruin and desolation which prevailed in Europe sixty years later, it *was* the case that many acute observers in the late nineteenth century sensed the direction in which the dynamics of world power were driving. Intellectuals and journalists in particular, but also day-to-day politicians, talked and wrote in terms of a vulgar Darwinistic world of struggle, of success and failure, of growth and decline. What was more, the future world order was already seen to have a certain shape, at least by 1895 or 1900.

The most noticeable feature of these prognostications was the revival of de Tocqueville's idea that the United States and Russia would be the two great World Powers of the future. Not surprisingly, this view had lost ground at the time of Russia's Crimean disaster and its mediocre showing in the 1877 war against Turkey, and during the American Civil War and then in the introspective decades of reconstruction and westward expansion. By the late nineteenth century, however, the industrial and agricultural expansion of the United States and the military expansion of Russia in Asia were causing various European observers to worry about a twentieth-century world order which would, as the saying went, be dominated by the Russian knout and American moneybags. Perhaps because neomercantilist commercial ideas were again prevailing over those of a peaceful, Cobdenite, free-trading global system, there was a much greater tendency than earlier to argue that changing economic power would lead to political and territorial changes as well. Even the usually cautious British prime minister Lord Salisbury admitted in 1898 that the world was divided into the "living" and "dying" powers. The recent Chinese defeat in their 1894–1895 war with Japan, the humiliation of Spain by the United States in their brief 1898 conflict, and the French retreat before Britain over the Fashoda incident on the Upper Nile (1898–1899) were all interpreted as evidence that the "survival of the fittest" dictated the fates of nations as well as animal species. The Great Power struggles were no longer merely over European issues—as they had been in 1830 or even 1860—but over markets and territories that ranged across the globe.

But if the United States and Russia seemed destined by size and population to be among the future Great Powers, who would accompany them? The "theory of the Three World Empires"—that is, the popular belief that only the three (or, in some accounts, four) largest and most powerful nation-states would remain independent—exercised many an imperial statesman. "It seems to me," the British minister for the colonies, Joseph Chamberlain, informed an 1897 audience, "that the tendency of the time is to throw all power into the hands of the greater empires, and the minor kingdoms—those which are nonprogressive—seem to fall into a secondary and subordinate place. . . ." It was vital for Germany, Admiral Tirpitz urged Kaiser Wilhelm, to build a big navy, so that it would be one of the "four World Powers: Russia, England, America and Germany." France, too, must be up there, warned a Monsieur Darcy, for "those who do not advance, go backwards and who goes back goes under." For the long-established powers, Britain, France, and Austria-Hungary, the issue was whether they could maintain themselves in the face of these new challenges to the international status quo. For the new powers, Germany, Italy, and Japan, the problem was whether they could break through to what Berlin termed a "world-political freedom" before it was too late.

It need hardly be said that not every member of the human race was obsessed with such ideas as the nineteenth century came to a close. Many were much more concerned about domestic, social issues. Many clung to the liberal, laissez-faire ideals of peaceful cooperation. Nonetheless there existed in governing elites, military circles, and imperialist organizations a prevailing view of the world order which stressed struggle, change, competition, the use of force, and the organization of national resources to enhance state power. The less-developed regions of the globe were being swiftly carved up, but that was only the beginning of the story; with few more territories to annex, the geopolitician Sir Halford Mackinder argued, efficiency and internal development would have to replace expansionism as the main aim of modern states. There would be a far closer correlation than hitherto "between the larger geographical and the larger historical generalizations"; that is, size and numbers would be more accurately reflected in the international balances, provided that those resources were properly exploited. A country with hundreds of millions of peasants would count for little. On the other hand, even a modern state would be eclipsed also if it did not rest upon a large enough industrial, productive foundation. "The successful powers will be those who have the greatest industrial base," warned the British imperialist Leo Amery. "Those people who have the industrial power and the power of invention and science will be able to defeat all others."

Much of the history of international affairs during the following half-century turned out to be a fulfillment of such forecasts. Dramatic changes occurred in the power balances, both inside Europe and without. Old empires collapsed, and new ones arose. The *multipolar* world of 1885 was replaced by a *bipolar* world as early as 1943. The international struggle intensified, and broke into wars totally different from the limited clashes of nineteenth-century Europe. Industrial productivity, with science and technology, became an ever more vital component of national strength. Alterations in the international shares of manufacturing production were reflected in the changing international shares of military power and diplomatic influence. Individuals still counted—who, in the century of Lenin, Hitler, and Stalin, could say they did not?—but they counted in power politics only because they were able to control and reorganize the productive forces of a great state. And, as Nazi Germany's own fate revealed, the test of world power by war was ruthlessly uncaring to any nation which lacked the industrial-technical strength, and thus the military weaponry, to achieve its leader's ambitions.

If the broad outlines of these six decades of Great Power struggles were already being suggested in the 1890s, the success or failure

The Corliss Engine at the Philadelphia Centennial Exposition, 1876. This huge machine symbolized the industrial might that was deemed so essential to the United States' becoming a major power in the world. (*The Metropolitan Museum of Art*)

of *individual* countries was still to be determined. Obviously, much depended upon whether a country could keep up or increase its manufacturing output. But much also depended, as always, upon the immutable facts of geography. Was a country near the center of international crises, or at the periphery? Was it safe from invasion? Did it have to face two or three ways simultaneously? National cohesion, patriotism, and the controls exercised by the state over its inhabitants were also important; whether a society withstood the strains of war would very much depend upon its internal makeup. It might also depend upon alliance politics and decision-making. Was one fighting as part of a large alliance bloc, or in isolation? Did one enter the war at the beginning, or halfway through? Did other powers, formerly neutral, enter the war on the opposite side?

Such questions suggest that any proper analysis of "the coming of a bipolar world, and the crisis of the 'middle powers' " needs to consider three separate but interacting levels of causality: first, the changes in the military-industrial productive base, as certain states became materially more (or less) powerful; second, the geopolitical, strategical, and sociocultural factors which influenced the responses of each *individual* state to these broader shifts in the world balances; and third, the diplomatic and political changes which also affected chances of success or failure in the great coalition wars of the early twentieth century. . . .

Of all the changes which were taking place in the global power balances during the late nineteenth and early twentieth centuries, there can be no doubt that the most decisive one for the future was the growth of the United States. With the Civil War over, the United States was able to exploit . . . rich agricultural land, vast raw materials, and the marvelously convenient evolution of modern technology (railways, the steam engine, mining equipment) to develop such resources; the lack of social and geographical constraints; the absence of significant foreign dangers; the flow of foreign and, increasingly, domestic investment capital—to transform itself at a stunning pace. Between the ending of the Civil War in 1865 and the outbreak of the Spanish-American War in 1898, for example, American wheat production increased by 256 percent, corn by 222 percent, refined sugar by 460 percent, coal by 800 percent, steel rails by 523 percent, and the miles of railway track in operation by over 567 percent. "In newer industries the growth, starting from near zero, was so great as to make percentages meaningless. Thus the production of crude petroleum rose from about 3,000,000 barrels in 1865 to over 55,000,000 barrels in 1898 and that of steel ingots and castings from less than 20,000 long tons to nearly 9,000,000 long tons." This was not a growth which stopped with the war against Spain; on the contrary, it rose upward at the same meteoric pace throughout the early twentieth century. Indeed, given the advantages listed above, there was a virtual inevitability to the whole process. That is to say, only persistent human ineptitude, or near-constant civil war, or a climatic disaster could have checked this expansion—or deterred the millions of immigrants who flowed across the Atlantic to get their share of the pot of gold and to swell the productive labor force.

The United States seemed to have *all* the economic advantages which *some* of the other powers possessed *in part*, but *none* of their disadvantages. It was immense, but the vast distances were shortened by some 250,000 miles of railway in 1914 (compared with Russia's 46,000 miles, spread over an area two and a half times as large). Its agricultural yields per acre were always superior to Russia's; and if they were never as large as those of the intensively farmed regions of western Europe, the sheer size of the area under cultivation, the efficiency of its farm machinery, and the decreasing costs of transport (because of railways and steamships) made American wheat, corn, pork, beef, and other products cheaper than any in Europe. Technologically, leading American firms like International Harvester, Singer, Du Pont, Bell, Colt, and Standard Oil were equal to, or often better than, any in the world; and they enjoyed an enormous domestic market and economies of scale, which their German, British, and Swiss rivals did not. "Gigantism" in Russia was not a good indicator of industrial efficiency; in the United States, it usually was. For example, "Andrew Carnegie was producing more steel than the whole of England put together when he sold out in 1901 to J. P. Morgan's colossal organization, the United States Steel Corporation." When the famous British warship designer Sir William White made a tour of the United States in 1904, he was shaken to discover fourteen battleships and thirteen armored cruisers being built simultaneously in American yards (although, curiously, the U.S. merchant marine remained small). In industry *and* agriculture *and* communications, there was both efficiency and size. . . .

The role of foreign trade in the United States' economic growth was small indeed (around 8 percent of its GNP derived from foreign trade in 1913, compared with Britain's 26 percent), but its economic impact upon other countries was considerable. Traditionally, the United States had exported raw materials (especially cotton), imported finished manufactures, and made up the usual deficit in "visible" trade by the export of gold. But the post–Civil War boom in industrialization quite transformed that pattern. Swiftly becoming the world's largest producer of manufactures, the United States began to pour its farm machinery, iron and steel wares, machine tools, electrical equipment, and other products onto the world market. At the same time, the Northern industrialists' lobby was so powerful that it ensured that foreign products would be kept out of the home market by higher and higher tariffs; raw materials, by contrast, or specialized goods (like German dyestuffs) were imported in ever-larger quantities to supply American industry. But while the surge in the country's industrial exports was the most significant change, the "transportation revolution" also boosted American farm exports. With the cost of carrying a bushel of wheat from Chicago to London plummeting from 40 cents to 10 cents in the half-century before 1900, American agricultural produce streamed across the Atlantic. Corn exports peaked in 1897 at 212 million bushels, wheat exports in 1901 at 239 million bushels; this tidal wave also included grain and flour, meat and meat products.

The consequences of this commercial transformation were, of course, chiefly economic, but they also began to affect international relations. The hyperproductivity of American factories and farms caused a widespread fear that even its enormous domestic market might soon be unable to absorb these goods, and led powerful interest groups (midwestern farmers as well as Pittsburgh steel producers) to press the government to give all sorts of aid to opening up, or at least keeping open, markets overseas. The agitation to preserve an "open door" in China and the massive interest shown in making the United States the dominant economic force in Latin America were only two of the manifestations of this concern to expand the country's share of world trade. Between 1860 and 1914 the United States increased its exports more than sevenfold (from $334 million to $2.365 billion), yet because it was so protective of its own market, imports increased only fivefold (from $356 million to $1.896 billion). Faced with this avalanche of cheap American food, continental European farmers agitated for higher tariffs—which they usually got; in Britain, which had already sacrificed its grain farmers for the cause of free trade, it was the flood of American machines, and iron and steel, which produced alarm. While the journalist W. T. Stead wrote luridly of "the Americanization of the world"—the phrase was the title of his book of 1902—Kaiser Wilhelm and other European leaders hinted at the need to combine against the "unfair" American trading colossus.

Perhaps even more destabilizing, although less well understood, was the impact of the United States upon the world's financial system and monetary flows. Because it had such a vast surplus in its trade with Europe, the latter's deficit had to be met by capital transfers—joining the enormous stream of direct European investments into U.S. industry, utilities, and services (which totaled around $7 billion by 1914). Although some of this westward flow of bullion was reversed by the returns on European investments and by American payments for services such as shipping and insurance, the drain was a large one, and constantly growing larger; and it was exacerbated by the U.S. Treasury's policy of accumulating (and then just sitting on) nearly one-third of the world's gold stock. Moreover, although the United States had by now become an integral part of a complete global trading system—running a deficit with raw-materials-supplying countries, and a vast surplus with Europe—its own financial structure was underdeveloped. Most of its foreign trade was done in sterling, for example, and London acted as the lender of last resort for gold. With no central bank able to control the financial markets, with a stupendous seasonal outflow and inflow of funds between New York and the prairie states conditioned solely by the grain harvest and that by a volatile climate, and with speculators able to derange not merely the domestic monetary system but also the frequent calls upon gold in London, the United States in the years before 1914 was already becoming a vast but unpredictable bellows, fanning but also on occasions dramatically cooling the world's trading system. . . .

This growth of American industrial power and overseas trade was accompanied, perhaps inevitably, by a more assertive diplomacy and by an American-style rhetoric of *Weltpolitik* [world politics]. Claims to a special moral endowment among the peoples of the earth which made American foreign policy superior to those of the Old World were intermingled with Social Darwinistic and racial arguments, and with the urging of industrial and agricultural pressure groups for secure overseas markets. The traditional, if always exaggerated, alarm about threats to the Monroe Doctrine was accompanied by calls for the United States to fulfill its "Manifest Destiny" across the Pacific. While entangling alliances still had to be avoided, the United States was now being urged by many groups at home into a much more activist diplomacy—which, under the administrations of McKinley and (especially) Theodore Roosevelt, was exactly what took place. The 1895 quarrel with Britain over the Venezuelan border dispute—justified in terms of the Monroe Doctrine—was followed three years later by the much more dramatic war with Spain over the Cuban issue. Washington's demand to have sole control of an isthmian canal (instead of the older fifty-fifty arrangement with Britain), the redefinition of the Alaskan border despite Canadian protests, and the 1902–1903 battlefleet preparations in the Caribbean following the German actions against Venezuela were all indications of U.S. determination to be unchallenged by any other Great Power in the western hemisphere. As a "corollary" of this, however, American administrations showed themselves willing to intervene by diplomatic pressure *and* military means in Latin American countries such as Nicaragua, Haiti, Mexico, and the Dominican Republic when their behavior did not accord with United States norms.

But the really novel feature of American external policy in this period were its interventions and participation in events *outside* the western hemisphere. Its attendance at the Berlin West Africa Conference in 1884–1885 had been anomalous and confused: after grandiose speeches by the U.S. delegation in favor of free trade and open doors, the subsequent treaty was never ratified. Even as late as 1892 the *New York Herald* was proposing the abolition of the State Department, since it had so little business to conduct overseas. The war with Spain in 1898 changed all that, not only by giving the United States a position in the western Pacific (the Philippines) which made it, too, a sort of Asiatic colonial power, but also by boosting the political fortunes of those who had favored an assertive policy. Secretary of State Hay's "Open Door" note in the following year was an early indication that the United States wished to have a say in China, as was the commitment of 2,500 American troops to the international army sent to restore order in China in 1900. Roosevelt showed an even greater willingness to engage in *grosse Politik* [international politics], acting as mediator in the talks which brought an end to the Russo-Japanese War, insisting upon American participation in the 1906 conference over Morocco, and negotiating with Japan and the other Powers in an attempt to maintain the "Open Door" in China. . . .

Along with these diplomatic actions went increases in arms expenditures. Of the two services, the navy got the most, since it was the front line of the nation's defenses in the event of a foreign attack (or a challenge to the Monroe Doctrine) and also the most useful instrument to support American diplomacy and commerce in Latin America, the Pacific, and elsewhere. Already in the late 1880s, the rebuilding of the fleet had commenced, but the greatest boost came at the time of the Spanish-American War. Since the easy naval victories in that conflict seemed to justify the arguments of Admiral Mahan and the "big navy" lobby, and since the strategists worried about the possibility of a war with Britain and then, from 1898 onward, with Germany, the battle fleet was steadily built up. The acquisition of bases in Hawaii, Samoa, the Philippines, and the Caribbean, the use of naval vessels to act as "policemen" in Latin America, and Roosevelt's dramatic gesture of sending his "great white fleet" around the world in 1907 all seemed to emphasize the importance of sea power.

Consequently, while the naval expenditures of $22 million in 1890 represented only 6.9 percent of total federal spending, the $139 million allocated to the navy by 1914 represented 19 percent. Not all of this was well spent—there were too many home fleet bases (the result of local political pressures) and too few escort vessels—but the result was still impressive. Although considerably smaller than the Royal Navy, and with fewer *Dreadnought*-type battleships than Germany, the U.S. Navy was the third largest in the world in 1914. Even the construction of a U.S.-controlled Panama Canal did not stop American planners from agonizing over the strategical dilemma of dividing the fleet, or leaving one of the country's coastlines exposed: and the records of some officers in these years reveal a somewhat paranoid suspicion of foreign powers. In fact, given its turn-of-the-century *rapprochement* with Great Britain, the United States was immensely secure, and even if it feared the rise of German sea power, it really had far less to worry about than any of the other major powers.

The small size of the U.S. military was in many ways a reflection of that state of security. The army, too, had been boosted by the war with Spain, at least to the extent that the public realized how minuscule it actually was, how disorganized the National Guard was, and how close to disaster the early campaigning in Cuba had come. But the tripling of the size of the regular army after 1900 and the additional garrisoning tasks it acquired in the Philippines and elsewhere still left the service looking insignificant compared with that of even a middle-sized European country like Serbia or Bulgaria. Even more than Britain, the United States clung to a laissez-faire dislike of mass standing armies and avoided fixed military obligations to allies. Less than 1 percent of its GNP went to defense. Despite its imperialist activities in the period 1898–1914, therefore, it remained what the sociologist Herbert Spencer termed an "industrial" society rather than a "military" society like Russia. Since many historians have suggested that "the rise of the superpowers" began in this period, it is worth noting the staggering *differences* between Russia and the United States by the eve of the First World War. The former possessed a front-line army about ten times as large as the latter's; but the United States produced six times as much steel, consumed ten times as much energy, and was four times larger in total industrial output (in per capita terms, it was six times more productive). No doubt Russia seemed the more powerful to all those European general staffs thinking of swiftly fought wars involving masses of available troops; but by all other criteria, the United States was strong and Russia weak.

The United States had definitely become a Great Power.

Michael H. Hunt

AMERICAN IDEOLOGY: VISIONS OF NATIONAL GREATNESS AND RACISM

The great powers of the late nineteenth century developed modern navies and industrialized economies. Michael Hunt argues, however, that material strength alone does not explain why the United States annexed Hawaii, Puerto Rico, and the Philippines; insisted upon dominating Cuba, Panama, and the Caribbean; and sent merchants and missionaries to China and other distant lands. In his book *Ideology and U.S. Foreign Policy*, from which this essay is selected, Hunt makes the case that ideas matter in foreign policy. In Hunt's view, Americans were so aggressively proud of their nation and so racist toward nonwhite peoples that they believed they could remake foreign societies. Americans looked at their liberty and economic growth as signs that they were destined to be great and to lead others

From *Ideology and U.S. Foreign Policy*, pp. 17–18, 36–39, 41–42, 48, 51–52, 58–62, 77–81, 90–91, by Michael H. Hunt. Footnotes omitted. Copyright © 1987. Reprinted by permission of Yale University Press.

whom they judged racially inferior. Ideas pushed the United States outward and justified the tutelage of others. In the American ideology, national greatness, racial supremacy, commercial prosperity, military security, and territorial expansion went hand in hand. Professor Hunt, a historian at the University of North Carolina, has also written two studies of U.S. relations with China: *Frontier Defense and the Open Door* (1973) and *The Making of a Special Relationship* (1983).

By the early twentieth century, three core ideas relevant to foreign affairs had emerged, and they collectively began to wield a strong influence over policy. The capstone idea defined the American future in terms of an active quest for national greatness closely coupled to the promotion of liberty. It was firmly in place by the turn of the century, after having met and mastered a determined opposition on three separate occasions—in the 1790s, the 1840s, and the 1890s. A second element in the ideology defined attitudes toward other peoples in terms of a racial hierarchy. Inspired by the struggle of white Americans to secure and maintain their supremacy under conditions that differed from region to region, this outlook on race was the first of the core ideas to gain prominence. The third element defined the limits of acceptable political and social change overseas in keeping with the settled conviction that revolutions, though they might be a force for good, could as easily develop in a dangerous direction. Attitudes toward revolution, like those toward race, were fairly consistent through the formative first century, but unlike views on race, they were only sporadically evoked in that period. It was not until the 1910s, in response to an outburst of revolutionary activity abroad, that the power and the place of this element in the ideological construct was confirmed.

Now tightly interrelated and mutually reinforcing, these core ideas could provide national leaders with a clear and coherent vision of the world and the American place in it. In other words, by the early twentieth century those ideas had assumed the status of an informal but potent ideology that would point the direction for subsequent foreign policy, as well as set the tone and define the substance of American life to an unprecedented degree. . . .

After four decades of national immobility the old vision of greatness and liberty regained its hold on policy in the 1880s and 1890s. The end of Reconstruction together with sectional reconciliation finally removed a prime source of national controversy and division.

At the same time, the extension of European imperial rivalries into the Pacific, East Asia, and the Americas began to evoke in the United States both alarm and calls for imitation. New technology applied to weaponry, ships, and communications suddenly made the world seem smaller and more threatening. The vogue enjoyed by the competitive ethic of social Darwinism strengthened this perception that the world was rapidly pressing in. Americans were also discovering that they needed new spiritual and commercial frontiers abroad to replace an exhausted continental frontier and a saturated home market. Recurrent economic crises—first in the 1870s, again in the 1880s, and finally most severely in the 1890s—made foreign markets seem, at least to some, indispensable to the nation's future prosperity.

The dramatic transformation of American life in the post–Civil War decades, some historians have speculated, may also have prepared the way psychologically for this return to an active policy. Industrialization, urbanization, and the arrival of millions of immigrants created internal pressures (or at least elite anxieties) that were ultimately vented in overseas adventures. These trends, as reflected in the troubling fragmentation of the nation into antagonistic blocs of capital and labor and diverse ethnic and regional cultures, may have made the unifying effect of an assertively nationalist foreign policy particularly attractive. Whatever the causes, Washington began to build up the navy in the late 1880s and to move toward a more active role in both Latin America and the Pacific.

The siren call of national greatness was again being loudly and clearly heard. In a widely read book of 1885, the evangelist Josiah Strong gave voice to the expansionist strain common among mission-minded Protestants. He promised his countrymen that God was "preparing mankind to receive our impress." As successors to the British and beneficiaries of the westward movement of civilization, this generation of Americans would turn commerce, missionary work, and colonization toward shaping "the destinies of mankind." Alfred Thayer Mahan, who was embarked on writing the classic text on naval strategy, saw Americans irrevocably caught in a wary, strife-torn world. "Everywhere nation is arrayed against nation; our own no less than others." The United States would have to have a large navy, overseas bases, and a Central American canal if it were to protect its commercial and strategic interests. Henry Cabot Lodge, prominent Massachusetts senator and influential Republican, sought to awaken Americans to their place "as one of the great nations of the world." With "a record of conquest, colonization, and territorial expansion unequalled by any people in the nineteenth century," they should not hesitate now to join other powers in the current race for "the waste places of the earth." National honor, power, and profits as well as racial fitness and pride were the watchwords of these commentators. . . .

Once more a president precipitated a major debate by seizing the opportunities created by a one-sided war. William McKinley, an Ohio politician of few words and a keen political sense, was an effective proponent of the dynamic republic. After accepting war with Spain in 1898 to free Cuba, he quickly put through Congress the long-delayed annexation of Hawaii and ordered American forces to occupy Cuba, Puerto Rico, Guam, and the Philippines. He followed in 1899 with fresh initiatives: the passage of a treaty annexing the latter three islands and the conclusion of an agreement with Germany on the partition of Samoa. That same year he oversaw the dispatch of the open-door notes in response to a feared partition of China and in 1900 sent troops to help put down the Boxers.

These decisions reveal not a master plan but rather a consistent devotion to those ends that publicists had already linked to national greatness—commercial prosperity, territorial expansion, and military security. The president himself defended his policy in September 1898 with a reference to "obligations which we cannot disregard." The next month, during a swing through the Midwest, he called on Americans to be faithful to "the trust which civilization puts upon us." Echoing the liturgy of foreign-policy activists earlier in the decade, McKinley claimed for the United States a right and duty to establish colonies, help "oppressed peoples," and generally project its power and influence into the world. Americans would benefit, and so would all humanity. To a Boston audience in February 1899 he described control of the Philippines, Cuba, and Puerto Rico as a "great trust" that the nation carried "under the providence of God and in the name of human progress and civilization." He reassured doubters with the claim that "our priceless principles undergo no change under a tropical sun. They go with the flag."

Supporters of the president played on the same range of themes. Americans were "a people imperial by virtue of their power, by right of their institutions, by authority of their Heaven-directed purposes." Such were the views of the young Indiana Republican Albert J. Beveridge, whose perfervid and popular speech given in September 1898 helped prepare the Midwest for McKinley's visit. The United States was "henceforth to lead in the regeneration of the world." He and others made much of the trade and strategic advantages derived from overseas possessions. The Philippines in particular were lauded as a base for promoting the "vast" China trade and protecting growing interests throughout the Pacific. In a world made small by electricity and steam, those islands were not remote but were rendered virtually contiguous to the continental United States by an easily crossed ocean. . . .

By the turn of the century the keystone of U.S. foreign-policy ideology had fallen securely in place. Americans had succumbed to the temptations of an assertively nationalist foreign policy. [Alexander] Hamilton had first dangled it before them, [Thomas] Jefferson himself had fallen to its charms, [James K.] Polk and [William] McKinley had warmly embraced it. Step by step foreign-policy activists had come to occupy the patriotic high ground, defeating doubters and defying critics ever more decisively along the way. Activist leaders embraced a broad definition of national security that would carry the nation toward greatness in the world. In this endeavor they ultimately brought Americans to terms with colonies and naval bases, spheres of influence and protectorates, a powerful blue-water navy, and an expeditionary army.

A multiplicity of arguments justified the search for international greatness. Foreign powers hostile to the United States had to be met and thrown back. Crusading abroad would elevate the national character, strengthen national unity and pride, and smooth the workings of the economy. American energy and vision were too great to confine within fixed domestic bounds. But of all the arguments developed in behalf of a foreign policy of greatness none was to be as fateful as those that invoked liberty.

A policy devoted to both liberty and greatness, activists contended, was far from being a dangerous and unstable union of incompatibles. Instead, greatness abroad would glorify liberty at home. As success followed success and the boundaries of the American enterprise extended steadily outward, a free people's faith in their special destiny would be confirmed and deepened. Secure in their faith in liberty, Americans would set about remaking others in their own image while the world watched in awe.

At the same time liberty sanctified greatness. A chosen people could lay claim to special rights and obligations that rendered irrelevant the Cassandras who spoke of imperialism and the demise of republics. Let the fainthearted cry that the annals of history were filled with those who had reached for greatness and thereby lost liberty. Had they forgotten that the same laws of history need not govern Americans, a special people with a unique destiny? Thus the ascendant nationalists argued that the American pursuit of lofty ambitions abroad, far from imperiling liberty, would serve to invigorate it at home while creating conditions favorable to its spread in foreign lands. In other words, the United States could transform the world without itself being transformed.

By inextricably entangling liberty with greatness, proponents of activism not only met and matched their critics on the critics' favorite ground but also developed an argument with broad appeal. For a people in flux the rhetoric of liberty and greatness established reassuring ties to the nation's mythic beginnings. A nation born out of a struggle against tyranny still held to the ideals of its founders and kept in sight the old promise "to begin the world all over again." Foreign policy could thus supply a sense of national continuity that the domestic sphere was less and less able to sustain. . . .

[The second element in the ideology was racism, by which Americans] drew distinctions among the various peoples of the world on the basis of physical features, above all skin color and to a lesser extent head type . . . and guided by those distinctions they ranked the various types of peoples in the world. Those with the lightest skin were positioned on the highest rung of the hierarchy, and those with the darkest skin were relegated to the lowest. In between fell the "yellow" Mongolians and Malays, the "red" American Indian, and the racially mixed Latino. Each color implied a level of physical, mental, and moral development, with white Americans setting themselves up as the unquestioned standard of measurement. "Superior peoples" thus spoke English or some language akin to it, responsibly exercised democratic rights, embraced the uplifting influence of Protestant Christianity, and thanks to their industry enjoyed material abundance. Those toward the bottom were woefully deficient in each of these areas. . . .

This conception of race, defined by the poles of black and white, carried over into American foreign policy. By its grip on the thinking of the men who debated and determined that policy, by its influence over the press, and by its hold on the electorate, race powerfully shaped the way the nation dealt with other peoples. This included not just the Indian even before [Benjamin] Franklin's day but also the peoples of Latin America, East Asia, and Europe as Americans developed their own independent foreign policy.

The idea of a racial hierarchy proved particularly attractive because it offered a ready and useful conceptual handle on the world. It was reassuringly hardy and stable in a changing world. It was also accessible and gratifyingly easy to apply. Rather than having to spend long hours trying—perhaps inconclusively—to puzzle out the subtle patterns of other cultures, the elite interested in policy had at hand in the hierarchy of race a key to reducing other peoples and nations to readily comprehensible and familiar terms. It required no more than an understanding of easily grasped polarities and superficial characteristics. Races were different and unequal. Some were more civilized or progressive, others were more barbaric or backward. By locating white Americans of old stock among the most advanced peoples, the racial hierarchy had the incidental attraction of flattering that elite's ego and lending credence to that other major pillar of American foreign policy, the commitment to greatness.

From the perspective of the chosen few who made and followed policy, the idea of a racial hierarchy had the additional virtue of being congruent with popular attitudes. Americans high and low absorbed an awareness of race in their schooling, in their homes, and in their work place. As a central point of cultural reference on which all were agreed, race could be applied to foreign problems without fear that the concept itself would arouse domestic controversy. . . .

Latinos, the Spanish-speaking peoples of the Americas, occupied a position midway up the hierarchy of race. Their position there was fixed by the hold on the American imagination of the "black legend" with its condemnatory view of Spanish character. That legend had been part of the intellectual baggage that the English colonists had brought to the New World, and it was subsequently amplified by American merchants and diplomats who made direct contact with the newly independent Latin American states early in the nineteenth century. The resulting critique of Latin culture was perpetuated by school texts, kept fresh in cartoons, retailed in political rhetoric, and even incorporated into the views of policymakers, so that by the early twentieth century it had come to exercise a pervasive influence on the American approach to Latin America.

Narrowly construed, the black legend highlighted the cruelty with which Spanish conquerors had dealt with native-American populations. Driven by a taste for "carnage and plunder" (in the words of a 1794 text), these adventurers had overcome the Indians by a combination of brutality and deception and then exploited them unmercifully.

More broadly understood, the legend stood for all those undesirable characteristics that were Spain's unfortunate legacy to much of the New World. An 1898 account written to justify the war against Spain drew on what had become a widely accepted notion of that legacy. "Spain has been tried and convicted in the forum of history. Her religion has been bigotry, whose sacraments have been solemnized by the faggot and the rack. Her statesmanship has been infamy: her diplomacy, hypocrisy: her wars have been massacres: her supremacy has been a blight and a curse, condemning continents to sterility, and their inhabitants to death." Henry Cabot Lodge, an outspoken proponent of that war, characterized the foe as "mediaeval, cruel, dying" and "three hundred years behind all the rest of the world." Returning from a tour of Cuba, Redfield Proctor delivered a major Senate speech in March 1898 flatly accusing Spain of "the worst misgovernment of which I ever had knowledge."

From this legacy derived those qualities that Americans most often associated with Latinos—servility, misrule, lethargy, and bigotry. Latin governments were but parodies of the republican principles that they claimed to embody. John Randolph, a Virginia congressman, had looked south in 1816 and morosely observed that South Americans struggling for liberty would end up under "a detestable despotism. You cannot make liberty out of Spanish matter." Secretary of State John Quincy Adams agreed. Latin Americans, he observed in 1821, "have not the first elements of good or free government. Arbitrary power, military and ecclesiastical, was stamped upon their education, upon their habits, and upon all their institutions." The somnolent populations of that region, debilitated by their heritage and enervated by a tropical climate, neglected their rich natural resources, while the Catholic faith lulled them into intellectual passivity. "A priest-ridden people," Jefferson had predicted in 1813, were beyond "maintaining a free civil government."

Color-conscious Americans came to incorporate yet another element into their view of Latinos, a horror over the wholesale miscegenation that had further blackened that people both literally and figuratively. With appalling freedom, white Spaniards had mixed with enslaved blacks and native Indians to produce degenerate mongrel offspring. This sexual license among the races set an example particularly disturbing to Americans dedicated to defending the color line at home. The woeful consequences of crossing that line were everywhere apparent in Latin America. All Latin countries fell under censure for lax racial standards and indifference to the social consequences of polluting the blood of whites. But the darker the complexion of the people in question, the sharper was the attack. In this respect Haiti, populated by descendants of African slaves, was repeatedly singled out as an example of what happened when dark-skinned people were left to run wild and to murder their masters and then each other.

The black legend provided Americans with the basis for a wide array of negative stereotypes. These were usually assigned—so far as the gender can be determined—to the Latin male. He was depicted, depending on the circumstances and the prejudice of the observer, as superstitious, obstinate, lazy, cowardly, vain, pretentious, dishonest, unclean, impractical, and corrupt. However, alongside this dominant conception of Latin incapacity and the image of the swarthy if not black Latin male that accompanied it, there developed a more positive picture of the Latino as an imminently redeemable, even desirable white. In this alternative embodiment, the Latin usually took the form of a fair-skinned and comely senorita living in a mongrelized society yet somehow escaping its degrading effects. This distinction so favorable to Latin women was drawn by early firsthand American observers, invariably males traveling alone, and it stuck in the minds of those at home, to be summoned up when the times called for saving Latins either from themselves or from some outside threat. A macho Uncle Sam would rush in and sweep the Latin lady off her feet, save her from her half-breed husband or from some sinister intruder from outside the hemisphere, and introduce her to the kind of civilized life she deserved.

Americans could thus choose their images of Latin Americans to fit the circumstances. During the period of continental expansion, the negative image of the male fated to give way before his betters was the most serviceable. Denigration of the Mexican, for example, developed apace with American interest in his land. The first wave of Americans to visit Mexico in the 1820s reported that they found a dark-complected, cowardly, and cruel people addicted to gambling and plagued by loose morals. A visitor to Mexico City early in the decade concluded that most of its people "want nothing but tails to be more brute than the apes." Early Anglo settlers in Texas were quick to accept this harsh estimate. The folklore about "niggers" and "redskins" that many of them had brought from their homes along the Southern frontier predisposed them to a low regard for another dark-skinned people, the Mexicans, who stood in their way. As the contest for control of Texas and the Southwest proceeded, fellow Southerners and other Americans picked up and developed this theme of Mexican inferiority as a justification for American claims. Such a "colored mongrel race" had no claim to Texas, the influential senator from Mississippi, Robert J. Walker, insisted in 1836. A decade later, in the debate over Texas annexation, Pennsylvania's Senator James Buchanan, soon to become Polk's secretary of state, called for pushing aside "the imbecile and indolent Mexican race."

Once war began, James K. Polk and his expansionist supporters justified their aggressive course by denouncing the enemy in the conventional and contemptuous terms as "ignorant, prejudiced, and perfectly faithless." In this same spirit a New York paper declared, "The Mexicans are *aboriginal Indians*, and they must share the destiny of their race." So widely accepted had this negative stereotype become that even those who resisted the call of conquest and regeneration characterized the Mexican as a "half-savage" who would be difficult if not impossible to improve or assimilate. Whig critics of Polk's policy freely derided the Mexicans as a race that was "mongrel," "a sad compound," "slothful, indolent, ignorant," or simply "miserable."

When by contrast Americans saw themselves acting benevolently, they liked to picture the Latino as a white maiden passively awaiting salvation or seduction. During the Mexican War proponents of sweeping annexation indulged this fantasy. One patriotic poet imagined a union between "The Spanish maid, with eye of fire," and the Yankee, "Whose purer blood and valiant arms, / Are fit to clasp her budding charms." Cuba, which had awakened the interest of territorially acquisitive Americans as early as Jefferson's day, even more strikingly evoked this tendency to feminize the Latin. For example, in the 1850s, when calls for acquiring the island were frequently sounded, one enthusiast rhapsodized about Cuba as Uncle Sam's beloved "Queen of the Antilles . . . breathing her spicy, tropic breath, and pouting her rosy, sugared lips." Later in the century, Spanish atrocities committed in an effort to suppress a Cuban independence movement reawakened the vision of a feminine Cuba not so much ready for the taking as ravaged and desperate for rescue from her Spanish master, who fairly bristled with traits associated with the black legend.

The American drive for hemispheric preeminence at the turn of the century brought to the fore yet a third image: The Latino as a black child. Americans had intervened in Cuba to oust the Spaniards, appropriated Puerto Rico as their own, and encouraged a Panamanian secessionist movement against Colombia in order to obtain canal rights. The unexpected resentment and sullen defiance which these supposedly benevolent actions evoked proved puzzling and irritating. To compound the problem, Americans soon found themselves up against the psychologically troubling implications of continuing to portray the Latinos as mates. The picture of Uncle Sam in close proximity to a female Latin America carried strong sexual overtones and suggested the disturbing possibility of racial mixing. Americans uncomfortable over this prospect yet unwilling to surrender claims to dominion found a way out by making the Latino into a black child. This new image was a hybrid, drawing on the chief characteristics of the two previously dominant stereotypes, the racially degenerate male and the dependent woman.

Again Cuba can serve as an example. The Cubans were initially pictured as hapless victims of Spanish brutality and colonial oppression. Cartoons that appeared during the Cuban insurrection played on the theme of womanhood outraged, while the reconcentration policy pressed by the Spanish commander ("Butcher" Wyler) and the sinking of the *Maine* were depicted as entirely consistent with the cruel and treacherous Spanish character. But criticism of Spain did not in the end translate into respect for the insurgents. That the Cubans were not to be taken as even approximate equals was clear in the response of Anglo policymakers even before the war began. Both the Cleveland and McKinley administrations expressed a preference for the possibility of ordered Spanish rule over the certainty of anarchic Cuban self-government. Once the war came McKinley denied the Cubans recognition as a belligerent and afterward placed them under the control of an American military government. Closer contact now impressed on Americans the fact that many Cubans were swarthy, even black. Their army was a contemptible ragtag band ("made up very considerably of black people, only partially civilized") whose leaders were insufficiently grateful for American succor. They might wish independence but were certain to mismanage it if left on their own.

These discoveries quickly transformed the cartoon Cuban into a petulant child whose place on the racial hierarchy was made clear by his stereotypical black features and his minstrel drawl. This picture of

Cuban infantilism helped Americans to ignore the protests of this obviously immature and turbulent people against outside intervention and control, and it provided justification for a policy of keeping them in an appropriately dependent relationship to the United States. Thus the Cuban as mistress gave way to the Cuban as Southern black, "very poor and densely ignorant," as a text of 1900 quick to adopt the new imagery observed, but "capable of advancement under proper guidance."

Americans thus entered the twentieth century with three images of Latin Americans at their disposal. One, the Latin as half-breed brute, could be invoked to justify a contemptuous aloofness or a predatory aggressiveness. The second, of the feminized Latin, allowed the United States to assume the role of ardent suitor or gallant savior. The third, of an infantile and often negroid Latin, provided the justification for Uncle Sam's tutelage and stern discipline. In each case Americans stood in relation to Latinos as superiors dealing with inferiors.

These images, which had already helped rationalize the drive to expel Spain from North America and then push to the Mexican border south, also supported the ripening claim of the United States to the role of natural leader and policeman of an American system of states. That claim was embodied in the Monroe Doctrine, which began its career in 1823 as a bold but only partially enforceable pronouncement against the extension of European influence in the Western Hemisphere. By the 1890s it had evolved into a major principle of American policy, which not even Britain could safely ignore. With Europe fenced out, American policymakers with inherited pretensions to superiority over Latinos, and with ever-increasing power to make good on those pretensions, moved steadily toward making the hemisphere a U.S. preserve. Cubans, Puerto Ricans, and Colombians had already learned the practical implications of dominance by a people gripped by the black legend. Other Latin Americans, similarly stigmatized, would soon be subjected to the same hard education. . . .

In the structure of American race thinking, Anglo-Saxonism—the belief that Americans and the British were one people united by uncommon qualities and common interests—occupied a central position. By the first half of the nineteenth century Americans had begun to claim with pride their place in a trans-Atlantic community of English-speaking people. Dimming memories of fratricidal conflict set off by the American revolution created the conditions favorable to the rise of Anglo-Saxonism in an increasingly firm national consciousness. School texts began to celebrate the trans-Atlantic tie. A poetic paean to "America and Britons" often reproduced in the 1830s and 1840s proclaimed, "The voice of blood shall reach, / More audibly than speech, / WE ARE ONE." At the same time the proud American racial lineage assumed an honored position as a standard topic in public rhetoric. "Out of all the inhabitants of the world . . . a select stock, the Saxon, and out of this the British family, the noblest of the stock, was chosen to people our country."

By the end of the nineteenth century the Anglo-Saxon spell had further strengthened its hold. Race thinking, widely retailed in properly impressive pseudoscientific terms, had given added plausibility to an older ethnocentric notion of Anglo solidarity and superiority. The racial traits of both peoples, as they were now defined, included prominently industry, intelligence, a keen sense of moral purpose, and a talent for government. Together they stood preeminent in world affairs. Already the British had achieved much: their empire embraced one-fifth of the world's surface and one-quarter of its people, and their navy dominated the seas. Americans basked in the reflected glory of these accomplishments but they also knew that they, the child and heir of imperial Britain, were well on their way to eclipsing the parent in wealth and power. The United States was bound to become "a greater England with a nobler destiny," proclaimed Albert J. Beveridge, one of the more nationalistic of the Anglo-Saxonists.

The arrival of large numbers of disturbingly foreign immigrants sharpened the sensitivity to racial differences even within the circle of European whites. The nativism of the antebellum period had revealed early on the determination of ethnic Anglos to preserve their cultural hegemony against alien newcomers, then chiefly Irish and Germans. The concerns felt during that era proved mild, however, compared to the anxiety provoked by an even greater influx of still more foreign peoples, from southern and eastern Europe, at the end of the century. From the racial comparisons then drawn by a defensive but culturally dominant Anglo elite, there emerged a clear and fixed pecking order even for whites.

The elite's preoccupation with the differences among whites carried over into the fabric of thinking on world affairs. Anglo-Saxons clearly dominated the international stage. The Germans came next. They had the same qualities as their racial cousins save one—they had lost their love of liberty. This single serious defect set Germans just beyond the Anglo-Saxon pale and made this still-formidable people into a threatening global competitor, to be closely watched. By the turn of the century they were increasingly pictured as latter-day Huns, prone to the aggressive, even brutal behavior characteristic of a militaristic and autocratic system. The Slavs, half European and half Asiatic, were also formidable racial competitors on the international stage. Highly regimented and of rugged peasant stock, they had displayed great endurance, patience, and strength (if not intelligence and a knack for innovation) as they had slowly but irresistibly extended their control over much of the Eurasian land mass.

Lower down in the hierarchy were the Latin peoples of Europe, defined to include the French as well as Italians and Spaniards. They lacked vigor; they were sentimental, undisciplined, and superstitious; and consequently they were of small account in international affairs. Still farther back among the ranks of the unworthy appeared the Jews, depicted in explicitly racial, antisemitic terms. Predictably, farthest back were the peoples of Africa. In the popular literature of the late nineteenth century the "dark continent" began to emerge as the fascinating home of "savage beasts and beastly savages." Above all other places Africa invited white dominion.

The popular vogue enjoyed by Darwinism further accentuated the tendency for Americans to think of themselves as a race in comparative and competitive terms and to locate themselves in an Anglo-Saxon community of interests. Given an optimistic twist, Darwinian notions served to reinforce preexisting ideas of Anglo-Saxon superiority. By the standards of industrial progress, military prowess, and international influence and control, Anglo-Saxons had an incontestable claim to the top of the racial heap. From that eminence they would point the way toward an era of unprecedented world peace and prosperity. Lesser races, awed and grateful, could follow the lead of the Anglo-Saxon—or drop to the bottom of the heap to meet their fate, ultimate extinction.

But Darwinism also led some contemporary Anglo-Saxonist observers to more somber conclusions. In international competition among the races victory might not go to the refined and peaceful peoples but rather to the amoral, the cunning, the fecund, and the power hungry. Anglo-Americans might then need to cultivate a sense of solidarity and a capacity for cooperation in order to hold at bay the hard forces of barbarism that might overwhelm them singly.

This world view dominated by a belief in the shared superiority of Americans and Englishmen is nicely illustrated in the outlook of Alfred Thayer Mahan, naval historian and influential strategist. Through the 1880s and 1890s Mahan steadily advocated Anglo-American cooperation, for "in political traditions as well as by blood we are kin, the rest alien." He saw "the best hope of the world" in the union of the two branches of the race and the extension of their control over the multitude of peoples still in "the childhood stage of race development" and hence unfit for self-government. Of the Europeans Mahan regarded the Germans as the most progressive, though by 1897 Germany's international misbehavior began to plant doubts. Slavs, he was certain, were cruel and barbarous, and the Russians, who combined that "remorseless energy" of their race with the "unscrupulous craft of the Asiatic," particularly troubled him. He censured the French as fickle and false and the Latino (save for the entrancing women) as backward. The Chinese he viewed as both pitifully inert and dangerously barbaric, thus justifying on the one hand missionary ministrations and on the other strict exclusion from the outposts of civilization in Hawaii and the West Coast. He classified Filipinos as children and after some hesitations endorsed their annexation. Of the "Orientals" only the westernizing Japanese won his respect; they were "repeating the experience of our Teutonic ancestors." Blacks stood at the bottom of Mahan's racial hierarchy. They had been "darkies" and "niggers" since his youth, and even conversion to abolitionism had not shaken his conviction that they were the most primitive of all the races.

The appeal of Anglo-Saxonism and the related notions about the racial inferiority of other peoples, especially those of color, became dramatically apparent in the 1890s. At home the Southern effort to create a caste system fixing blacks in a place of permanent inferiority intensified; Congress passed new laws against Chinese immigrants and began to debate doing the same to some Europeans; the executive snuffed out the last embers of Indian resistance. Abroad involvement in Cuba and China both betrayed, as suggested above, the workings of deep-seated racial assumptions. In Hawaii and the Philippines, where a policy of intervention gave way to one of outright annexation, the issue of race emerged in more explicit form. Indeed, so prominent and pervasive an influence was race thinking that it figured in the armory of arguments of Americans on both sides of the question. Then, as in the debates of the 1840s and 1850s, race served equally as a reason for a cautious, self-limiting policy and as justification for a bold, assertive one.

In the case of Hawaii, whose future had been argued intermittently in Congress since the 1850s, racial considerations had proven as important as economic, strategic, and constitutional ones. The vigor and superiority of Anglo-Saxons, one side contended, was evident in the way New England merchants, sea captains, and missionaries had gained a foothold on the islands and in the way their offspring, even though a minority, had won commercial and political dominance. The racially deficient natives had simply given way like the Indians. Annexationists saw as the logical next step acceptance by the United States of the white islanders' wish for union and of the remaining native Hawaiians' need for civilization. Critics, repelled by the prospect of incorporating masses of nonwhites, warned against the perils of miscegenation that would produce a feeble, half-breed race on the islands and stressed that the inherent inferiority of native peoples prevented them from rising to the level of full and responsible citizenship. They would remain mere subjects, unassimilable and forever a millstone around the national neck. In the first major contest over Hawaii's annexation in 1893, the critics prevailed—only to find themselves reversed in the summer of 1898 when racial imperialism, brought to fever pitch by war with Spain, easily won out. . . .

The racial views embraced by Benjamin Franklin and carried forward by generations of his countrymen had not been an American invention, nor was race thinking an American monopoly. The American experience with race, and the closely related and formative experience with slavery, deserve to be seen as an extension of a variegated pattern of beliefs and practices extending back millennia and across cultures around the globe. There are, however, no easy generalizations to make about the American case or comparisons to draw between it and other cases. Only the obvious point remains—Americans were hardly unique. Gripped by ethnocentric impulses of seemingly universal force, Americans used race to build protective walls against the threatening strangeness of other people and to legitimize the boundaries and terms of intergroup contact. Moved no less by exploitative impulses, Americans followed other "master classes" in employing racial attributes to justify subordination of "inferior peoples," whether as black slaves, Indian wards, or Filipino subjects. Finally, Americans betrayed their common humanity by using the resulting collection of racial notions as an arena for the exercise of libidinous and other fantasies normally held in close confinement.

Americans inherited a rich legacy of racial thought from their immediate European ancestors. Westerners coming into contact with peoples of the "Third World" in the fifteenth century had already betrayed signs of racism. Well before Englishmen took that first step on the North American continent, they had absorbed Elizabethan myths about blacks and easily extrapolated them to other nonwhite peoples. These inherited views were greatly sharpened as Anglos began to contend with other expatriate Europeans, native Americans, and even Asians for a place on the new continent. For ambitious yet initially isolated British colonists, a picture of the world's peoples in which lightness of skin was tied to innate worth proved understandably attractive. Had there existed no ready-made Elizabethan notions about race, these colonists would surely have had to invent them. They used the racial hierarchy to underwrite their claim to lands they wanted and, once possession was secure, to justify the imposition of Anglo cultural values and institutions as well as the expulsion or political and economic subordination of lesser peoples. Race also provided a balm for the pangs of conscience over the inevitable instances of false dealing and the broader patterns of exploitation and dehumanization that attended this process of achieving white (and above all, Anglo) hegemony.

The attitudes toward race that developed in domestic affairs from black-white relations, and in the interstice between foreign and domestic affairs where the Indian and the immigrant were to be found, were in one sense a mosaic made up of pieces from different regions of the country. Each region had fought the war for racial supremacy in its own way and in accord with the economic prize in question, the nature of the opposing people, and the power disparities between them. Seizing Indian land in New England in the 1680s differed from holding a black population under control in the antebellum South, just as evicting Mexico from the Southwest and subordinating the resident Latino population differed from the struggle to control the immigrant tide washing the urban East at the turn of the century.

But the overall pattern of the mosaic was clear enough. Americans of light skin, and especially of English descent, shared a loyalty to race as an essential category for understanding other peoples and as a fundamental basis for judging them. They had, in other words, fixed race at the center of their world view. Public policy in general and foreign policy in particular had from the start of the national experience reflected the central role that race thinking played. As Americans came into closer contact with an ever-widening circle of foreign peoples in the last decade of the nineteenth century, racial assumptions continued to guide their response. Those crying for a strenuous foreign policy invoked the need to enhance the racial vitality of the Anglo-Saxon stock and to honor the tutelary obligations superior races owed lesser ones, while those skeptical about foreign crusades and colonies either labored to repel charges that they were traitors to their kind or recoiled in horror from races they considered irredeemably backward. Accepted by the turn of the century as an important ingredient in a demonstrably successful foreign policy no less than in the established domestic order, race would pass to subsequent generations as a well-nigh irresistible legacy.

Richard Hofstadter

THE DEPRESSION OF THE 1890s AND PSYCHIC CRISIS

Notwithstanding their material strength, national pride, and belief in racial superiority, Americans became deeply troubled in the 1890s. Political-protest movements, violent labor confrontations, and a brutal economic depression rocked the decade. The late historian Richard Hofstadter (1916–70) suggests in the following essay that Americans suffered a national psychic crisis that helped generate their imperialism. Hofstadter, for more than twenty years a teacher of American intellectual and political history at Columbia University, devoted much of his scholarship to the irrational behavior of Americans. He admitted that his assumptions were speculative and that delving into the psychology of the past is difficult. Yet this essay, from his book *The Paranoid Style in American Politics* (1965), adds another dimension to the study of imperialism and to an explanation of why, in the 1890s in particular, Americans became eager for foreign aggrandizement. Among Hofstadter's other works are *American Political Tradition* (1948), *Social Darwinism in American Thought* (1955) (which contains a chapter on racism and imperialism), *The Age of Reform* (1955), and *Anti-Intellectualism in American Life* (1962).

From *The Paranoid Style in American Politics and Other Essays*, pp. 147–51, 183–86, by Richard Hofstadter. Footnotes omitted. Copyright 1952, © 1964, 1965 by Richard Hofstadter. Reprinted by permission of Random House, Inc.

The taking of the Philippine Islands from Spain in 1899 marked a major historical departure for the American people, a breach in their traditions and a shock to their established values. To be sure, from their national beginnings they had constantly engaged in expansion, but almost entirely into contiguous territory. Now they were extending themselves to distant extra-hemispheric colonies. They were abandoning a strategy of defense hitherto limited to the continent and its appurtenances, in favor of a major strategic commitment in the Far East. Thus far their expansion had been confined to the spread of a relatively homogeneous population into territories planned from the beginning to develop self-government; now control was to be imposed by force on millions of ethnic aliens. The acquisition of the islands, therefore, was understood by contemporaries on both sides of the debate, as it is readily understood today, to be a turning point in our history.

To discuss the debate in isolation from other events, however, would be to deprive it of its full significance. America's entrance into the Philippine Islands was a by-product of the Spanish-American War. The Philippine crisis is inseparable from the war crisis, and the war crisis itself is inseparable from a larger constellation that might be called "the psychic crisis of the 1890s."

Central in the background of the psychic crisis was the great depression that broke in 1893 and was still very acute when the agitation over the war in Cuba began. Severe depression, by itself, does not always generate an emotional crisis as intense as that of the nineties. In the 1870s the country had been swept by a depression of comparable acuteness and duration which, however, did not give rise to all the phenomena that appeared in the 1890s or to very many of them with comparable intensity and impact. It is often said that the 1890s, unlike the 1870s, form a "watershed" in American history. The difference between the emotional and intellectual impact of these two depressions can be measured, I believe, not by the difference in severity, but rather by reference to a number of singular events that in the 1890s converged with the depression to heighten its impact upon the public mind.

First in importance was the Populist movement, the free-silver agitation, the heated campaign of 1896. For the first time in our history a depression had created a protest movement strong enough to capture a major party and raise the specter, however unreal, of drastic social convulsion. Second was the maturation and bureaucratization of

American business, the completion of its essential industrial plant, and the development of trusts on a scale sufficient to stir the anxiety that the old order of competitive opportunities was approaching an eclipse. Third, and of immense symbolic importance, was the apparent filling up of the continent and the disappearance of the frontier line. We now know how much land had not yet been taken up and how great were the remaining possibilities for internal expansion both in business and on the land; but to the mind of the 1890s it seemed that the resource that had engaged the energies of the people for three centuries had been used up. The frightening possibility suggested itself that a serious juncture in the nation's history had come. As Frederick Jackson Turner expressed it in his famous paper of 1893: "Now, four centuries from the discovery of America, at the end of one hundred years of life under the Constitution, the frontier has gone, and with its going has closed the first period of American history."

To middle-class citizens who had been brought up to think in terms of the nineteenth-century order, the outlook seemed grim. Farmers in the staple-growing region had gone mad over silver and [William Jennings] Bryan; workers were stirring in bloody struggles like the Homestead and Pullman strikes; the supply of new land seemed at an end; the trust threatened the spirit of business enterprise; civic corruption was at a high point in the large cities; great waves of seemingly unassimilable immigrants arrived yearly and settled in hideous slums. To many historically conscious writers, the nation appeared overripe, like an empire ready for collapse through a stroke from outside or through internal upheaval. Acute as the situation was for all those who lived by the symbols of national power—for the governing and thinking classes—it was especially poignant for young people, who would have to make their careers in the dark world that seemed to be emerging.

The symptomatology of the crisis would record several tendencies in popular thought and behavior that had previously existed only in pale and tenuous form. These symptoms were manifest in two quite different moods. The key to one of them was an intensification of protest and humanitarian reform. Populism, utopianism, the rise of the Christian Social gospel, the growing intellectual interest in socialism, the social settlement movement that appealed so strongly to the college generation of the nineties, the quickening of protest and social criticism in the realistic novel—all these are expressions of this mood. The other mood was one of national self-assertion, aggression, expansion. The motif of the first was social sympathy; of the second, national power. During the 1890s far more patriotic groups were founded than in any other decade of our history; the naval theories of Captain [Alfred] Mahan were gaining in influence; naval construction was booming; there was an immense quickening of the American cult of Napoleon and a vogue of the virile and martial writings of Rudyard Kipling; young Theodore Roosevelt became the exemplar of the vigorous, masterful, out-of-doors man; the revival of European imperialism stirred speculation over what America's place would be in the world of renewed colonial rivalries, and in some stirred a demand to get into the imperial race to avoid the risk of being overwhelmed by other powers. But most significant was the rising tide of jingoism, a matter of constant comment among observers of American life during the decade.

Jingoism, of course, was not new in American history. But during the 1870s and 1880s the American public had been notably quiescent about foreign relations. There had been expansionist statesmen, but they had been blocked by popular apathy, and our statecraft had been restrained. [Ulysses S.] Grant had failed dismally in his attempt to acquire Santo Domingo; our policy toward troubled Hawaii had been cautious; in 1877 an offer of two Haitian naval harbors had been spurned. In responding to Haiti, Secretary of State [Frederick T.] Frelinghuysen had remarked that "the policy of this Government . . . has tended toward avoidance of possessions disconnected from the main continent." Henry Cabot Lodge, in his life of George Washington published in 1889, observed that foreign relations then filled "but a slight place in American politics, and excite generally only a languid interest." Within a few years this comment would have seemed absurd. In 1895, Russell A. Alger reported to Lodge, after reading one of Lodge's own articles to a Cincinnati audience, that he was convinced by the response that foreign policy, "more than anything else, touches the public pulse of today." The history of the 1890s is the history of public agitation over expansionist issues and of quarrels with other nations. . . .

Since Julius W. Pratt published his *Expansionists of 1898* in 1936, it has been obvious that any interpretation of America's entry upon the paths of imperialism in the nineties in terms of rational economic motives would not fit the facts, and that a historian who approached the event with preconceptions no more supple than those, say, of Lenin's *Imperialism* would be helpless. This is not to say that markets and investments have no bearing; they do, but there are features of the situation that they do not explain at all. Insofar as the economic factor was important, it can be better studied by looking at the relation between the depression, the public mood, and the political system.

The alternative explanation has been the equally simple idea that the war was a newspapers' war. This notion, once again, has some point, but it certainly does not explain the war itself, much less its expansionist result. The New Deal period, when the political successes of F. D. R. [Franklin D. Roosevelt] were won in the face of over-whelming newspaper opposition, showed that the press is not power-ful enough to impose upon the public mind a totally uncongenial view of public events. It must operate roughly within the framework of public predispositions. Moreover, not all the papers of the nineties were yellow journals. We must inquire into the structure of journalistic power and also into the views of the owners and editors to find out what differentiated the sensational editors and publishers from those of the conservative press.

There is still another qualification that must be placed upon the role of the press: the press itself, whatever it can do with opinion, does not have the power to precipitate opinion into action. That is something that takes place within the *political* process, and we cannot tell that part of the story without examining the state of party rivalries, the origin and goals of the political elites, and indeed the entire political context. We must, then, supplement our story about the role of the newspapers with at least two other factors: the state of the public tem-per upon which the newspapers worked, and the manner in which party rivalries deflected domestic clashes into foreign aggression. Here a perennial problem of politics under the competitive two-party system became manifest again in the 1890s. When there is, for whatever rea-son, a strong current of jingoism running in the channels of public sentiment, party competition tends to speed it along. If the party in power is behaving circumspectly, the opposition tends to beat the drums. For example, in 1896, with Cleveland still in office, the Republican platform was much more exigent on the Cuba issue. When McKinley came into office and began to show reluctance to push toward intervention, the Democratic party became a center of inter-ventionist pressure; this pressure was promptly supplemented by a large number of Republicans who, quite aside from their agreement on the issue, were concerned about its effect on the fate of their party.

When we examine the public temper, we find that the depression, together with such other events as the approaching completion of the settlement of the continent, the growth of trusts, and the intensification of internal social conflict, had brought to large numbers of people intense frustrations in their economic lives and their careers. To others they had brought anxiety that a period of stagnation in national wealth and power had set in. The restlessness of the discontented classes had been heightened by the defeat of Bryan in 1896. The anxieties about the nation's position had been increased among statesmen and publicists by the revival of world imperialism, in particular by the feeling that America was threatened by Germany, Russia, and Japan. The expansionist statesmen themselves were drawn largely from a restless upper-middle-class elite that had been fighting an unrewarding battle for conservative reform in domestic politics and looked with some eagerness toward a more spacious field of action.

Men often respond to frustration with acts of aggression, and allay their anxieties by threatening acts against others. It is revealing that the underdog forces in American society showed a considerably higher responsiveness to the idea of war with Spain than the groups that were satisfied with their economic or political positions. Our entry into the Philippines then aroused the interest of conservative groups that had been indifferent to the quixotism of freeing Cuba but were alert to the possibility of capturing new markets. Imperialism appealed to members of both the business and the political elites as an enlargement of the sphere of American power and profits; many of the underdogs also responded to this new note of national self-assertion. . . .

Clearly this attempt to see the war and expansion in the light of social history has led us onto the high and dangerous ground of social psychology and into the arena of conjecture. But simple rationalistic explanations of national behavior will also leave us dissatisfied. What I have attempted here is merely a preliminary sketch of a possible explanatory model. Further inquiry might make it seem more plausible at some points, more questionable at others.

Lewis L. Gould

PRESIDENT McKINLEY'S STRONG LEADERSHIP AND THE ROAD TO WAR

In this essay from his book *The Spanish-American War and President McKinley*, Lewis L. Gould sharply rejects the view that the United States succumbed to war hysteria or a psychic crisis in 1898. He argues instead that William McKinley was a tenacious diplomat who gave Spain every chance to avoid war over Cuba, which had been in revolt against its imperial master since 1895. The quest for national security and humanitarianism, not irrationality, compelled the United States to resolve the Cuban issue. Gould also counters the once-popular charge that McKinley was a weak, manipulated leader who had few talents or ideas of his own. In his scholarship, Professor Gould, of the University of Texas at Austin, holds that McKinley was the first truly modern president and, as an architect of important departures in U.S. foreign policy, a key historical figure. Among Gould's other books are *The Presidency of William McKinley* (1980) and *Reform and Regulation: American Politics, 1900 1916* (1978).

The climactic phase of the Cuban problem began on March 19, 1898, when four members of the *Maine* inquiry board met with McKinley. They told him that the court would conclude that an external explosion, probably a submarine mine, had caused the *Maine* to sink [on February 15]. The physical evidence regarding the vessel's keel and bottom plates, which had been driven upward, as an explosion from outside would do, persuaded the court to reject the hypothesis of an internal explosion. Knowing that the court's verdict would have a profound influence on the popular mind when the report officially reached him four or five days later, McKinley sent a stern message to [Minister Stewart] Woodford [in Spain] on March 20, which conveyed the board's findings and warned: "This report must go to Congress soon." The president indicated that the *Maine* issue could be handled through a payment of reparations by Spain, but "general conditions in Cuba which can not be longer endured, and which will demand action on our part," required positive steps in Madrid. "April

From *The Spanish-American War and President McKinley*, pp. 41–47, 49–53, by Lewis L. Gould. Footnotes omitted. Copyright © 1982. Reprinted by permission of the University of Kansas Press.

15 is none too early date for accomplishment of these purposes." At home, McKinley began a round of meetings with congressional leaders of both parties to offset the impact of the *Maine* report and to retain control of events. He agreed that Congress would receive diplomatic papers on Cuba by April 20, but still, in the face of a deadline for Spain and Congress, he hoped "that something may yet happen to avert hostilities." On the day that these words appeared in the *New York Herald*, the spiral into war commenced.

The *Maine* report, blaming an external cause, arrived at the White House during the evening of March 24. The next day the president, the cabinet, and some military advisors digested the lengthy document. The report, with a message from McKinley, would go to Capitol Hill on Monday, March 28. Meanwhile, McKinley prepared a message to Woodford, which went out over [Assistant Secretary of State William R.] Day's signature shortly after midnight on March 26. This telegram briefly reviewed McKinley's policy and then stated: "The President suggests that if Spain will revoke the reconcentration order [that forced Cubans into debilitating and death-dealing concentration camps] and maintain the people until they can support themselves and offer to the Cubans full self-government, with reasonable indemnity, the President will gladly assist in its consummation. If Spain should invite the United States to mediate for peace and the insurgents would make like request, the President might undertake such office of friendship." Woodford received the wire late on March 26 and immediately asked if "full self-government" meant "actual recognition of independence, or is nominal Spanish sovereignty over Cuba still permissible?" Day responded that "full self-government with indemnity would mean Cuban independence."

By Sunday, March 27, the president apparently had decided that Congress would not act hastily on the *Maine* report. At the same time, Woodford was reporting that Spain had made tentative feelers toward an armistice in Cuba. With the prospect of a slight breathing space, McKinley had Day wire the American minister: "See if the following can be done: First. Armistice until October 1. Negotiations meantime looking for peace between Spain and insurgents through friendly offices of President United States." Second, the president sought the revocation of the reconcentration order. Finally, Woodford was told to add, if possible, that if peace terms between Spain and the rebels were not reached by October 1, McKinley would be the final arbiter between the parties.

McKinley's second proposal offered Spain a more measured path toward Cuban independence, but both the March 26 and the March 27 messages assumed, as an end result, a Cuba that would be free of Spanish rule. There was no outright demand for independence, because the Spanish government would have peremptorily rejected it. Imprecision in diplomacy would offer a slim chance to avoid war, if Spain were to yield. Categorical ultimatums at any point in the negotiating process would have meant hostilities.

In Madrid, Woodford submitted the American proposals to Spain on March 29. Faced with intense congressional pressure after McKinley's *Maine* message, the administration wanted a prompt response. Thursday, March 31, became the deadline. The Sagasta government found that the Spanish army was opposed to an armistice, and Woodford reported that the tender of an armistice would cause a revolution. In its formal answer, Spain agreed to submit the *Maine* question to arbitration and revoked the reconcentration order. On McKinley's principal demands, however, it yielded nothing. The Cuban problem would be turned over to that island's parliament, "without whose intervention it will not be able to arrive at the final result." Spain would accept an armistice if the rebels asked for it, but its length and extent would be up to the Spanish commander in Cuba. Spain had gone to the limit of its domestic political resources, but Cuban independence, either immediately through submission or eventually through American mediation, was an impossibility. Madrid was now seeking time in order to mobilize European support against the United States. . . .

The negative reply reached the White House at 10:30 P.M. on March 31. Its unsatisfactory character was clear, and it left little room for additional negotiation. Without abandoning his hope that Spain might still recognize the necessity of relinquishing Cuba, McKinley now moved to put the nation on a war footing. On April 1 the navy stepped up its preparations, including night patrols; the administration explored taxation problems that a war would bring; and the president began to work on his message to Congress. "That the President has less confidence in a peaceable outcome," wrote a reporter in the *New York Tribune* on April 1, "was apparent from the views he expressed to several of his closest friends." Congress expected to receive the message on April 4, and influential Republicans wanted the president to "lead and not be pushed." Then, on April 3, the White House announced that the message would go in two days later, on April 6.

This brief delay may have been connected to a final presidential initiative to gain concessions from Spain. Through Archbishop John Ireland of Minnesota, an informal papal envoy, McKinley was exploring the prospects of having the Vatican use persuasion with Spain. The president's remark that he would welcome help from the Holy See meant that he wanted assistance in obtaining Spain's acquiescence. Madrid interpreted these words as an invitation to use papal mediation and as evidence of a relaxation of American pressure. Woodford received proposals that, in return for an armistice that Spain would grant, the United States would withdraw its navy from Cuban waters. He cabled Washington that "when armistice is once proclaimed hostilities will never be resumed and . . . permanent peace will be secured." The White House denied the Spanish interpretation as soon as it became public, and Day wired to Woodford: "Would the peace you are so confident of securing mean the independence of Cuba?" The more the administration learned of what Spain meant in its note of March 31, the less it liked the substance of it. The manifesto regarding the autonomous government, said Day on April 4, "is not armistice" but only "an invitation to the insurgents to submit," pending further Spanish action. . . .

Spain's decision to ask for a suspension of hostilities in Cuba, not an armistice, was directed at the European powers rather than at McKinley and Washington. Knowing that capitulation to the Americans was politically impossible, the government saw the truce as a negotiating ploy in its efforts to find foreign support. Even so, there was strong opposition within the cabinet to a move that might alienate the armed forces. Proponents contended that the suspension would buy time so that Cuba could be defended against the United States. The cabinet deadlock ended on April 9, when the queen arranged for the ambassadors of the European powers to call in Madrid, as they had in Washington. The diplomats favored an armistice, in the interests of peace, and Spain could now consent, to placate potential friends. Within the cabinet, advocates of the move stressed that it would not be a prelude to surrender, and they noted that the suspension of hostilities, instead of an armistice, would not involve recognizing the rebel regime.

Woodford believed, as he wired the president, that "the present Government is going, and is loyally ready to go, as fast and as far as it can." A closer reading of Spain's statement, which reached McKinley on April 10, revealed the true character of this "capitulation." The

William McKinley Campaign Poster, 1896. The Republican presidential candidate's themes captured two U.S. foreign policy goals: spurring overseas commerce and "civilizing" other peoples around the world. (*Division of Political History, Smithsonian Institution*)

Spanish commander in Cuba could determine how long and under what conditions hostilities would stop. The insurgents were offered autonomy, with "the franchise and liberties" extended to such an extent "that no motive or pretext is left for claiming any fuller measure thereof." Whatever changes might take place in autonomy would be "within the bounds of reason and of the national sovereignty." Spain also revoked its policy of reconcentration and offered to submit the *Maine* question to arbitration. Of American mediation, a true armistice, and Cuba's independence, Spain said nothing. To Day's inquiry about whether Spain would give Cuba its independence if the United States deemed it necessary, the minister in Washington said only no.

McKinley's critics place less weight on these considerations; they contend that Spain, once the fighting stopped, could not have resumed the struggle. Time would have been on the side of a peaceful solution. Such a result was, of course, possible, but now remains only a might-have-been. It is doubtful, however, that the rebels would have accepted the suspension, and it is even more unlikely that Spanish opinion would have endorsed a move toward peace. Announcement of the suspension brought public disturbances in Madrid. More important, the passage of time, after an American diplomatic concession, would have strengthened not only the Spanish will to fight but also the military power at its disposal. The minister of war told the Cuban commander, for example, that the cabinet had opted for the suspension in order to remedy "a scarcity of resources with which to defend our indisputable rights." The Spanish proposal was a last-minute diplomatic gambit that, from an American perspective, revived old questions about Madrid's good faith in the negotiating process.

The belief that Spain submitted rests on a misreading of the evidence and owes much to retrospective guilt about the impact which the war had on American history. The hypothetical scenario that has McKinley risking the prestige of his office, the future of his party, and what Americans saw as the nation's honor in exchange for a settlement of the Cuban issue without war is an attractive one. Its advocates must recognize, however, the greater likelihood that after placing these elements at risk, McKinley would have been confronted with Cuban opposition, a rebellion in Congress, and mounting indications that the Spanish had abused his good will and trust. The devastating effect that such a humiliation would have had on the presidency and the government should not be weighed lightly.

After the last message from Spain came to the White House on the morning of April 10, the administration decided to take no action beyond adding the information that it contained to the president's address on the situation in Cuba. The document had been ready for a week. . . .

Congress listened to the message on April 11 "with intense interest and profound silence" as the clerks droned through its seven thousand words. It was not a call to arms. McKinley began with a historical narrative of the nation's involvement with the Cuban issue. He reviewed the negotiations with Spain up to the action of the Sagasta government on March 31 in response to his note of March 27. "With this last overture in the direction of immediate peace, and its disappointing reception by Spain, the Executive is brought to the end of his effort." The absence here of any reference to Cuban independence disturbed legislators who had been assured that the administration had demanded it of Spain. Once again, categorical assertion of this goal in a presidential statement would have ensured that Spain would reject it.

McKinley next turned to what the United States should do. He came out against a recognition of Cuban belligerency that would "accomplish nothing toward the one end for which we labor—the instant pacification of Cuba and the cessation of the misery that afflicts the island." American recognition of the Cuban Republic's independence was also ruled out as not being necessary "in order to enable the United States to intervene and pacify the island. To commit this country now to the recognition of any particular government in Cuba might subject us to embarrassing conditions of international obligation toward the organization so recognized." When a government appeared "capable of performing the duties and discharging the functions of a separate nation," the United States could adjust its position.

At this point in his message, McKinley weighed the alternatives of intervention as an impartial neutral or as an ally, presumably of the Cubans. He chose the former course, setting out four reasons to justify the American action. Humanitarian grounds were listed first: "It is no answer to say that this is all in another country, belonging to another nation, and is therefore none of our business. It is specially our duty, for it is right at our door." The citizens of Cuba required protection that no government currently afforded them. Therefore, "the very serious injury to the commerce, trade, and business of our people," as well as "the wanton destruction of property and devastation of the island," constituted the third ground for action. Finally, "the present condition of affairs in Cuba is a constant menace to our peace, and entails upon this Government an enormous expense." The president cited the *Maine* as "a patent and impressive proof of a state of things in Cuba that is intolerable." After quoting from Presidents Grant and Cleveland on the Cuban question and from his own annual message in 1897, McKinley asserted: "In the name of humanity, in the name of civilization, in behalf of endangered American interests which give us the right and the duty to speak and to act, the war in Cuba must stop." That sentence produced a wave of applause in the House chamber.

McKinley then asked the lawmakers to "authorize and empower the President to take measures to secure a full and final termination of hostilities between the Government of Spain and the people of Cuba." He also sought authority to establish a stable government in Cuba, and "to use the military and naval forces of the United States as may be necessary for these purposes." Following two paragraphs that closed the original version of the message came two more that alluded to Spain's suspension of hostilities. "If this measure attains a successful result," the president wrote, "then our aspirations as a Christian, peace-loving people will be realized. If it fails, it will be only another justification for our contemplated action."

McKinley had not submitted a war message. The possibility of further negotiations with Spain remained alive, and the language about Cuba's belligerency and independence ensured that Congress would debate the issue for several days. The executive had also requested large discretionary power to use the nation's military force short of actually going to war. Even at this moment of greatest crisis for his administration, McKinley was broadening the scope of presidential power. . . .

The president signed the congressional resolution [declaring Cuba free and independent and directing the president to use force to remove Spanish authority from the island] on April 20. Spain broke diplomatic relations at once. In Madrid, Woodford was informed of Spain's action before he could convey the resolution formally, and he asked for his passports. On April 22 a naval blockade of Cuba was imposed, and two days later, Spain declared war as American ships moved into position. The action of their government was popular with the Spanish people, a response that underlined how little room there had actually been for carrying on negotiations over Cuba. On April 25

McKinley asked Congress to declare war, and it complied by passing a resolution that said that war had existed since April 21.

Of the two dominant explanations for McKinley's Spanish-Cuban diplomacy, the view that he was a weak, indecisive executive, who yielded at last to war hysteria, has commanded more adherents than the view that he was a wily expansionist, who in the end, wanted "what only a war could provide: the disappearance of the terrible uncertainty in American political and economic life, and a solid basis from which to resume the building of the new American commercial empire." The first hypothesis assumes several considerations: that the Spanish would ultimately have submitted peacefully, that they virtually gave in, in April 1898, and that McKinley lacked the courage and vision to seize the real chances for peace. The evidence from Spanish diplomatic sources does not provide much support for the first two assumptions. Madrid did not see itself as being on a road from which no backward step was possible. With resolve and purpose, it maneuvered to maintain its grip on Cuba to the end, and its celebrated concessions of April 9, 1898, were, in fact, last-minute efforts to buy more time to keep the island.

The allegation of presidential weakness remains the most damning indictment of McKinley. When seen in the light of Spanish tenacity, however, what is remarkable is how long the president was able to obtain time for the conducting of peaceful diplomacy. At any point in the process from November 1897 onward, the two countries were likely to begin fighting. Through this morass of crisis and danger, McKinley worked his way for five months in order to allow Spain the chance to submit peacefully. Finally, in April 1898, it was obvious that diplomacy had failed, that Spain would not yield, and that war was the only alternative to the prolongation of an intolerable foreign-policy situation. His conduct up to that point reveals a subtlety of action, a fortitude of will, and a simple courage that belie the easy stereotypes of his historical reputation.

The second school of McKinley's critics presents a more sophisticated bill of particulars. They question whether the motives behind the nation's concern with Cuba were genuine or whether they sprang from less attractive premises. Behind the stated reasons for American interest in Cuba lay economic causes—the tensions within a society that was emerging from a prolonged depression, an industrial machine that was glutted with its products and was seeking foreign markets, and statesmen who, unwilling to confront internal problems, preferred to export their social difficulties. The often unstated theses of this approach seem to be that the United States had, at most, marginal interests in the Cuban crisis beyond economic ones and that McKinley took his cues from the business community. On the latter point the image of the president as the tool of capitalists has confused the situation. McKinley operated within the framework of the economic system that he knew, in pursuit of the national interest of a society whose values, he thought, were basically healthy. He sought the counsel of successful businessmen on many issues, but the ostensible connections between their advice on Cuba and his actions remains ephemeral and inferential. Though the business community and its spokesmen responded to foreign policy, they did not make it.

It is possible to visualize Americans turning away from the horrors of the Cuban conflict, rejecting anything beyond the most modest role in foreign affairs, and addressing the society's inequities through some form of democratic socialism in 1898, but this is an improbable vision. The nation's historic traditions, humanitarian impulses, and economic calculations gave the Cuban problem a strong grip on the emotions of a majority of American citizens. It would have taken a revolution in attitudes, outside the existing political consensus, to have produced any other result than intense absorption in the fate of Cuba. To that foreign-policy commitment, Americans brought motives at once cynical and elevated, crass and noble. When economic causes are omitted, the picture lacks clarity, but excessive emphasis on them reduces foreign affairs to a crude equation that misreads the national character.

But was Cuba any business of the United States? Perhaps not; but it is hard to see how the effects of the rebellion could have been escaped. Few scholars advocate that the president should have joined Spain in suppressing the uprising. Another position contends that all the United States had to do was to recognize Cuba's independence, since the rebels had won militarily. Spain would have questioned whether the verdict on the war was that clear, and recognition would have meant war in any case, as 1898 showed. An independent Cuba, free from outside influence, is a laudable goal; and a unilateral defense of the American presence there during this century is difficult. It takes a great faith in the benevolent workings of international politics in these years, however, to maintain that Cuba would not, in the absence of United States involvement, have at least been the object of attention from nations such as Germany which had a larger capacity to assert their will than did Spain.

Like most wars, the Spanish-American War occurred when two nations, both convinced that they were right, pursued their national interests to an ultimate conclusion. Spain tried to defend its territorial integrity and sense of nationhood with the limited means open to it. In order to end a bloody conflict, the United States, under the leadership of William McKinley, went to war in 1898 against a foe that had resisted all attempts at peaceful compromise. The nation's motives owed far more to the better side of American life than posterity has recognized. If the war that ensued was not splendid, it had come in a way that dishonored neither the two countries involved nor the presidency of William McKinley.

Walter LaFeber

THE BUSINESS COMMUNITY'S PUSH FOR WAR

Walter LaFeber accepts the depiction of President William McKinley as a determined leader who surrendered to neither public opinion nor an unruly Congress, but LaFeber refutes the familiar thesis that jingoistic yellow journalism stampeded leaders into war. Instead, this Cornell University historian emphasizes that McKinley was a conservative capitalist closely connected to businesspeople who wanted to build a commercial empire in Asia and Latin America. Unlike Lewis Gould, LaFeber argues that the American business community helped push McKinley to a war decision. By going to war against Spain, McKinley could end uncertainty at home and pursue expansionism abroad. Professor LaFeber's many works include *The New Empire* (1963) (from which this essay is chosen), *Inevitable Revolutions* (1983), *The Panama Canal* (1978), and *America, Russia, and the Cold War* (1991).

The President did not want war; he had been sincere and tireless in his efforts to maintain the peace. By mid-March, however, he was beginning to discover that, although he did not want war, he did want what only a war could provide: the disappearance of the terrible uncertainty in American political and economic life, and a solid basis from which to resume the building of the new American commercial empire. When the President made his demands, therefore, he made the ultimate demands; as far as he was concerned, a six-month period of negotiations would not serve to temper the political and economic problems in the United States, but only exacerbate them.

To say this is to raise another question: why did McKinley arrive at this position during mid-March? What were the factors which limited the President's freedom of choice and policies at this particular time? The standard interpretations of the war's causes emphasize the yellow journals and a belligerent Congress. These were doubtlessly

Reprinted from Walter LaFeber, *The New Empire: An Interpretation of American Expansion, 1860–1898*, pp. 400–406. Footnotes omitted. Copyright © 1963 by the American Historical Association. Used by permission of the publisher, Cornell University Press.

crucial factors in shaping the course of American entry into the conflict, but they must be used carefully. A first observation should be that Congress and the yellow press, which had been loudly urging intervention ever since 1895, did not make a maiden appearance in March, 1898; new elements had to enter the scene at that time to act as the catalysts for McKinley's policy. Other facts should be noted regarding the yellow press specifically. In areas where this press supposedly was most important, such as New York City, no more than one-third of the press could be considered sensational. The strongest and most widespread prowar journalism apparently occurred in the Midwest. But there were few yellow journals there. The papers that advocated war in this section did so for reasons other than sensationalism; among these reasons were the influence of the Cuban Junta and, perhaps most important, the belief that the United States possessed important interests in the Caribbean area which had to be protected. Finally, the yellow press obviously did not control the levers of American foreign policy. McKinley held these, and he bitterly attacked the owners of the sensational journals as "evil disposed . . . people." An interpretation stressing rabid journalism as a major cause of the war should draw some link to illustrate how these journals reached the White House or the State Department. To say that this influence was exerted through public opinion proves nothing; the next problem is to demonstrate how much public opinion was governed by the yellow press, how much of this opinion was influenced by more sober factors, and which of these two branches of opinion most influenced McKinley.

Congress was a hotbed of interventionist sentiment, but then it had been so since 1895. The fact was that Congress had more trouble handling McKinley than the President had handling Congress. The President had no fear of that body. He told [his friend and Chicago banker] Charles Dawes during the critical days of February and March that if Congress tried to adjourn he would call it back into session. McKinley held Congress under control until the last two days of March, when the publication of the "Maine" investigation forced Thomas B. Reed, the passionately antiwar Speaker of the House, to surrender to the onslaughts of the rapidly increasing interventionist forces. As militants in Congress forced the moderates into full retreat, McKinley and Day were waiting in the White House for Spain's reply to the American ultimatum. And after the outbreak on March 31

McKinley reassumed control. On April 5 the Secretary of War, R. A. Alger, assured the President that several important senators had just informed him that "there will be no trouble about holding the Senate." When the President postponed his war message on April 5 in order to grant [U.S. consul in Havana, Cuba] Fitzhugh Lee's request for more time, prowar congressmen went into a frenzy. During the weekend of April 8 and 9, they condemned the President, ridiculed Reed's impotence to hold back war, and threatened to declare war themselves. In fact, they did nearly everything except disobey McKinley's wishes that nothing be done until the following week. Nothing was done.

When the Senate threatened to overrule the President's orders that the war declaration exclude recognition of the Cuban insurgent government, McKinley whipped the doubters into line and forced the Senate to recede from its position. This was an all-out battle between the White House and a strong Senate faction. McKinley triumphed despite extremely strong pressure exerted by sincere American sentiment on behalf of immediate Cuban independence and despite the more crass material interests of the Junta's financial supporters and spokesmen. The President wanted to have a free hand in dealing with Cuba after the war, and Congress granted his wishes. Events on Capitol Hill may have been more colorful than those at the White House, but the latter, not the former, was the center of power in March and April, 1898.

Influences other than the yellow press or congressional belligerence were more important in shaping McKinley's position of April 11. Perhaps most important was the transformation of the opinion of many spokesmen for the business community who had formerly opposed war. If, as one journal declared, the McKinley administration, "more than any that have preceded it, sustains . . . close relations to the business interests of the country," then this change of business sentiment should not be discounted. This transformation brought important financial spokesmen, especially from the Northeast, into much the same position that had long been occupied by prointerventionist business groups and journals in the trans-Appalachian area. McKinley's decision to intervene placated many of the same business spokesmen whom he had satisfied throughout 1897 and January and February of 1898 by his refusal to declare war.

Five factors may be delineated which shaped this interventionist sentiment of the business community. First, some business journals emphasized the material advantages to be gained should Cuba become a part of the world in which the United States would enjoy, in the words of the New York *Commercial Advertiser*, "full freedom of development in the whole world's interest." The *Banker's Magazine* noted that "so many of our citizens are so involved in the commerce and productions of the island, that to protect these interests . . . the United States will have eventually to force the establishment of fair and reasonable government." The material damage suffered by investors in Cuba and by many merchants, manufacturers, exporters, and importers, as, for example, the groups which presented the February 10 petition to McKinley, forced these interests to advocate a solution which could be obtained only through force.

A second reason was the uncertainty that plagued the business community in mid-March. This uncertainty was increased by [Senator Redfield] Proctor's powerful and influential speech and by the news that a Spanish torpedo-boat flotilla was sailing from Cadiz to Cuba. The uncertainty was exemplified by the sudden stagnation of trade on the New York Stock Exchange after March 17. Such an unpredictable economic basis could not provide the springboard for the type of overseas commercial empire that McKinley and numerous business spokesmen envisioned.

Third, by March many businessmen who had deprecated war on the ground that the United States Treasury did not possess adequate gold reserves began to realize that they had been arguing from false assumptions. The heavy exports of 1897 and the discoveries of gold in Alaska and Australia brought the yellow metal into the country in an ever widening stream. Private bankers had been preparing for war since 1897. *Banker's Magazine* summarized these developments: "Therefore, while not desiring war, it is apparent that the country now has an ample coin basis for sustaining the credit operations which a conflict would probably make necessary. In such a crisis the gold standard will prove a bulwark of confidence."

Fourth, antiwar sentiment lost much strength when the nation realized that it had nothing to fear from European intervention on the side of Spain. France and Russia, who were most sympathetic to the Spanish monarchy, were forced to devote their attention to the Far

East. Neither of these nations wished to alienate the United States on the Cuban issue. More important, Americans happily realized that they had the support of Great Britain. The *rapprochement* which had occurred since the Venezuelan incident now paid dividends. On an official level, the British Foreign Office assured the State Department that nothing would be accomplished in the way of European intervention unless the United States requested such intervention. The British attitude made it easy for McKinley to deal with a joint European note of April 6 which asked for American moderation toward Spain. The President brushed off the request firmly but politely. On an unofficial level, American periodicals expressed appreciation of the British policy on Cuba, and some of the journals noted that a common Anglo-American approach was also desirable in Asia. The European reaction is interesting insofar as it evinces the continental powers' growing realization that the United States was rapidly becoming a major force in the world. But the European governments set no limits on American dealings with Spain. McKinley could take the initiative and make his demands with little concern for European reactions.

Finally, opposition to war melted away in some degree when the administration began to emphasize that the United States enjoyed military power much superior to that of Spain. One possible reason for McKinley's policies during the first two months of 1898 might have been his fear that the nation was not adequately prepared. As late as the weekend of March 25 the President worried over this inadequacy. But in late February and early March, especially after the $50,000,000 appropriation by Congress, the country's military strength developed rapidly. On March 13 the Philadelphia *Press* proclaimed that American naval power greatly exceeded that of the Spanish forces. By early April those who feared a Spanish bombardment of New York City were in the small minority. More representative were the views of Winthrop Chanler who wrote Lodge that if Spanish troops invaded New York "they would all be absorbed in the population . . . and engaged in selling oranges before they got as far as 14th Street."

As the words of McKinley's war message flew across the wires to Madrid, many business spokesmen who had opposed war had recently changed their minds, American military forces were rapidly growing more powerful, banks and the United States Treasury had secured themselves against the initial shocks of war, and the European powers were divided among themselves and preoccupied in the Far East. Business boomed after McKinley signed the declaration of war. "With a hesitation so slight as to amount almost to indifference," *Bradstreet's* reported on April 30, "the business community, relieved from the tension caused by the incubus of doubt and uncertainty which so long controlled it, has stepped confidently forward to accept the situation confronting it oweing to the changed conditions." "Unfavorable circumstances . . . have hardly excited remark, while the stimulating effects have been so numerous and important as to surprise all but the most optimistic," this journal concluded. A new type of American empire, temporarily clothed in armor, stepped out on the international stage after a half century of preparation to make its claim as one of the great world powers.

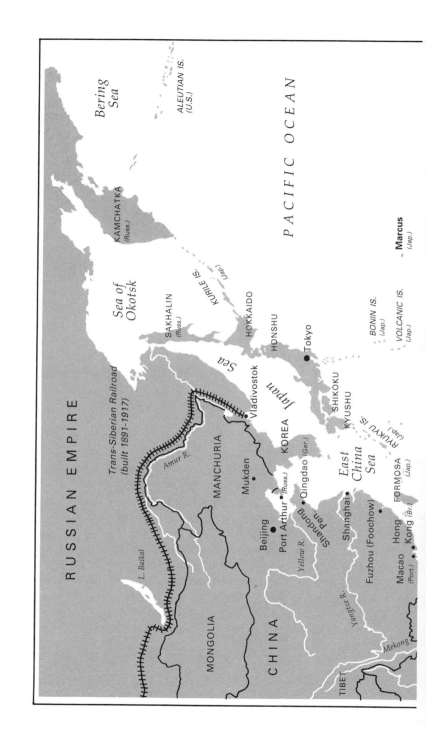

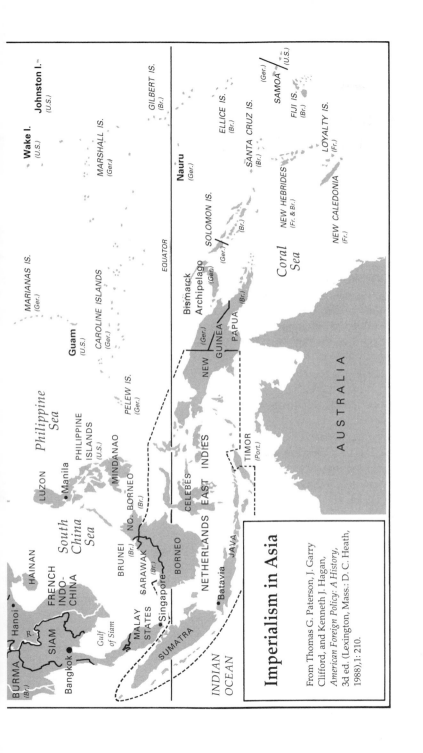

Imperialism in Asia

From Thomas G. Paterson, J. Garry Clifford, and Kenneth J. Hagan, *American Foreign Policy: A History,* 3d ed. (Lexington, Mass.: D. C. Heath, 1988),1: 210.

BURMA *(Br.)*
HAINAN
Hanoi
FRENCH INDO-CHINA
South China Sea
Philippine Sea
Wake I. *(U.S.)*
Johnston I. *(U.S.)*
SIAM
Bangkok
Gulf of Siam
LUZON
Manila
PHILIPPINE ISLANDS *(U.S.)*
MINDANAO
MARIANAS IS. *(Ger.)*
MARSHALL IS. *(Ger.)*
GILBERT IS. *(Br.)*
MALAY STATES
Singapore
BRUNEI *(Br.)*
SARAWAK *(Br.)*
NO. BORNEO *(Br.)*
CAROLINE ISLANDS *(Ger.)*
Guam *(U.S.)*
PELEW IS. *(Ger.)*
SUMATRA
Batavia
JAVA
BORNEO
CELEBES
NETHERLANDS EAST INDIES
TIMOR *(Port.)*
NEW GUINEA *(Ger.)*
PAPUA *(Br.)*
Bismarck Archipelago *(Ger.)*
EQUATOR
Nauru *(Ger.)*
SOLOMON IS. *(Ger.)* *(Br.)*
SANTA CRUZ IS. *(Br.)*
ELLICE IS. *(Br.)*
SAMOA *(Ger.)* *(U.S.)*
FIJI IS. *(Br.)*
NEW HEBRIDES *(Fr. & Br.)*
LOYALTY IS. *(Fr.)*
NEW CALEDONIA *(Fr.)*
Coral Sea
AUSTRALIA
INDIAN OCEAN

Thomas J. McCormick

INSULAR POSSESSIONS FOR THE CHINA MARKET

Thomas J. McCormick, a historian at the University of Wisconsin, Madison, agrees with Walter LaFeber that U.S. diplomats and members of the business community in the late 1890s were intensely concerned about America's commercial future. They grew alarmed when the European powers and Japan began to carve out spheres of influence in China's maritime areas and to impose discriminatory trade rules. In this selection from his book *China Market* (1967), McCormick argues that America's Pacific acquisitions of 1898—Hawaii, Wake, Guam, and the Philippines—were a means to an end. Americans coveted the large profits expected from the sale of American goods to the Chinese. In order to reach the China market, the United States needed "steppingstones" across the Pacific; the Philippines became central to this objective. Professor McCormick has also written *America's Half-Century: United States Foreign Policy in the Cold War* (1989).

America's insular acquisitions of 1898 were not products of "large policy" imperialism. Hawaii, Wake, Guam, and the Philippines were not taken principally for their own economic worth, or for their fulfillment of Manifest Destiny, or for their venting of the "psychic crisis." They were obtained, instead, largely in an eclectic effort to construct a system of coaling, cable, and naval stations for an integrated trade route which could help realize America's overriding ambition in the Pacific—the penetration and ultimate domination of the fabled China market.

From the very beginning of the Spanish-American War, the McKinley administration intended to retain a foothold in the Philippines as an "American Hong Kong," a commercial entrepôt to the China market and a center of American military power. Formulation of this policy commitment began seven months before hostilities with Spain, when McKinley examined a Navy Department memorandum written by Assistant Secretary Theodore Roosevelt. This multipurpose

From *China Market: America's Quest for Informal Empire, 1893–1901*, pp. 107–15, 117–20, 122–25, by Thomas J. McCormick. Footnotes omitted. Copyright © 1967 by Thomas J. McCormick. Reprinted by permission of Random House, Inc.

paper made one especially bold suggestion: in the event of war with Spain, the Asiatic Squadron "should blockade, and if possible take Manila." Historical myth notwithstanding, it was a suggestion that fell on already prepared ground, for the influential Senator from Connecticut, Orville Platt, had earlier taken pains to impress upon the President "that Manila had become one of the most important ports of the Orient and that the importance of that station demanded most careful attention."

Temporarily put in abeyance by a short-lived détente with Spain in late 1897, the proposal was revived and made the basis of Roosevelt's famous February 25 orders instructing Commodore George Dewey to "start offensive operations in the Philippines" after eliminating the Spanish fleet. The view that this was simply a conspiratorial effort by "large policy" extremists misses two more significant facts: first, Roosevelt's superiors accepted his orders for the Philippine operations even though they unceremoniously countermanded nearly two-thirds of the other miscellaneous orders issued concurrently by the Assistant Secretary; second, the administration had already accepted the substance of Dewey's orders in principle and thereafter permitted the Naval War Board to incorporate the February 25 orders into overall strategy plans for the Pacific. Clearly, while Roosevelt's actions may have been precipitate, they fell within the main lines of the "large policies" of the administration. Of these, Roosevelt, as he privately admitted, was largely "ignorant."

With the outbreak of war the McKinley administration rushed (with almost unseemly haste) to implement its designs upon the likeliest entrepôt, Manila, by determining to send an army of occupation to the Philippine capital. It made this decision on May 2 *before* fully credible news of Dewey's victory at Manila Bay reached Washington and it formally issued the call for Philippine volunteers on May 4, three days *before* an anxious, jittery Secretary of the Navy received authoritative word that the Asiatic Squadron was safe—not immobilized by heavy damages, as he feared. The size of the Army force was to be "not less than twenty thousand men"—quadruple the number recommended by Dewey "to retain [Manila] and thus control the Philippine Islands." It was a move that confirmed Roosevelt in his belief that "the Administration is now fully committed to the large policy." It also persuaded the *San Francisco Chronicle*, on May 4, to splash across its front page the prophetic headline: "WE WILL HOLD THE PHILIPPINES."

On May 11, in one of the most important (and overlooked) decision-making sessions in American history, McKinley and his cabinet gave definite form to their war aims in the Pacific by approving a State Department memorandum calling for Spanish cession to the United States of a suitable "coaling station," presumably Manila. The islands as a whole, however, were to remain with Spain. Acting within the framework of this decision, McKinley on May 19 endowed the commander of the expeditionary force with sufficiently broad powers to effect "the severance of the former political relations of the inhabitants and the establishment of a new political power." Simultaneously, he instructed his Secretary of the Treasury to undertake a study of the islands with an eye "to substitut[ing] new rates and new taxes for those now levied in the Philippines." The stated purpose of both orders, as well as a similar one to Dewey (which he was to "interpret . . . liberally"), was to "[give] to the islands, while in the possession of the United States, that order and security which they have long since ceased to enjoy." Shortly thereafter, on June 3, when it became apparent that the great distance between Manila and Honolulu demanded an intermediate coaling and cable station, the President broadened the American position to include "an island in the Ladrones" (Marianas). The choice made was Guam, and the United States Navy promptly seized it.

As of early June, then, the administration envisioned postwar control only of Manila and Guam as way stations to the orient. But dramatic events swiftly undercut this limited resolve and for a critical fortnight set American policy aimlessly adrift. First of all, as the State Department itself noted, the emergence of the Philippine "insurgents" as "an important factor" made it increasingly doubtful that the islands—minus Manila—could be returned to effective Spanish sovereignty. What then—bestow the largess of Philippine independence but with the stipulation of American control in Manila? Certainly it was within American power to impose such a solution upon the insurgents, by force if necessary. Moreover, the revolutionaries might even have accepted it peacefully, especially since they themselves had offered (as far back as November 1897) to turn over "two provinces and the Custom House at Manila" in exchange for an alliance against Spain (though theoretically these would not be permanent cessions but simply collateral pledges against eventual Filipino repayment for American aid). Nevertheless, relinquishing the rest of the islands ran counter to the administration belief that "if we evacuate, anarchy rules"; (as Dewey later noted) "The natives appear unable to govern."

This presumption that an independent Philippines would be strife-ridden and unstable raised, in turn, the most frightening spectre of all: European intervention, especially by Germany, who considered herself heir-apparent to Spain's insular empire in the Pacific. Actually, the threat was not to American designs on Manila—notwithstanding the Continental feeling that an American foothold in the islands would "complicate the Eastern Question" or the seemingly hostile presence of the German squadron in Manila harbor. Given Germany's diplomatic isolation, Europe's divisiveness, and England's pro-American stance, there was little likelihood of another 1895-type intercession to deprive the victor of his spoils. Germany herself made this clear on several fronts by mid-July. In Berlin one high-ranking German official assured Ambassador White "that Germany does not want large annexations and could not afford to take the Philippine Islands if they were offered her." And in London the German Ambassador told [Ambassador John] Hay that his government had "no disposition to interfere with or deprive [the United States] of [her] rights of conquest in any direction." It was on the basis of this and other collaborating evidence that Hay advised the President that he could "now make war or make peace without danger of disturbing the equilibrium of the world."

The real and continuing danger was German intervention against a weak, fledgling republic that might well render the isolated American position in Manila more vulnerable than useful. *This* was no chimera! By mid-June, Andrew White had already confirmed what the State Department feared: that Germany would use the expected "anarchy, confusion and insecurity under a 'Philippine Republic' " as an excuse "to secure a stronghold and centre of influence in that region." Less than a month later, Germany informed White (and Hay as well) that she expected "a few coaling stations" and "a naval base" in the Philippines (not to mention control of the Carolines and "predominant" influence in Samoa). Nor did the passage of time and the solidification of American intentions eliminate such German ambitions. Even after the armistice with Spain, rumors flowed freely that Germany still sought "the Sulu islands" in the southern Philippines—rumors given great credence by Assistant Secretary of State John Bassett Moore. And in late October the State Department continued to receive "trustworthy information" that if the United States failed to take all the Philippines, Germany has "every intention to establish a foothold there."

Rival intervention or nationalistic revolution: either could undermine American plans for Manila. Unable to decide on a course of action, American policy lay momentarily immobilized—at a time when the growing crisis in China itself least afforded the luxury of prolonged indecision. On the one hand, intensified rumors that Russia would close Talienwan to foreign commerce and that she regarded her southern Manchurian leases as "integral portions of Russian territory" weakened the already shaky underpinnings of the open door in that key commercial area. At the same time England's extension of her Hong Kong settlement and her monopolistic approach to Yangtze Valley developments seemed to indicate that nation's growing estrangement from her traditional open door approach, and threatened to leave American policy in China diplomatically isolated. In this deteriorating framework, any sustained impasse over Philippine policy incurred the risk of letting American hopes in China go by default. Against the formidable hosts of Philippine insurgency, German antagonism, and crisis in China, the limited American policy commitment of June 3 (for Manila and Guam) seemed an ineffectual one indeed. Realizing the situation, the McKinley administration in mid-June made a determined effort to break the bind by initiating three dramatic and interrelated moves in Hawaii, China, and the Philippines, designed to increase American influence and leverage in the western Pacific. . . .

By early June . . . the Philippine question and the general Far Eastern situation made it both propitious and imperative that the Hawaiian project be revived in the hope of strengthening America's hand in the Pacific basin (on the long-standing belief held by Mahan and many Americans that Hawaii was the key to "commercial and military control of the Pacific"). The ensuing debate on the joint congressional resolution was something of a dress rehearsal for the "great debate" that lay seven months ahead. It was predicated clearly on the assumption that passage of the Hawaiian annexation resolution made retention of the Philippines both possible and likely, while a defeat might foreshadow a similar fate for any territorial aspirations in the oriental archipelago. Congressman William Alden Smith made these and other links explicit with his statement, "If we will take the Hawaiian Islands, hold on to the Philippines, and cultivate good neighborship with the Orient, to which they are the key, the expansion of our commerce will be augmented a thousandfold."

In the actual debate, administration spokesmen hammered the same theme: "we must have Hawaii to help us get our share of China." America needed Hawaii not only for its own economic or cultural worth but also for its commercial and military value as a stepping-stone to the China market. The influential Iowa Representative, William P. Hepburn, captured the theme best when he declared: "I can distinguish between a colonial policy and a commercial policy. I can distinguish between the policy that would scatter colonies all over the islands of the sea and the lands of the earth and that policy which would secure to us simply those facilities of commerce that the new commercial methods make absolutely essential." . . .

Strikingly, even the opposition accepted the annexationists' chief premise that America needed commercial expansion into Asia. As one Democratic opponent on the House Foreign Affairs Committee put it, he favored "as earnestly as any man can the legitimate extension of our commerce"; nor was he "unmindful that the excessive production of our fields and factories must have an outlet." Some even admitted the modern necessity of commercial-military bases as accoutrements to marketplace expansionism, but they argued that the Pearl Harbor lease of 1886 and the Kiska holding in the Aleutians already gave "all the advantages, everything required." Most, however, stressed the laissez-faire, free-trade approach that "commercial expansion" could best be realized "by competition of quality and price," not by "annexation of territory"; in the words of the Minority Report of the House Foreign Affairs Committee: "Political dominion over the islands is not commercially necessary." But the point did not carry. On June 15 the House passed the annexation resolution by an overwhelming vote, 209 to 91. Three weeks later, after redundant and one-sided discussion (annexationists remained silent to hurry the process), the Senate affirmed the measure by a similar ratio. Thus, on July 8, with McKinley's signature, America acquired her halfway house to the Philippines and China. The acquisitions followed by only four days the American occupation of Wake Island, a move intended to meet the technological necessities of an additional cable base between Hawaii and Guam.

Synchronous with the push on Hawaiian annexation, the administration initiated the first step in an American economic offensive in China itself by proposing a government commission to China to recommend measures for trade expansion. Secretary of State

William R. Day's supporting letter to Congress made it pointedly clear that an industrial production "of large excess over home consumption" demanded "an enlargement of foreign markets." He also made clear his conviction that "American goods have reached a point of excellence" which made fulfillment of that demand quite feasible. Analyzing the world market situation, he concluded that underdeveloped areas offered the best export outlets and that "nowhere is this consideration of more interest than in its relation to the Chinese Empire." Aware that "the partition of commercial facilities" in China threatened America's "important interests," the Secretary still contended that "the United States . . . is in a position to invite the most favorable concessions to its industries and trade . . . provided the conditions are thoroughly understood and proper advantage is taken of the present situation."

Congress failed to appropriate the necessary monies for the China commercial commission—as it would again fail in 1899 and 1900. But the chief reason was most revealing. Most who opposed the measure did so because they considered such one-shot missions to be ineffectual and an inadequate substitute for a thoroughgoing reform of our consular representative in China (and elsewhere as well). Nevertheless, the administration proposal—when coupled with subsequent prodding of Minister [Edwin H.] Conger to gain more "Precise knowledge . . . of the large and grave questions of commercial intercourse," and with intensive questioning of American consuls as to specific means to expand the China trade—served clear notice of American intent to take "proper advantage . . . of the present situation" in order to play a more active role in China.

Simultaneously, on June 14 the administration capped its trio of dramatic moves by shelving the earlier decision to return the Philippines to Spain, thus opening the disposition of the islands to further examination. Thereafter, despite uneasiness over increased military and administrative burdens, there began a progressive redefinition of the desired area of American sovereignty: from Manila, to Luzon, and finally to the entire group. Significantly, this redefinition involved no real change in the focus of political power; those who influenced and made policy in June 1898 still did so at year's end. What changed was men's minds. . . .

In this evolution of Philippine policy, America's commercial stake in China played the primary role in the thinking of the business and government elite that chiefly shaped and supported McKinley's decisions. It also played a significant, though not paramount, part in the outlook of the military advisers who exercised a more limited but still crucial influence upon the President's policies.

Between June and October, economic and political leaders united vigorously in support of retaining all or a large part of the Philippines. But they de-emphasized the intrinsic worth of the islands and stressed instead their strategic relationship to China—both as a commercial stepping-stone and a political-military lever. Moreover, they increasingly affirmed that Manila alone would not suffice for these purposes, that the United States would have to take Luzon and perhaps the whole group. In part this support for enlarged control reflected the already pervasive fear that native revolution or European penetration might undermine the viability of American power in Manila. But it also indicated a growing belief, born of newly accumulated information, that the economic interdependence of the archipelago made efficient division most difficult. Charles H. Cramp, that renowned Philadelphia shipbuilder, aptly illustrated the impact of all these factors upon influential Americans when he asserted: "[Manila] is the emporium and the capital of the Philippines . . . and it exists because of that fact. . . . Can anyone suppose that with Manila in our hands and the rest of the Philippine territory under any other Government, that city would be of any value?"

In the business world many associations, journals, and prominent individuals accepted and propagated the analysis that commercial ambitions in China *demanded* American control in the Philippines. Led by the NAM [National Association of Manufacturers] and the American Asiatic Association, special business organizations urged retention of the islands "for the protection and furtherance of the commercial interests of our citizens in the Far East." In a survey of the trade journals of the country, the *Chicago Inter-Ocean* found it "remarkable with what unanimity they have advocated the retention of the Philippines." Even more remarkable was the unanimity of their reasoning: that (in the words of the *Insurance Advocate*) it would encourage "the teeming millions of the Middle Kingdom" to "buy largely from us"; that with "one-third of the human race within easy distance of us, coaling stations on the road, and Manila as the Hong Kong of Uncle Sam's alert and keen merchant trader," the result was preordained. Finally, save for a few prominent dissenters like Andrew Carnegie and Chauncey Depew, McKinley's many personal friends in the corporate world espoused similar viewpoints. . . .

Most of McKinley's close associates in the federal government (many of whom were themselves products of the business community) pressed similar views upon their chief. There were exceptions, of course. Worthington C. Ford, head of the Bureau of Statistics, appeared to feel (like former Minister to China George F. Seward) that *"We do not want the Philippines at any price or under any circumstances."* A few others like Judge Day held largely to the position (as Carl Schurz summarized it for the President) that "all desirable commercial facilities" and "all naval stations needed could be secured without the annexation of populous territories," without "dangerous political entanglements and responsibilities." But most thought and counseled otherwise. The redoubtable Mark Hanna, State Department economic expert Frederic Emory, Charles Denby and his successor Edwin Conger, Comptroller of the Currency Charles G. Dawes, Assistant Secretary of the Treasury Frank A. Vanderlip, to name a few, all shared in general the conviction (as Vanderlip stated) that an American-controlled Philippines would be "pickets of the Pacific, standing guard at the entrances to trade with the millions of China and Korea, French Indo-China, the Malay Peninsula, and the islands of Indonesia." By October, McKinley's cabinet—led by his new Secretary of State, John Hay—was nearly as one in voicing that sentiment. . . .

Exerting a more narrow influence upon McKinley's Philippine policy was a third group, the military. In general the President's military advisers shared the widespread concern over the strategic relationship of the archipelago to the Asian mainland. Yet, attracted by the siren's call of *imperium* (in which they would play a prominent role), many military spokesmen also promoted retention of the Philippines as the first step toward an expansive territorial imperialism. These hopes were dashed as McKinley refused to heed their advice for a general American advance into Micronesia and the islands of the South China Sea. But military advice could claim one significant result: it resolved the President's ambivalence (shared by the business and government elite) between taking Luzon or the entire group by convincing him that the islands were an indivisible entity; that strategically and economically they were interdependent and inseparable. Especially persuasive were the lengthy and articulate reports of Commander R. B. Bradford and General Francis V. Greene. Coming in late September and early October, they were a decisive fact in broadening McKinley's instructions. . . .

There can be no doubt that the Chinese question, illuminated by the opinion of business, government, and the military and by the growing crises in China, had a progressive impact upon the shaping of America's Philippine policy. Nowhere is this more dramatically apparent than in the private, candid, and lengthy exchange between McKinley and his peace commissioners at a White House meeting on September 16. The President, speaking somberly and with none of his frequent evasiveness, explained his reasons for retaining all or part of the islands. Almost all of them were negative, embraced with obvious reluctance. The *only* positive and assertive determinant was his conviction that "our tenure in the Philippines" offered the "commercial opportunity" to maintain the open door, a policy which McKinley defined as "no advantages in the Orient which are not common to all." "Asking only the open door for ourselves," he told his commissioners, "we are ready to accord the open door to others." Explaining further, he made it clear that retention of the Philippines was no first step in an orgy of imperialism and jingoism, but simply a limited though important accoutrement to commercial expansion. "The commercial opportunity . . . associated with this opening," he declared, "depends less on large territorial possessions than upon an adequate commercial basis and upon broad and equal privileges."

This last statement was more than mere rhetoric, and nothing proved it more than the President's policy in Micronesia during the last stages of peace negotiations with Spain. Acting on the advice of the Pacific Cable Company that Wake Island had certain technical drawbacks, the administration instructed its peace commissioners to negotiate for the purchase of "one of the Caroline Islands"—preferably Ualan (Kusaie)—"for cable purposes." Despite strong German protests that "Kusaie lies in the midst of German sphere" and that "Germany regards herself as the only competitor for the acquisition of the Carolines," the United States pressed on with its effort, offering Spain $1 million for the island and "cable-landing rights in other Spanish territory" (an offer which, in turn, provoked an even stronger German denunciation of the American "policy of seeking islands all over the world for coaling stations").

What happened next is most revealing. Declining the American offer, Spain made an even more dramatic counterproposal—the cession of *all* the Carolines and *all* the Marianas in exchange for open door status for Spain in Cuba and Puerto Rico. In so doing, Spain appeared to be playing directly into the hands of the Reid-Frye-Davis group (and some of the American military) who had favored total American control in those islands all along. (Indeed, Reid and Frye implied at one juncture a hope that Spain would break off peace negotiations, giving America an excuse to take the islands.) These three commissioners gave their enthusiastic endorsement to the project and asked for permission to negotiate along the lines of the Spanish proposal (though perhaps with a time limit on the open door for Spain). But McKinley and Hay refused to pay such a price for something they neither needed nor desired. Seeking only individual cable and coaling stations for limited purposes, they were in no way disposed to exercise indiscriminate sovereignty over numerous, widely dispersed islands; to plant the Stars and Stripes on every ocean-bound rock and pebble they could get. Hay rejected the Spanish offer out-of-hand by return cable on December 4, and there the matter died. . . .

Thus the peace negotiations with Spain, initiated in September within the conscious framework of the Chinese question, concluded three months later on an identical note. Article IV of the treaty made clear the intimacy that bound Philippine and China policy: McKinley would keep his earlier promise to accord the open door in the Philippines, provided the United States received reciprocal treatment elsewhere in the orient. In actuality, this American open door was limited in time and scope, and it later vanished in the midst of emerging American economic aspirations in the Philippines themselves. But for the moment administration spokesmen regarded the proviso as *key* to future American policy in the Far East. Assistant Secretary of State A. A. Adee, that permanent fixture in the Department, stated unequivocally that "the open door paragraph is the most important"; and Whitelaw Reid, the peace commission's most powerful figure, insisted the open door for the Philippines "enables Great Britain and the United States to preserve a common interest and present a common front in the enormous development in the Far East that must attend the awakening of the Chinese Colossus."

The final treaty arrangements on the Philippines were the outgrowth of an evolving set of circumstances dating back to 1895, when the combined impact of the American depression and the Sino-Japanese War offered both the need and the hope that China might become the great absorber of America's industrial surplus. Subsequent developments, culminating in the partitioning of late 1897 and early 1898, critically threatened the hope but in no way dissipated the need. They did, however, dictate the desirability of finding some vigorous means of safeguarding America's present and future commercial stake in the Chinese Empire. Fortunately, the Spanish-American War provided just such an opportunity, and the McKinley administration was quick to exploit it. The result was the effective thrust of American influence into the far Pacific. From Honolulu through Wake and Guam to Manila stretched a chain of potential coaling, cable, and naval stations to serve as America's avenue to Asia. Only the construction of an isthmian canal remained to complete the system.

The grand scheme was not imperial—in the narrow sense of the word. The insular possessions in the Pacific were not pieces of empire, per se, but stepping-stones and levers to be utilized upon a larger and more important stage—China. Paradoxically, American expansion was designed in part to serve an anti-imperial purpose of preventing the colonization of China and thus preserving her for open door market penetration: *the imperialism of anti-imperialism* ("neo-colonialism" in today's parlance). All this McKinley captured in his Presidential Message of December 5, 1898, when he declared that our "vast commerce . . . and the necessity of our staple production for Chinese uses" had made the United States a not "indifferent spectator of the extraordinary" partitioning in China's maritime provinces. Nevertheless, he continued, so long as "no discriminatory treatment of American . . . trade be found to exist . . . the need for our country becoming an actor in the scene" would be "obviated." But, he concluded, the fate of the open door would not be left to chance; it would be, he said, "my aim to subserve our large interests in that quarter by all means appropriate to the constant policy of our government." Quite obviously, the fruits of the Spanish-American War had enormously multiplied the "appropriate . . . means" available to American policy-makers and had completed the setting for America's illusory search after that holy commercial grail—the China market.

William Appleman Williams

THE OPEN DOOR POLICY AND CHINA

The late William Appleman Williams (1921–1990) was one of the first historians to argue that the United States acquired imperial outposts in the
Pacific to facilitate access to the China market. In the following essay from
his highly influential book *The Tragedy of American Diplomacy*, Williams
analyzes how the United States, having obtained strategic bases, formulated a new policy designed to protect China and U.S. trade from the imperial European powers and Japan. In the Open Door Notes of 1899 and
1900, the United States called for the preservation of China's territorial
integrity and for equal commercial opportunity for all nations. Williams
considers the Open Door policy a very sophisticated and calculated effort
to make China part of America's "informal empire" of free trade and
investment. Through the use of its preponderant economic power, Americans forecast, the United States would overawe foreign competitors and
extend the American way of life throughout China. In Williams's view,
moreover, in the twentieth century the Open Door policy of equal trade
opportunity became the driving ideological force behind U.S. expansionism
into what is now called the Third World. Williams taught at the University
of Wisconsin and Oregon State University. Among his many books are
America Confronts a Revolutionary World, 1776 1976 (1976), *The Roots of
the Modern American Empire* (1969), and *The Contours of American History* (1961).

American leaders went to war with Spain as part of, and as the consequence of, a general outlook which externalized the opportunity and
the responsibility for America's domestic welfare; broadly in terms of
vigorous overseas economic expansion into Latin America and Asia;
and specifically in terms of Spain's inability to pacify Cuba by means
(and within time limits) acceptable to the United States, and the separate but nevertheless related necessity of acting in Asia to prevent the
exclusion of American interests from China.

This basic *Weltanschauung* [world view] underlying American
diplomacy led directly to the great debate of 1898–1901 over the
proper strategy and tactics of such expansion, a debate that was

resolved by the promulgation of the famous Open Door Notes of 1899 and 1900. This national argument is usually interpreted as a battle between imperialists led by Roosevelt and Lodge and anti-imperialists led by William Jennings Bryan, Grover Cleveland, and Carl Schurz. It is far more accurate and illuminating, however, to view it as a three-cornered fight. The third group was a coalition of businessmen, intellectuals, and politicians who opposed traditional colonialism and advocated instead a policy of an open door through which America's preponderant economic strength would enter and dominate all underdeveloped areas of the world. This coalition won the debate, and the Open Door Policy became the strategy of American foreign policy for the next half-century.

Discounted in recent years as a futile and naive gesture in a world of harsh reality, the Open Door Policy was in fact a brilliant strategic stroke which led to the gradual extension of American economic and political power throughout the world. If it ultimately failed, it was not because it was foolish or weak, but because it was so successful. The empire that was built according to the strategy and tactics of the Open Door Notes engendered the antagonisms created by all empires. . . .

In particular, the long "Review of the World's Commerce," prepared by the State Department's Bureau of Foreign Commerce and dated April 25, 1898, made it apparent that the McKinley Administration understood quite clearly the basic features of the expansionist outlook advocated by Brooks Adams and other unofficial spokesmen. The central and common assumptions as phrased by the Department of State were that "the ability of the United States to compete successfully with the most advanced industrial nations in any part of the world, as well as with those nations in their home markets, can no longer be seriously questioned," and that "every year we shall be confronted with an increasing surplus of manufactured goods for sale in foreign markets if American operatives and artisans are to be kept employed the year around."

This meant very simply that "the enlargement of foreign consumption of the products of our mills and workshops has, therefore, become a serious problem of statesmanship." The "zealous co-operation" of government officials acting under "special instructions" to help private companies was naturally necessary, and had already been undertaken. But the essence of the problem was to devise a strategy that would prevent other industrial powers from pre-empting the underdeveloped areas of the world. "We ourselves have become a competitor in the world-wide struggle for trade," the Department emphasized, and proceeded to define the regions of crucial importance.

China was of course given first attention: it "has, for many years, been one of the most promising fields for American enterprise, industry, and capital." Access to that market, "under conditions which would secure equality of opportunity to the United States, would doubtless result in immense gains to our manufacturers." Thus it was mandatory to prevent Japan and the European powers from excluding the United States: that was an "immediate and most important" objective. But any similar partition of Africa raised "considerations of an economic character of almost equal magnitude," as did any drive by the nations of Europe to enlarge their economic position in Latin America.

Feeling that "nowhere else" were such matters "of more interest" than in China, and very worried about the "large excesses above the demands of home consumption," Secretary of State [William R.] Day initiated, in June 1898, a special study of the China situation. As such actions indicated, the McKinley Administration was very pointedly and vigorously dealing with the issue of overseas economic expansion without waiting for the end of the debate about imperialism.

All of the elements that went into the making of the Open Door Policy converged within the McKinley Administration as the President appointed his commission to make peace with Spain. Acting individually, and through groups such as the American Asiatic Association and the N. A. M., private economic operators pressured the government with their desires and recommendations. John Hay was appointed Secretary of State in the fall of 1898, and that gave the Adams-Lodge-Roosevelt group an additional lever of influence for their ideas. And McKinley himself made it obvious that the administration already had the central idea of the final policy it was to evolve. For in his instructions to the peace commission of September 16, 1898, he specifically defined the broad issue as "the enlargement of American trade" in the Orient. Then, after discounting the necessity of acquiring "large territorial possessions," in order to win such trade, he explicitly used the phrase "the open door for ourselves" to describe the preferred strategy.

This is of course significant as well as striking, for the first of the Open Door Notes was not written until 1899. It remains so even after recalling that the central idea of obtaining "equality with all competing nations in the conditions of access to the markets" had provided the basis of American policy at the time of the International Conference on the Congo held in Berlin during the winter of 1884–85. For in that situation, as in Asia in 1897–99, the United States confronted rivals who already had spheres of influence or formal colonies. In any event, the point is not to provide some artificial birthday for the policy of the open door, but rather to indicate how the policy emerged from the interplay between private and public leaders.

Perhaps nothing illustrates this as neatly as the way that the arguments inside McKinley's peace commission brought out almost every shade of opinion. Even so, everyone agreed that the United States had at the very least to retain a port and a naval base. Three considerations seem to have convinced the administration to keep all the Philippines. For one thing, the crisis caused by the native rebellion was most easily—though by no means most successfully—resolved in that fashion. In another way, the serious inherent difficulties of keeping the main island of Luzon, or the key city of Manila, without disrupting the political economy of the remainder of the islands soon became apparent even to those who originally favored that kind of solution. And finally, the vigor of German and other expansionism in China exerted considerable influence on the thinking of the administration.

Though many of them felt that they had suffered a terrible defeat in the decision to retain the Philippines, the anti-imperialists actually won their domestic war over fundamental policy with the issuance of the Open Door Notes. Hay's dispatches of 1899 and 1900 distilled the conglomeration of motives, pressures, and theories into a classic strategy of non-colonial imperial expansion. Based on the assumption of what Brooks Adams called "America's economic supremacy," the policy of the open door was designed to clear the way and establish the conditions under which America's preponderant economic power would extend the American system throughout the world without the embarrassment and inefficiency of traditional colonialism. As Hay indicated with obvious anticipation and confidence in September 1899, the expectation was that "we shall bring the sweat to their brows."

Hay's first note of September 6, 1899, asserted the proposition that American entrepreneurs "shall enjoy perfect equality of treatment for their commerce and navigation" within all of China—*including the spheres of interest held by foreign powers*. That principle was soon extended to other underdeveloped areas. His second note of July 3, 1900, was designed to prevent other nations from extending the formal colonial system to China. That axiom was also applied to other regions in later years. Hay also circulated a third dispatch among the powers. Though rarely linked with the first two in discussions of the Open Door Notes, it was nevertheless an integral part of the general policy statement. In that document, Hay made it plain that the United States considered loans to be an inherent part of commerce. The connection was always implicit, if not rather obvious. "It is impossible to separate these two forms of business activity," as one businessman remarked at the time, "since it is axiomatic that trade follows the loan." The relationship was also and without any question in the minds of American policy-makers when the first notes were written, since such loans were being sought and discussed as early as 1897. Hay's purpose was to close every formal loophole through which America's competitors might seek to counter the strategy of the open door.

The Open Door Notes took the substance out of the debate between the imperialists and the anti-imperialists. The argument trailed on with the inertia characteristic of all such disagreements, but the nation recognized and accepted Hay's policy as a resolution of the original issue. Former Secretary of State John W. Foster summarized this point quite accurately in the *Independent* at the end of 1900. "Whatever difference of opinion may exist among American citizens respecting the policy of territorial expansion, all seem to be agreed upon the desirability of commercial expansion. In fact it has come to be a necessity to find new and enlarged markets for our agricultural and manufactured products. We cannot maintain our present industrial prosperity without them."

It took some years (and agitation) to liquidate the colonial status of the territory seized during the war against Spain. It also required time to work out and institutionalize a division of authority and labor between economic and political leaders so that the strategy could be put into operation on a routine basis. And it was necessary to open the door into existing colonial empires as well as unclaimed territories. . . .

Americans of that era and their European competitors were basically correct in their estimate of the Open Door Policy. It was neither an alien idea foisted off on America by the British nor a political gesture to disarm domestic dissidents. Latter-day experts who dismissed the policy as irrelevant, misguided, or unsuccessful erred in two respects. They missed its deep roots in the American past and its importance at the time, and they failed to realize that the policy expressed the basic strategy and tactics of America's imperial expansion in the twentieth century. When combined with the ideology of an industrial Manifest Destiny, the history of the Open Door Notes became the history of American foreign relations from 1900 to 1958.

The most dramatic confluence of these currents of ideological and economic expansion did not occur until the eve of American entry into World War I. For this reason, among others, it is often asserted that the United States did not take advantage of the Open Door Policy until after 1917, and some observers argue that the policy never led to the rise of an American empire. In evaluating the extent to which Americans carried through on the strategy of the Open Door Notes, there are two broad questions at issue with regard to statistics of over-seas economic expansion, and they cannot be mixed up without confusing the analysis and the interpretation. One concerns the over-all importance of such expansion to the national economy. The answer to that depends less upon gross percentages than upon the role in the American economy of the industries which do depend in significant ways (including raw materials as well as markets) on foreign operations. Measured against total national product, for example, the export of American cars and trucks seems a minor matter. But it is not possible at one and the same time to call the automobile business the key industry in the economy and then dismiss the fact that approximately 15 per cent of its total sales in the 1920s were made in foreign markets.

The other major point concerns the role of such foreign enterprises and markets in the making of American foreign policy. This effect can be direct in terms of domestic political pressure, or indirect through the results of the American overseas economic activity on the foreign policy of other nations. In the broadest sense of gross statistics, moreover, the overseas economic expansion of the United States from 1897 to 1915 is more impressive than many people realize. Loans totaled over a billion dollars. Direct investments amounted to $2,652,300,000. While it is true that the nation also owed money abroad during the same period, that point is not too important to an understanding of American foreign policy. For the loans and the investments had a bearing on American foreign policy even though balance of payment computations reduce the net figure. Businessmen with interests in Mexico or Manchuria, for example, did not stop trying to influence American policy (or cease having an effect on Mexican or Asian attitudes) just because their investments or loans or sales were arithmetically canceled out by the debt incurred by other Americans in France.

Another misleading approach emphasizes the point that America's overseas economic expansion amounted to no more than 10 or 12 per cent of its national product during those years. But 10 per cent of any economic operation is a significant proportion; without it the enterprise may slide into bankruptcy. In that connection, the most recent studies by economists reveal that exports did indeed spark recovery from the depression of the 1890s. In any event, the businessmen and other economic groups *thought* the 10 per cent made a crucial difference, and many of them concluded that they could not get it in any way but through overseas expansion.

Other considerations aside, the conviction of these groups would make the figure important if it were only one per cent. Or, to make the point even clearer (and historically accurate), it would still be significant if all an entrepreneur did was to pressure the government to support an effort that failed. In that case the economic indicators would be negative, but the relevance to foreign policy might be very high. Such was precisely the case, for example, with the America-China Development Company. It ultimately disappeared from the scene, but before it died it exerted an extensive influence on American policy in Asia during the first decade of the twentieth century.

In another way, overseas economic operations which seem small on paper may mean the difference between survival and failure to a given firm. Faced by the near-monopoly control over key raw materials exercised by the United States Steel Corporation after 1903, Charles Schwab had to go to Chile to get the ore supplies that were necessary to sustain the Bethlehem Steel Company. Schwab's investment was only 35 million dollars, but it played a vital role in his own affairs and exercised a significant influence on Chilean-American relations. Or, to reverse the example, economic activity which seems incidental judged by American standards is often fundamental to a weaker economy. This aspect of the problem can be illustrated by the situation in Manchuria between 1897 and 1904, where approximately one-tenth of one per cent of America's national product gave the Americans who were involved a major role in the affairs of that region, and provoked them to agitate vigorously for official American support. Their efforts were successful and led to crucial developments in American foreign policy.

This facet of the Open Door Policy bears directly on the argument that the open door did not actually create an American empire. Leaving aside the question-begging approach which evades the issue by defining empire solely and narrowly in terms of seventeenth- or nineteenth-century colonialism, the problem is not very difficult to resolve. When an advanced industrial nation plays, or tries to play, a controlling and one-sided role in the development of a weaker economy, then the policy of the more powerful country can with accuracy and candor only be described as imperial.

The empire that results may well be informal in the sense that the weaker country is not ruled on a day-to-day basis by resident administrators, or increasingly populated by emigrants from the advanced country, but it is nevertheless an empire. The poorer and weaker nation makes its choices within limits set, either directly or indirectly, by the powerful society, and often does so by choosing between alternatives actually formulated by the outsider. And not only was the Open Door Policy designed to establish the conditions whereby the economic and political power of the United States could be deployed in that manner, it was exercised in that pattern in Asia, Latin America, and Africa. In Canada and Europe, too, for that matter.

Even the implicit dynamic of the policy worked to create the imperial relationship. Let it be assumed, for example, that American policy-makers were not at the time conscious of their superiority or of the expected consequences of that advantage. Then it could be argued that all they wanted was an open marketplace in the tradition of laissez faire; and that such a marketplace would reproduce a relatively pluralistic and balanced political economy in the poorer and weaker societies. But even under the most favorable circumstances, as in the United States during the nineteenth century, the competition of laissez faire produced giant entrepreneurs who dominated the little operators or squeezed them out of the marketplace.

In the case of the underdeveloped nations, furthermore, the conditions were anything but ideal for laissez faire, even in the short-run. For not only were the outside operators already giants both absolutely and relatively, but they worked with and through the most powerful elements in the weaker country. This served, as in Asia and Latin America, to create anything but a pluralistic and balanced society. In all respects, therefore, it seems accurate and fair to describe the strategy of the Open Door Notes as imperial in nature, and as leading to the rise of a modern American empire. That the empire had some positive features is not to be denied; its existence is the issue under discussion at this point.

It is impossible, in short, to judge the bearing of overseas economic expansion upon American diplomacy—and thus to judge the importance and efficacy of the Open Door Policy—in terms of gross statistics. The important factors are the relative significance of the activity and the way it is interpreted and acted upon by people and groups who at best are only vaguely symbolized by abstract aggregate statistics. And by these criteria there is no question about the great relevance for diplomacy of America's proposed and actual overseas economic expansion between 1893 and 1915—and throughout the rest of the twentieth century.

Still another interpretation which discounts the significance of the Open Door Policy is based upon America's failure to exercise full control over Japanese and Russian activity in Asia. Though perhaps the strongest argument of its type, it nevertheless fails to establish its basic thesis. Three considerations undermine is conclusions: (1) the Open Door Policy was designed to secure and preserve access to China for American economic power, not to deny access to other nations; (2) America's difficulties with Russia and Japan between 1899 and 1918 stemmed from a failure of judgment concerning the execution of the policy, not from a flaw in the policy itself; and (3) the United States acted with considerable effectiveness between 1915 and 1918 to limit Japan's exploitation of America's earlier error.

In summation, the true nature and full significance of the Open Door Policy can only be grasped when its four essential features are fully understood.

First: it was neither a military strategy nor a traditional balance-of-power policy. *It was conceived and designed to win the victories without the wars.* In a truly perceptive and even noble sense, the makers of the Open Door Policy understood that war represented the failure of policy. Hence it is irrelevant to criticize the Open Door Policy for not emphasizing, or not producing, extensive military readiness.

Second: it was derived from the proposition that America's overwhelming economic power could cast the economy and the politics of the poorer, weaker, underdeveloped countries in a pro-American mold. American leaders assumed the opposition of one or many industrialized rivals. Over a period of two generations the policy failed because some of those competitors, among them Japan and Germany, chose to resort to force when they concluded (on solid grounds) that the Open Door Policy was working only too well; and because various groups inside the weaker countries such as China and Cuba decided that America's extensive influence in and upon their societies was harmful to their specific and general welfare.

Third (and clearly related to the second point): the policy was neither legalistic nor moralistic in the sense that those criticisms are usually offered. It was extremely hard-headed and practical. In some respects, at any rate, it was the most impressive intellectual achievement in the area of public policy since the generation of the Founding Fathers.

Fourth: unless and until it, and its underlying *Weltanschauung*, were modified to deal with its own consequences, the policy was certain to produce foreign policy crises that would become increasingly severe. The ultimate failures of the Open Door Policy, in short, are the failures generated by its success in guiding Americans in the creation of an empire.

Once these factors are understood, it becomes useful to explore the way that ideological and moralistic elements became integrated with the fundamentally secular and economic nature of the Open Door Policy. The addition of those ingredients served to create a kind of expansionism that aimed at the marketplace of the mind and the polls as well as of the pocketbook.

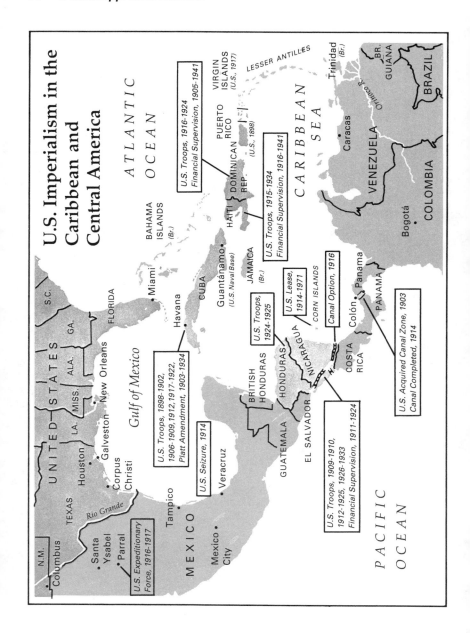

U.S. Imperialism in the
Caribbean and
Central America

David F. Healy

THE U.S. DRIVE TO HEGEMONY IN THE CARIBBEAN

In his discussion of the Open Door policy and China, William A. Williams argued that the United States used the war with Spain as a springboard for a vigorous foreign policy after 1900. The United States proclaimed especially bold, new policies in the circum-Caribbean area. In the following selection from his book *Drive to Hegemony*, David F. Healy explores how Americans began to transform the Caribbean into a U.S. lake. President Theodore Roosevelt, an ardent imperialist who believed that stability in the region was vital to U.S. security and economic growth, declared in 1904 that the United States would exercise "international police power" in the Western Hemisphere. This so-called Roosevelt Corollary to the Monroe Doctrine served to justify more than thirty armed interventions in the Caribbean during the following three decades. Professor Healy, who teaches history at the University of Wisconsin, Milwaukee, has also written *Gunboat Diplomacy in the Wilson Era: The U.S. Navy in Haiti, 1915 1916* (1976), *U.S. Expansionism: The Imperialist Urge in the 1890s* (1970), and *The United States in Cuba, 1898 1902* (1963).

The new strategic view of the Caribbean began to emerge clearly in a report submitted to the secretary of the navy by the navy's General Board in 1898, shortly after the Spanish-American War. The General Board was an advisory committee created during the war to do strategic analysis and planning, with Captain A. T. Mahan as its most prominent member. Though abandoned after the war, it was recreated on a permanent basis early in 1900 under the chairmanship of Admiral George Dewey, the victor of Manila Bay, and long remained the navy's chief center for strategic thought. The original board's final report in 1898 laid out some of the navy's basic thinking. The Caribbean, the board declared, was the most strategic single region for the United States, for it was there that hostile naval powers could most seriously threaten U.S. interests. From the first, naval strategists believed that no European power could defeat the United States in its own

From *Drive to Hegemony: The United States in the Caribbean, 1898–1917*, pp. 97–103, 106–109, by David F. Healy. Footnotes omitted. Copyright © 1988. Reprinted by permission of The University of Wisconsin Press.

hemisphere without securing a Caribbean base of operations. Furthermore, the report assumed that an isthmian canal was now a national necessity, and therefore certain to be built. Once such a canal existed, the Caribbean, already vital to the United States, would assume "surpassing influence" in the affairs of the rest of the world as well. Thus a completed isthmian canal would almost automatically draw in European rivalry and threats, the board members thought, while Germany soon emerged in American eyes as the leading European rival. The navy's top priorities were therefore to protect the future isthmian canal, and to prevent the appearance in the Caribbean of either European or local threats to the position of the United States.

The Caribbean is a landlocked sea, entered through a few main channels between the islands of the West Indies. By far the most important of these was the Windward Passage between Cuba and Hispaniola; others included the Yucatán Passage at the western end of Cuba, the Mona Passage between Hispaniola and Puerto Rico, and the Anegada Passage between the Virgin Islands and the Leeward Islands. In 1898 the General Board recommended the development of a chain of bases to guard these channels, plus the establishment of additional strong points along the isthmus and on the Pacific coast of Central America. The board's report suggested several acquisitions for this purpose: Saint Thomas in the Virgin Islands, then known as the Danish West Indies, or alternatively Samaná Bay in Santo Domingo; a base at Guantánamo Bay or Santiago in Cuba; Almirante Bay in Panamá; and a Pacific coast base yet to be selected. During the next decade, other possible base areas were added to the original list, including Port Elena in Costa Rica, the Pearl Islands in the Gulf of Panamá, Havana and Cienfuegos in Cuba, Chimbote in Peru, and Ecuador's Galápagos Islands, which lay some eight hundred miles out in the Pacific from Panamá.

Secretary of State John Hay gave serious attention to the navy's wishes, and for some years the exploration of possible base acquisitions was a routine chore at the State Department. Ultimately, the navy's chiefs had second thoughts about spreading their bases broadcast. Each would have to be defended, and the resulting dispersal of forces would contradict the fundamental principle of concentration. By 1903 the General Board, under the vigorous leadership of Admiral Dewey, was moving rapidly toward the concept of only a few bases in key positions. This essentially strategic decision was reinforced by the reluctance of Congress to appropriate funds for base development, and the board eventually narrowed its emphasis to Cuba. That island alone dominated two of the major outlets of the Caribbean, while the terms of the Platt Amendment already guaranteed the navy one or more bases there. Guantánamo Bay on the Windward Passage was by far the best base site in Cuba, but the General Board decided that the navy should have others at Havana, Cienfuegos, and Nipe Bay as well. Both John Hay and Theodore Roosevelt gave full support to these demands, but the Cubans were adamantly opposed to an American naval presence at Havana, while showing impressive skill at evading most of the other claims. In a 1903 treaty, Cuba finally ceded base rights at Guantánamo, and at Bahía Honda on the north coast west of Havana. Considering the latter site of little value, however, the Americans traded it off in the end for an enlarged naval reservation at Guantánamo Bay. Thus the result of several years of naval planning and diplomatic negotiation was one major Caribbean base at Guantánamo, and very little else. The quest for American bases had been largely converted to a determination to prevent the development of potentially hostile bases, especially on the part of Germany.

This did not mean that concern for canal security had abated; rather, thinking as to how to achieve that goal continued to evolve. The navy believed from the beginning that overall fleet strength was more important for canal defense than either regional naval bases or canal fortifications. American fleet strength had grown dramatically in the years after the war with Spain; sixteen new battleships were commissioned from 1899 to the end of 1906. These, with the four prewar battleships, gave the United States a total of twenty, to be supplemented by a continuing program of new construction. If these twenty American battleships looked modest in 1906 compared with Great Britain's forty-nine, they matched the strength of any other navy; Japan had eleven, France twelve, and Germany, like the United States, twenty. In the years after 1906, Germany and the United States vied for second place in fleet strength. Although the Germans would pull ahead by the First World War, the Americans still held the advantage in their own home waters. . . .

Military and naval thinking varied somewhat regarding the details of Caribbean defense, and both services changed their planning in some respects over time. The central themes were constant, however, and civilian policy makers were as loyal to them as service leaders. As Secretary of War Elihu Root wrote in 1902, "The great thing is to recognize the inevitable trend and consequences of American public policy in the large sense, which must certainly bring the West Indies . . . under the political and naval control of the United States." Root's view was to be the general one, as Americans assumed that the United States had become, and must remain, supreme in the Caribbean.

Washington was not long, however, in perceiving a new challenge to its Caribbean supremacy. During the very months in which the Roosevelt administration was negotiating the abortive Hay-Herrán Treaty with Colombia in its attempt to acquire the Panama Canal Zone, it became involved in the second Venezuelan crisis. As the first Venezuelan crisis, that of 1895–96, had reflected American fears of an expansionist Britain, this 1902 crisis was closely tied to burgeoning suspicions of Germany, as well as generalized American security fears in the Caribbean. The episode forced Theodore Roosevelt into some rapid policy formulation, and ultimately resulted in a formal claim of United States hegemony in the region. Like so many Caribbean crises, it stemmed from the failure of a local government to pay its European debts, and the consequent resort to gunboat diplomacy by the Europeans involved.

Venezuela's foreign obligations took several forms. Its government had floated large loans in London in 1881 and in Berlin in 1896, together totaling over five and one quarter million pounds sterling, which went into complete default in 1901. There were also snowballing damage claims by foreign citizens who had suffered harm in person or property from the civil strife which regularly erupted in that country. Also, from 1901 on, Venezuelan gunboats seized a number of small British-flag coasters from Trinidad which plied local waters, charging them with smuggling and revolutionary activity. And finally, railroad promoters and other European businessmen were increasingly involved in disputes with the Venezuelan government. Mounting British and German protests about these issues were rebuffed by Venezuela's feisty and xenophobic President Cipriano Castro, who ruled his country with a strong hand and showed open contempt for the rest of the world. The German government was considering forcible measures by 1901, and made a point of getting an early clearance from Theodore Roosevelt. Sounded out by his old friend Hermann Speck von Sternberg of the kaiser's diplomatic service, Roosevelt warned against any attempt at territorial aggrandizement, but had no objection to the proper punishment of Castro's misdeeds. "If any South American State misbehaves toward any European country," he wrote Sternberg, "let the European country spank it; but I do not wish the United States or any other country to get additional territory in South America."

The British government, which was also considering forcible action against Castro's regime, repeatedly inquired in Berlin about German intentions. In the summer of 1902 the Germans proposed a joint naval intervention by the two powers, and since Castro had now refused even to acknowledge any of the numerous British notes of protest, London agreed. The new allies decided not to seize Venezuelan customhouses for fear of antagonizing the United States. Instead they would seize or immobilize the gunboats which constituted Venezuela's navy, and if necessary impose a naval blockade of that country's coast. The powers duly notified the United States government of their intention, giving assurance that they would seize no territory. Secretary of State Hay replied in November 1902 that his government could not object to the redress of injury, though it regretted the need to use force, and repeated the usual strictures against taking possession of territory.

By December 7 the two capitals had agreed upon parallel ultimata and delivered them to Caracas. Anglo-German naval forces were already at hand, and when the twenty-four-hour deadline for the satisfaction of demands expired without an answer, the Europeans launched their campaign against the Venezuelan navy. On December 20 the powers implemented a full coastal blockade, while the government of Italy presented its own demands to Castro and withdrew its diplomats from the capital. Rather than giving in to the formidable coalition ranged against him, President Castro astutely asked the United States to arbitrate the dispute. Though Castro was as unpopular in the United States as in Europe, and faced protests from Washington too, he rightly guessed that the Americans would be uneasy at the allies' use of force, and would prefer to substitute their own initiatives for those from across the Atlantic. A German cruiser had already sunk two Venezuelan gunboats, while a pair of warships, one belonging to each ally, had shelled and destroyed a coastal fort with the aid of landing parties. The American press had fully reported these events, while public opinion in the Great Republic grew restive.

President Roosevelt too reacted strongly, though he had given the punitive enterprise his prior approval. While no one seemed seriously alarmed about British motives, the navy had been suspicious from the first of German designs in Venezuela. Beginning early in

"Room for All, if They're Careful," 1904. An athletic President Theodore Roosevelt demanded order in Latin America to ensure U.S. hegemony. (*New York Herald, 1904*)

1901, naval commanders in the Caribbean had forwarded persistent reports of a German scheme to acquire the island of Margarita, which lay near the Venezuelan coast about one hundred and fifty miles west of Trinidad. The State Department made official inquiries about these rumors, but the navy remained unconvinced by Berlin's denial that they were true. So, presumably, did the president, who ordered the navy to prepare a base of operations at Culebra, a small island belonging to Puerto Rico, "in case of sudden war."

When word reached America of plans for an Anglo-German intervention in Venezuela, naval commanders reacted with alarm. In a memorandum to the president written in late November 1902, Admiral Henry C. Taylor drew some grim conclusions about the action's probable results. The forcible debt-collecting action, Taylor believed, was likely to lead to war between Germany and Venezuela. While the Germans did not seek such a war, it might well be thrust upon them by the fiery Castro, and to preserve their prestige they must win a clear-cut victory. Having done so, they would probably demand indemnity, and given Venezuela's empty treasury this must necessarily take the form either of territory or a lien on Venezuelan revenues, both equally unacceptable to the United States. The result would be a dangerous confrontation between the United States and Germany.

In light of these risks, the memo argued, Washington must not tolerate Germany's occupation of any Venezuelan port or fortification which could be useful to her in a war with the United States. Furthermore, the navy should maintain a force in readiness at Culebra large enough to match the German forces in the Caribbean. If Germany sent troops to the region, American troops in corresponding strength should be sent to Puerto Rico. "Our aim must be at all times to be in a better state of preparation for war than Germany is, and her every move must be met by corresponding preparatory action on our part."

A combination of these naval warnings and his own deep-seated suspicions led Roosevelt to regret his approval of the Venezuelan intervention almost as soon as it got under way, and to push for the arbitration which Castro had requested. Late in December he wrote a friend that "the chances of complication from a long and irritating little war between the European powers and Venezuela were sufficiently great to make me feel most earnestly that the situation should be brought to a peaceful end if possible." By a useful coincidence, large-scale fleet exercises had already been scheduled in the Caribbean for December of 1902, and a rapid naval buildup soon found the North Atlantic Squadron, with most of the navy's battleships, gathered at Culebra. The Caribbean Squadron joined the heavy ships there, while the South Atlantic and European squadrons rendezvoused at Trinidad. Thus the bulk of the United States fighting fleet rapidly concentrated in the eastern Caribbean, while Admiral Dewey, the navy's top-ranking commander, sailed on December 1 to take personal command. Clearly, the presence of so much naval force in the immediate area gave Roosevelt a unique advantage in the Venezuelan situation.

Events peaked on December 16, after Washington learned that a full blockade of the Venezuelan coast was imminent. On that day, Hay formally called upon the governments of Great Britain and Germany to accept arbitration of their dispute with Venezuela. On the same

day, Roosevelt ordered four battleships to move down to Trinidad and
two cruisers to Cura ao, both islands just off the Venezuelan coast and
within the blockade area. Two days later, London announced that the
British would yield to Hay's request, the Germans making a similar
announcement on the following day. The blockade would still go into
effect until the Venezuelans had agreed to the rather stringent conditions of the arbitration, including liability in principle for any claims
for injury or wrongful seizure of property. There would even be further armed clashes in January between Venezuela and the allies. For
the Americans, nevertheless, the crisis was almost over, and in fact the
blockade would end early in February. Admiral Dewey left the fleet for
home on January 5, though all of the fleet's battleships stayed on in
the Caribbean until April. . . .

Nor did the president's concern end when the danger of confrontation receded, for the policymakers of both Great Britain and
Germany helped to keep the issues alive in Roosevelt's mind. In a
public speech in February 1903, on the day the allies' naval blockade
of Venezuela ended, British Prime Minister Arthur J. Balfour called
for the United States to assume greater responsibility in the
Caribbean. He declared that "it would be a great gain to civilization if
the United States of America were more actively to interest themselves
in making arrangements by which these constantly recurring difficulties between European powers and certain States in South America
could be avoided. . . ." The Americans could be most helpful "by
doing their best to see that international law is observed, and by
upholding . . . the admitted principles of international comity." Behind
the prime minister's courteous phraseology lay a serious point: if
Washington was averse to the actions of European powers to redress
their legitimate grievances in the Americas, then Washington had better be prepared to redress such grievances itself.

The message from Germany was not quite the same. In March, a
month after Balfour's speech, Roosevelt was again visited by his friend
Hermann Speck von Sternberg. Sternberg proposed a scheme to create
an international syndicate to take over Venezuela's government
finances. This step, he said, would tend to stop the outbreak of revolutions there and make the country peaceful and prosperous, presumably because potential rebels could no longer hope to seize public
funds. It would also end the need for European punitive expeditions to
collect debts. The German proposed that the Americans take the lead
in such a movement. Roosevelt replied, as he promptly wrote Hay,

that "my judgment was very strongly that our people would view with the utmost displeasure any such proposal," for "it would pave the way for reducing Venezuela to a condition like that of Egypt, and . . . the American people interpreted the Monroe Doctrine as meaning of course that no European power should gain control of any American republic." In a forthcoming speech which he planned on the Monroe Doctrine, the president noted, he had better state plainly that his country would "never consent to allowing one of the American Republics to come under the control of a European power by any such subterfuge as . . . a pretense to the guaranteeing or collecting a debt."

Balfour had proposed that the United States make itself directly responsible for enforcing "international law" in the western hemisphere, with an obvious reference to debt collection; Sternberg had suggested that Washington join with the European powers to do so, as merely a partner in a multilateral enterprise. There could be no question as to which course Roosevelt preferred, though it would be another year before he was ready to express himself fully on the matter. He did so finally on May 20, 1904, through the medium of a letter to be read aloud at a banquet in New York celebrating the second anniversary of Cuban independence. Former Secretary of War Elihu Root, who had presided over the birth of the Cuban republic, read the letter to the assembled guests, who may not have realized that they were hearing the first announcement of the Roosevelt Corollary to the Monroe Doctrine.

The president began by denying that the United States entertained any ambition for further territory or dominion. "All that we desire is to see all neighboring countries stable, orderly and prosperous," he wrote.

> Any country whose people conduct themselves well can count upon our hearty friendliness. If a nation shows that it knows how to act with decency in industrial and political matters, if it keeps order and pays its obligations, then it need fear no interference from the United States.

If these conditions were not met, however, no such promise could be made. "Brutal wrongdoing, or an impotence which results in a general loosening of the ties of civilized society, may finally require intervention by some civilized nation, and in the Western Hemisphere the United States cannot ignore this duty. . . ."

This claim on behalf of the United States to a generalized right of intervention in its own hemisphere did not escape notice in the antiimperialist press. Three weeks after the Cuban dinner, Roosevelt wrote Root that he was "rather amused at the yell about my letter." It had stated, he insisted,

> the simplest common sense. . . . If we are willing to let Germany or England act as the policeman of the Caribbean, then we can afford not to interfere when gross wrongdoing occurs. But if we intend to say "hands off" to the powers of Europe, then sooner or later we must keep order ourselves. . . .

In December, after his reelection, the president expanded his statement somewhat and included it in his annual message to Congress. This revised version stated that "in the western hemisphere the adherence of the United States to the Monroe Doctrine" might force it "however reluctantly . . . to the exercise of an international police power." A year later, in his annual message for 1905, Roosevelt stated: "We must make it evident that we do not intend to permit the Monroe Doctrine to be used by any nation on this Continent as a shield to protect it from the consequences of its own misdeeds against foreign nations." By then the Rough Rider was deeply involved in a debt crisis in the Dominican Republic to which his letter of May 20, 1904, had an obvious relevance.

The question of unpaid debts, Roosevelt confessed in this latter message to Congress, was a thorny one. The United States itself had never been willing to use force in order to ensure the fulfillment of a foreign government's contracts to American citizens, and it was to be wished that other governments would show a similar forbearance. Unfortunately, they did not, which posed a dilemma.

> On the one hand, this country would certainly decline to go to war to prevent a foreign government from collecting a just debt; on the other hand, it is very inadvisable to permit any foreign power to take possession, even temporarily, of the custom houses of an American Republic in order to enforce the payment of its obligations, for such temporary occupation might turn into a permanent occupation.

There was only one solution: the United States must be ready at need to make the necessary arrangements for repayments and secure the agreement of the interested parties. This, the president wrote, was "the only possible way of insuring us against a clash with some foreign power."

As Roosevelt wrote a friend earlier in 1905, "I believe with all my heart in the Monroe Doctrine and have, for instance, formally notified Germany to that effect." But the doctrine, he said, must not "be used as a warrant for letting any of these republics remain as small bandit nests of a wicked and inefficient type. This means that we must in good faith try to help them . . . , and be ready if the worst comes to the worst to chastise them. . . ." By inventing an "international police power" to serve his purposes, Roosevelt drastically reshaped the Monroe Doctrine. What had been a declaration that Europe's powers must keep their hands off the independent states of the Americas became the justification for unilateral United States intervention in the hemisphere at its own discretion. In the name of security, the nation now claimed a regional hegemony.

Anti-Imperialism: The Rejected Alternative

Thomas J. Osborne

PRESIDENT CLEVELAND'S OPPOSITION TO THE ANNEXATION OF HAWAII

In January 1893, during the waning days of President Benjamin Harrison's administration, American sugar planters dethroned the native leader of Hawaii, Queen Liliuokalani. The insurgents were assisted by U.S. Minister to Hawaii John L. Stevens and U.S. marines from the warship USS *Boston*. In this essay from his book *Empire Can Wait*, Thomas J. Osborne of Santa Ana College explains why President Grover Cleveland denounced the planter-plotted revolution and withdrew a proposed Hawaiian annexation treaty from the Senate. In July 1898, however, President William McKinley persuaded Congress, via a joint resolution, to annex Hawaii. Professor Osborne argues that the debate over Hawaii foreshadowed the later controversy over the annexation of the Philippines and provides us with critical insights into both imperialism and its critics.

On December 4, 1893, [President Grover] Cleveland delivered his first annual message to Congress. Only a small segment of the address dealt with the Hawaiian problem, partly because the chief executive was awaiting fresh news from Honolulu about [Minister Albert S.] Willis's attempt to reinstate the queen [Liliuokalani]. The president alluded to the "serious embarrassment" which he had faced upon entering office as a result of having to deal with his predecessor's annexation treaty. He had withdrawn that convention from the upper house "for examination," said Cleveland, and had sent James H. Blount to the islands to conduct "an impartial investigation" into the Revolution and the annexation movement. Blount's findings showed "beyond all question" that the constitutional government of Hawaii was overthrown with the complicity of Minister Stevens and the American forces from the U.S.S. *Boston*. The only "honorable course" was to restore as far as possible the state of affairs existing at the time of Stevens' intervention. Pursuant to this goal the president reported that he was attempting, "within the constitutional limits of executive

From *Empire Can Wait: American Opposition to Hawaiian Annexation, 1893–1898*, pp. 60–63, 135–36, by Thomas J. Osborne. Footnotes omitted. Copyright © 1981. Reprinted with permission of The Kent State University Press.

power," to place the queen back upon her throne. He said that he had no definite results to report, but when he had more information he would send a special message to Congress.

The chief executive's message touched off a debate in Congress over Hawaii that continued intermittently until late May of the following year. Immediately after the address the Senate heard speeches for and against both annexation and restoration. Most important, as far as the preparation and timing of Cleveland's forthcoming Hawaiian message was concerned, was the introduction of George F. Hoar's resolution requesting the president to submit to the Senate copies of all instructions given to United States diplomatic representatives and naval officers assigned to Honolulu since March 4, 1893. Although there was doubtless some truth in the *New York Herald*'s charge that Hoar was attempting to gain partisan advantage by creating the false impression that the Republicans had to force Cleveland to disclose the facts, the resolution passed. The Senate debate then widened into a full-scale partisan conflict over the moral, historical, constitutional, racial, strategic, and commercial aspects of the Hawaiian question.

The House passed its own resolution of inquiry, drafted by Robert R. Hitt of Illinois. The measure asked the chief executive for copies of all the diplomatic correspondence to and from Honolulu since March 4, 1889. Cleveland complied with this request in mid-December 1893 and a lengthy House debate on Hawaii followed.

While Congress sought more information on Cleveland's policy toward the islands, the president gave close attention to his forthcoming Hawaiian message. He still did not know whether Willis's mission had succeeded. The most recent dispatches from the islands showed that an impasse had been reached. Liliuokalani still refused to grant full amnesty to the revolutionists; the provisional government had fortified the public buildings with sandbags and artillery, and had organized a thousand-man militia and a five-hundred-man reserve, in preparation for any attempt to reestablish the monarchy. Cleveland had first asked [Walter Q.] Gresham to prepare the message, but disliking Gresham's draft, he had turned to [Richard] Olney. The latter's draft proved satisfactory; it formed the largest part of the special message.

Cleveland's six-thousand-word communication, sent to Congress on December 18, emphasized at the outset that "right and justice should determine the path to be followed in treating this subject." The message reviewed at length the major findings of Commissioner

Blount and in a forceful and logical manner defended the administration's stand against the annexation treaty and in favor of the reestablishment of the monarchy. The president offered primarily moral, but also historical, reasons for his decision not to return the treaty to the Senate. He claimed that the American diplomatic representatives and naval forces had assisted in the overthrow of the Hawaiian queen and had established the provisional government "for the purpose of acquiring through that agency territory which we had wrongfully put in its possession." After questioning the right of the provisional government to transfer the sovereignty of Hawaii to another nation without the consent of the Polynesians, Cleveland announced his decision with respect to the treaty: "Believing, therefore, that the United States could not, under the circumstances disclosed, annex the islands without justly incurring the imputation of acquiring them by unjustifiable methods, I shall not again submit the treaty of annexation to the Senate for its consideration. . . ." The president mentioned that he opposed the convention also because "it contemplated a departure from unbroken American tradition in providing for the addition to our territory of islands of the sea more than two thousand miles removed from our nearest coast." However, Cleveland said that by itself, the latter objection might not justify the rejection of Harrison's accord.

Immediately after Cleveland gave his reasons for rejecting the compact, he discussed the ethical considerations that had prompted him to attempt to restore the queen. There was such a thing as "international morality" he insisted, and because "a substantial wrong" had been done to a weaker nation by the representatives of the United States, the latter incurred the obligation to repair the injury. In order to remedy the injustice committed against the Hawaiian monarch, the president said he had tried unsuccessfully to restore the status quo that existed before the "lawless landing" of the United States troops in Honolulu on January 16, 1893. He attributed the failure of his restoration policy to the queen's unwillingness to accept the conditions, especially the granting of full amnesty to the revolutionists, upon which is aid depended. Without making any recommendations for further action, the chief executive commended the entire Hawaiian matter to Congress. Altogether, Cleveland's Hawaiian message presented in a compelling manner the moral and anti-imperialist grounds for his opposition to annexation.

Significantly, the president had stated in this message that he declined the proffer of annexation "under the circumstances disclosed." Although Cleveland was an anti-imperialist by inclination, the above statement suggests that his moral repugnance to the particular circumstances surrounding the annexation movement of 1893 probably carried the most weight in his decision to reject Harrison's treaty. What the Democratic chief executive would have done respecting annexation had a different set of conditions prevailed is largely conjectural. However, the present writer believes that the president, for anti-imperialist reasons, probably would have opposed the acquisition of the islands even if the natives had given their consent to a transfer of sovereignty. . . .

It has been argued here that the anti-annexationists' struggle in the 1890s against the acquisition of Hawaii was based upon a reverence for America's republican tradition and an inveterate hostility to colonialism. The opposition of the sugar and labor interests to the annexation of the northern Pacific archipelago was by no means inconsiderable; it was secondary in importance, however.

Few of the anti-imperialists were irreconcilably antagonistic to the incorporation of the islands into the Union. Most of the opponents of annexation seemed to sense that at some time in the future Hawaii would probably become American territory but they remained hopeful that such an event could be postponed, if not entirely averted.

These hopes were dashed not so much by the military exigencies arising out of the war with Spain . . . but rather by the fear that Hawaii had to be annexed quickly to preclude possible foreign demands for compensation, and especially by the accelerated European partitioning of China in the spring of 1898—a partitioning that augured the loss of a vast potential market in the Far East for the surplus of American manufactures. Amid this charged atmosphere the reasoned warnings of the anti-imperialists seemed overdrawn. Although McKinley's treaty would not have been ratified in mid-1898, these events and fears made the passage of the Newlands [Resolution] a virtual certainty.

Yet why, over the years, was there such stubborn resistance to acquiring the Polynesian archipelago? To most anti-annexationists far more was at issue than the absorption of one small group of islands in the Pacific into the body politic. Generally, they believed that if Hawaii were annexed other accessions of distant territory would follow. To the domestic sugar interests this meant that in addition to having to compete with all grades of the Hawaiian product, the output of the Cuban and Philippine cane fields might further reduce the profits of the mainland producers if these former Spanish colonies were transferred to the United States. In addition to fearing the migration of Hawaii's Oriental toilers to the west coast and the reestablishment of virtual slavery as a result of annexation, American workingmen were concerned about having to contend with the products made by cheap native labor on the other islands that Uncle Sam might covet. Most importantly, however, the anti-imperialists were certain that Hawaii's acquisition constituted the "entering wedge" of a new imperialistic policy. For them the annexation of the insular nation symbolized America's loss of innocence. The opponents of empire viewed the United States as the archetype of the virtuous republic—a secularized "City upon a Hill." The possession of Hawaii signified the abandonment of America's time-honored mission of exemplifying the workings of self-government and augured the drift into colonialism with all its attendant embroilments and injustices. Because the Hawaiian controversy was the first to raise the specter of imperialism before the American public, the debate had about it a sense of poignancy that accounts for the relentless opposition to annexation from 1893 to 1898.

After Hawaii was brought into the Union it was easier to acquire other dependencies even though the difficult process of treaty ratification was involved. This point is illustrated by the fact that the Hawaiian debate of the 1890s lasted more than *five years* and was terminated by the approval of a joint resolution because a treaty would not pass the Senate. However, within approximately *seven months* of the passage of the Newlands measure the United States acquired Guam, the Philippines, Puerto Rico, and Wake Island. When the Hawaiian controversy is viewed in this manner if becomes evident that the "Great Debate" over empire did not begin in 1898, as so many historians have assumed, but in 1893.

Teodoro A. Agoncillo

THE FILIPINO PLEA FOR INDEPENDENCE

By January 1899, when Emilio Aguinaldo established a new Philippine government at Malolos, the United States and Spain had already signed the Treaty of Paris formalizing the annexation of the Philippines to the United States. Aguinaldo had been transported from Hong Kong to his country on the U.S. gunboat *McCulloch* at the start of the Spanish-American-Cuban-Filipino War, and he believed that U.S. officials had promised that if he helped to defeat Spain, his nation would realize independence. At war's end, Filipino nationalists futilely tried to dissuade American authorities from annexation, and they bristled when it became clear that one colonial master—Spain—was being replaced by another—the United States. In February 1899, war broke out between Filipino and U.S. soldiers. Before the Philippine Insurrection faltered in 1902, more than 5,000 Americans and 200,000 Filipinos lay dead. Teodoro A. Agoncillo, a scholar trained in the American-introduced Filipino public schools who became a professor of history at the University of the Philippines, has written a number of studies on the Filipino side of the story, including *History of the Filipino People* (1977, with Milagros C. Guerrero) and *The Revolt of the Masses* (1956). The following selection from *Malolos: The Crisis of the Republic* reveals Agoncillo's sympathy for the Filipino anti-imperialists who were defeated by occupying U.S. forces in a bloody war.

As early as June 10, 1898, [Felipe] Agoncillo [an aide to Emilio Aguinaldo] wrote Aguinaldo that a representative be sent to the United States in order to ascertain American intentions regarding the Philippines. Owing perhaps to this suggestion, the decree of June 23 provided for the creation of a committee to take charge of what may properly be called a propaganda corps. On August 7, Aguinaldo instructed Agoncillo to publish the "Act of Proclamation" and the "Manifesto to Foreign Governments" in the Hong Kong papers. Furthermore, he exhorted Agoncillo to exert all efforts in publicizing the Philippine situation, adding:

From *Malolos: The Crisis of the Republic*, pp. 311, 315–16, 322–25, 355–58, 362–65, 372, 429–34, 450–52, 532–36, by Teodoro A. Agoncillo. Copyright © 1960. Reprinted by permission of the University of the Philippines Press.

It is important that you should go [to the United States] as soon as possible, so that McKinley's Government would know the true situation. Show him that our people have their own Government, civil organizations in the provinces already exist, and soon the Congress of Representatives of these provinces will meet. Tell him that they cannot do with the Philippines what they like. . . . The policy that you will pursue in the United States is as follows: make them understand that whatever might be their intentions toward us it will not be possible for them to overrule the sentiments of the people represented by the government and so it cannot be ignored by them. . . .

In what may be regarded as final instructions to Agoncillo, Aguinaldo, on August 30, wrote:

It is said that General [Wesley] Merritt is going away to take part in the work of the Commission [Paris Peace Conference.] On this account, it is important that you proceed as quickly as possible to America, in order to know what will take place. If perchance we should go back to Spanish control, ask them [the Americans] to help us as the French helped them during their own revolution and ask also the terms. . . . In whatever agreement you will make you will insert as a condition the recognition of this government.

At almost the same time, Aguinaldo instructed the diplomatic representatives abroad to entangle the United States in the affairs of the Philippines so that she might be forced to prevent foreign Powers from dividing up the country. . . .

The ship docked in San Francisco on September 22. Since it had been known in the United States and in Europe that Agoncillo left Hong Kong on his way to America, the Americans, in their staggering ignorance of geography, expected that he would arrive on civilized American soil naked, except for the G-strings. They were, however, dumbfounded to see a highly educated man, complete with hat and well-pressed European suit, go down the gangplank with superior airs. On the same day, he and [General Francis V.] Greene took the train for Washington, D.C., where they arrived on September 27. It was during this land journey to the American capital that Agoncillo learned from the newspapers that he would not be officially received by Washington. He then requested Greene to make arrangements with President McKinley in order to confer with him officially. Greene, an understanding and accommodating man, did so upon their arrival in Washington, but the President expressed his regret that he could not see Agoncillo officially because it would be contrary to American understanding with Spain. However, he expressed his willingness to see Agoncillo unofficially. Disappointed, Agoncillo then sounded out the State Department regarding the acceptance of his credentials. He was met with a rebuff. At this point, he took it upon himself to see President McKinley at 10:00 A.M. of October 1. He was politely received in the official reception room. Agoncillo recounted to McKinley the Filipinos' struggles to be free. Although the President listened politely it was obvious that Agoncillo's mission to the United States was bound to fail. He then asked McKinley if he would be allowed to state the aims and purposes of the Philippine Government. McKinley answered that a secret note to this effect should be handed to him, a note, McKinley added, that should be personal and without Agoncillo's official designation. On October 3, Agoncillo handed the note to Assistant Secretary of State [Alvey A.] Adee, who in turn showed it to the President. The latter instructed Adee to accept Agoncillo's note on condition that he would agree to some amendments. Agoncillo, after conferring with Adee and learning that insistence on acceptance of his official note might result in its total rejection, gracefully accepted the amendments. The note, in its final form, reviewed the background of the Filipino-American relations, and then continued:

6. The lawful government of the natives now functioning in the Philippine Islands has been sanctioned by the only legitimate source of public power, the vote of its fellow-citizens, whose authority and representation it has, and it has in fact been recognized, not objected to, and utilized by the American nation. Said Government, in the performance of its duties, considers that it must address itself to the American public powers and remind them of its right, owing to its existence, its services, and its loyalty, to be consulted and considered and given a voice and decisive vote in all the questions to be finally settled in the Paris Conference or in consequence thereof, concerning the Philippines.

7. The present lawful Philippine Government of which the invincible leader General Emilio Aguinaldo is the president, also believes that the moment has come to remind and even notify, if proper, in a formal and precise manner, the Illustrious President and Government of Washington of its existence and normal and regular functioning, as well as of its relations of reciprocity with the authorities of the American Republic in the Philippine Islands.

8. It desires to state (in the same manner), that the Philippine people unanimously confirms its independence and confides that the American people will recognize the same, mindful of the offers made and obliga-

tions contracted in its name, proclaiming the principles of liberty, justice and right expressed in its famous, sacred Declaration of Independence for the benefit of the new nation which logically rises in that part of the globe under the impulse of its present beneficent and humanitarian action.

9. And the Philippine people hope that pending a permanent understanding for the evacuation of their territory, their present lawful *de facto* government will be accorded the rights of a belligerent and such other rights as may be proper, in order to compel Spain to submit to the just historical law which deprives her of the tutelage she has arrogated to herself over those Islands and which she was incapable of carrying on humanely and socially without detriment to the general interests. . . .

It was then agreed that Agoncillo's note be sent to the American commissioners in Paris. Agoncillo was further advised to hurry thither in order to have an interview with the commissioners. It is apparent that official Washington wanted to get rid of him in order to free itself from the possible embarrassment of dealing with the representative of the Philippine Government that the United States had no intention of recognizing. But Agoncillo thought that such show of assumed or studied sympathy was an invitation for the Philippines to send a representative to the Commission in Paris. While he thought that many Americans were for Philippine independence, yet Agoncillo clearly saw that he was fighting a lost cause and warned Aguinaldo that the people should be prepared for a possible conflict with the Americans. . . .

The deliberations of the commissioners were closely followed by the Filipino agents abroad, particularly by Agoncillo, whose duty it was to present before the conference the Filipino side of the Philippine question. As the deliberations dragged on and Agoncillo was not given a chance to air his views, the agents in Europe and in Hong Kong came to the conclusion that there was nothing more to do than to wait for developments. Agoncillo, however, upon learning of the conclusion of the treaty, submitted a memorandum to the Peace Commissioners, through General Greene, in which he said that the treaty "cannot be accepted as binding by my government inasmuch as the commission did not hear the Filipino people or admit them into its deliberations, when they have the undisputable right to intervene in all that might affect their future life." The commission merely shrugged its shoulders and ignored Agoncillo's protest. Agoncillo, as early as December 1, had admitted that the Philippines would be annexed to the United States. In the view of Agoncillo's failure to be heard in the

Paris conference, Ramon Abarca, treasurer of the Filipino Republican Committee of Paris, telegraphed [Dr. Galicano] Apacible on December 14 proposing the immediate return of Agoncillo to Washington. It was felt that Agoncillo's only hope was in preventing the ratification of the treaty by the American Senate. . . .

Aguinaldo, realizing the hopelessness of fighting for the recognition of an independent Philippines, now appealed to McKinley, proposing (1) that the Spanish possessions in Oceania be formed into a state and named "Republic of the Philippines" under the protection of the United States; (2) that the purpose of the protectorate under the United States was to make Spain abandon her possessions in Oceania and, too, to make the United States work for the recognition of the Republic by the foreign Powers; (3) that a commission composed of Filipinos and Americans be created to determine the period of protectorate and to formulate a treaty of alliance between the Philippines and the United States. McKinley, however, had no need for such an ambitious alliance, for he had already made up his mind that the Philippines should belong to the United States. . . .

The news of the annexation of the Philippines to the United States was received in the country with mixed feeling. To the vested interests, the Treaty of Paris was a wish fulfilled; to the idealistic patriots and nationalists, the news was the harbinger of dark days to come. In Pasig, the residents passed a resolution expressing their loyalty to the Philippine Government and to Aguinaldo and offering their lives in the interest of the country's freedom. Resolutions protesting the annexation of the Philippines to the United States were passed by the residents of Navotas, Pateros, San Pedro Makati, San Felipe Neri, then in Manila Province; by the people of Ilocos Sur, Batanes, Tayabas, Albay, Camarines, Zambales, Samar, Ilocos Norte, Cagayan, Cavite, Pampanga, Capiz, Pangasinan, and other places such as Malibay (now in Pasay), Sampaloc, San Mateo, Las Piäas, Antipolo, San Miguel (Manila), Tondo, and Kalumpit. It was obvious that the people, as distinguished from the intelligentsia and the wealthy, were for continuing the struggle for freedom and independence. . . .

Much has been made out of the alleged chaotic condition into which the countryside and the Malolos Government itself had fallen. It had been the American opinion in Manila that the second half of 1898 was a period that might be characterized as "something akin to anarchy." This opinion was held by the Americans of the imperialist type, such as Dean C. Worcester. It led to more misunderstandings between the Filipinos and the Americans and resulted in increased tension. Such opinions as were held by the more unprejudiced Americans as W. B. Wilcox and L. R. Sargent, who conducted a survey of existing conditions of northern Luzon in the second half of 1898, unfortunately did not reach the Filipino leaders and the masses. Yet their findings are important as throwing light on the actual conditions and the range of authority exercised by the Malolos Government. Thus Sargent:

> I can state unreservedly, however, that Mr. Wilcox and I found the existing conditions to be much at variance with this opinion. During our absence from Manila we traveled more than six hundred miles in a very comprehensive circuit through the northern part of the island of Luzon, traversing a characteristic and important district. In this way we visited seven provinces, of which some were under the immediate control of the central government at Malolos, while others were remotely situated, separated from each other and from the seat of government by natural divisions of land and accessible only by lengthy and arduous travel. As a tribute to the efficiency of Aguinaldo's government and to the law-abiding character of his subjects, I offer the fact that Mr. Wilcox and I pursued our journey to Manila with only the most pleasing recollections of the quiet and orderly life which we found the natives to be leading under the new regime.

Sargent then proceeded to tell of their pleasant trip to northern Luzon where they were royally dined and wined by the Filipinos and honored with presentations of Spanish plays. Concluding his estimate, Sargent said:

> I cannot see what better gage we can obtain at present of the intelligence and ambition of the whole Filipino race than the progress that has been made by its favored members with the limited opportunities at their command. Throughout the island a thirst for knowledge is manifested, and an extravagant respect for those who possess it. . . . The ruling Filipinos, during the existence of their provisional government, appreciated the necessity of providing public schools to be accessible to the poorer inhabitants. Had the events so shaped themselves as to have provided an opportunity for carrying into effect the plans formed on this point, it seems possible that the mental plane of the entire population might have been raised gradually to a surprising height.

A John Barrett, who argued for the retention of the Philippines on economic grounds, admitted that he had had a pleasant experience in his travels in the Philippines. Speaking of the Malolos Congress, he said:

> By the middle of October, 1898, he [Aguinaldo] had assembled at Malolos a congress of one hundred men who would compare in behavior, manner, dress and education with the average men of the better classes of other Asiatic nations, possibly including the Japanese. These men, whose sessions I repeatedly attended, conducted themselves with great decorum, showed knowledge of debate and parliamentary law that would not compare unfavorably with the Japanese Parliament. The executive portion of the government was made up of a ministry of bright men who seemed to understand their respective positions. Each general division was subdivided with reference to practical work. There was a large force of under-secretaries and clerks, who appeared to be kept very busy with routine labor.

Even Consul [Rounseville] Wildman [U.S. Consul at Hong Kong], realizing the unfairness of the common run of American opinion regarding the Filipinos and their government, officially warned the State Department of the futility of looking down upon the Filipino government and people with something akin to contempt. In a dispatch to John Basset Moore, Under-Secretary of State, he said:

> . . . the Insurgent Government of the Philippine Islands cannot be dealt with as though they were North American Indians willing to be removed from one reservation to another at the whim of their masters. If the United States decides not to retain the Philippine Islands, its ten million people will demand independence, and the attempt of any foreign nation to obtain territory or coaling stations will be resisted with the same spirit with which they fought the Spaniards.

The Filipino-American tension was not relieved by such professions of honesty on the part of some Americans. What appeared triumphant at the moment was the set opinions of the imperialists who looked upon the Filipinos as charges to be educated and civilized. The tension increased when President McKinley's Proclamation, which set forth for the first time the American policy toward the Philippines, was published. [Major General Elwell] Otis toned down the Proclamation in order to avoid exciting the Filipino leaders, for the original Proclamation contained phrases such as "sovereignty," "right of cession" and others, which, it was feared, might be used by Aguinaldo to incite the masses against the Americans. But General [Marcus P.] Miller, who received a copy of the original Proclamation, published it in Iloilo on January 4, 1899, and soon copies of this unedited version reached Malolos. The Proclamation was at once subjected to a heavy barrage of verbal fireworks, with Antonio Luna, the editor of the nationalistic *La Independencia*, leading the attack. Luna pointed out that the policy enunciated in the Proclamation was "merely a subterfuge to temporarily quiet the people until measures could be inaugurated and applied to put in practice all the odious features of government which Spain had employed" in the Philippines. On January 5, 1899, Aguinaldo issued a peppery counter-proclamation which, in effect, terminated the hitherto theoretical Filipino-American friendship. He summarized the American importunities and violations of the ethics of friendship, particularly the order to occupy Iloilo, and concluded:

> My government can not remain indifferent in view of such a violent and aggressive seizure of a portion of its territory by a nation which arrogated to itself the title champion of oppressed nations. Thus it is that my government is disposed to open hostilities if the American troops attempt to take forcible possession of the Visayan Islands. I denounce these acts before the world, in order that the conscience of mankind may pronounce its infallible verdict as to who are the true oppressors of nations and the tormentors of human kind.

Copies of this incendiary proclamation reached the masses and doubtless incensed them at what they thought, rightly or wrongly, to be the American perfidy. Aguinaldo himself must have realized its implications and promptly ordered the recall of the copies left undistributed. In its place, another proclamation was published in the *Heraldo de la Revolución* on the evening of the same day. He said partly:

> As in General [E. S.] Otis's proclamation he alluded to some instructions edited by His Excellency the President of the United States, referring to the administration of the matters in the Philippine Islands, I in the name of God, the root and fountain of all justice, and that of all the right which has been visibly granted to me to direct my dear brothers in the difficult work of our regeneration, protest most solemnly against this intrusion of the United States Government on the sovereignty of these islands.
>
> I equally protest in the name of the Filipino people against the said intrusion, because as they have granted their vote of confidence appointing me president of the nation, although I don't consider that I deserve such, therefore I consider it my duty to defend to death its liberty and independence.

To Otis, the two proclamations were tantamount to a call to arms. He met the situation by quietly taking precautionary measures. He strengthened the American observation posts and alerted his troops. The result was an apparent unconcern on his part and a dubious pacific intention on the part of the protagonists. But the tense atmosphere could be felt, and the Filipinos in and around Manila left for safer places. The exodus was so great that "all avenues of exit were filled with vehicles" and the railroad cars filled to capacity in transporting families to the north within the protective arm of the Filipino army. It was estimated that some 40,000 inhabitants fled "within a period of fifteen days." On the other hand, Aguinaldo's proclamations had the effect of drawing the masses together, so much so that some 20,000 Filipinos paraded at San Fernando, Pampanga, to show their loyalty to their President. . . .

Tension between the Filipinos and the Americans increased and only a slight incident was needed to break the relations completely. The Americans charged the Filipino soldiers with entering deep into American territory and with other alleged misdeeds calculated to break their relations. On February 1, a detachment of American engineers was arrested by the Filipino troops and sent to Malolos. The following day, Otis filed a protest with Aguinaldo. The latter replied that the five Americans belonging to the Corps of Engineers were merely detained and that they had already been released. They were arrested, according to Aguinaldo, because they were well within the Filipino lines on Solis Street, Tondo, and that the arrest was made in accordance with the decree of October 20, 1898 prohibiting foreigners from approaching the Filipino defensive works.

Misunderstanding continued. On February 2, General Arthur MacArthur protested the presence of Colonel Luciano San Miguel's soldiers within his territory. He wrote:

Sir: The line between my command and your command has been long established, and is well understood by yourself and myself.

It is quite necessary under present conditions that this line should not be passed by armed men of either command.

An armed party from your command now occupies the village in front of blockhouse No. 7, at a point considerably more than a hundred yards on my side of the line, and is very active in exhibiting hostile intentions. This party must be withdrawn to your side of the line at once.

> From this date, if the line is crossed by your men with arms in their hands they must be regarded as subject to such actions as I may deem necessary.

Colonial San Miguel wanted to avoid any conflict with the Americans and immediately wrote MacArthur:

> My very dear Sir: In reply to yours, dated this day, in which you inform me that my soldiers have been passing the line of demarcation fixed by agreement, I desire to say that this is foreign to my wishes, and I shall give immediate orders in the premises that they retire.

San Miguel promptly wrote an order, in the presence of Major Strong, directing his officers at the outpost to withdraw from the American side of the line in question. Strong himself delivered the order to the Filipino officers in the outpost. The following day, February 3, the Filipino troops inside MacArthur's territory withdrew. The tension seemed to have been relaxed. The following night, February 4, a patrol of the Nebraska Regiment was detailed to the village of Santol, near the Balsaham (San Juan) Bridge. It was instructed not to allow Filipino soldiers to enter the village or its vicinity. All armed persons coming from the Filipino lines were to be ordered back and arrested if they refused. Only upon failure to arrest them should they be shot. At about eight o'clock in the evening, Private Willie W. Grayson with two other members of the Patrol advanced beyond the village to ascertain whether there were Filipino soldiers in the vicinity. Suddenly four armed men appeared before Grayson.

> I yelled "halt" . . . . the man moved, I challenged with another "halt". Then he immediately shouted "Halto" to me. Well I thought the best thing to do was to shoot him. He dropped. Then two Filipinos sprang out of the gateway about fifteen feet from us. I called "Halt" and Miller fired and dropped one. I saw that another was left. Well I think I got my second Filipino that time. We retreated to where our six other fellows were and I said, "Line up fellows; the enemy are in here all through these yards." We then retreated to the pipe line and got behind the water work main and stayed there all night. It was some minutes after our second shots before Filipinos began firing.

The following day, General MacArthur issued his order to advance against the Filipino troops. No attempt was made to find out the cause of the shooting and to "see whether the former passive condition could be maintained."

The rift had widened into an armed conflict. The Filipino-American hostilities had begun. . . .

It is difficult to believe that the Americans came to the Philippines merely to expel the Spaniards and so defeat them in a war of their own making. There was, in the first place, Merritt's refusal to allow Aguinaldo and his men to participate in the conquest of Manila. The reason given, namely, that the Filipinos, if allowed to do so, might rape the Spanish women and kill their children and menfolk, had no justification in fact and served as a crude rationalization of his unjust act. No less than General [Thomas M.] Anderson, in his letter to the Adjutant General, dated December 24, 1898, testified that "they [the Filipinos] maintained good discipline." It is probable that Merritt, in pursuing a policy that was contrary to the interests of his ally, wanted to hog the limelight for himself, on the one hand, and, on the other, to consolidate his position militarily in preparation for an expected or possible conflict with the Filipinos. Whether he was acting on his own or whether he was officially instructed by Washington to act in the manner he did showed that there was from the very beginning an intention to take the Philippines or a part of it.

In the second place, the American Government, in sending a continuous stream of recruits to the Philippines, showed that it had no intention to help the Filipinos to their feet as it did to the Cubans. Since the American imperialists could not very well gobble up Cuba without arousing the moral ire of the world, particularly of Spain, Germany, and France, they had to get compensation elsewhere. The Philippines, then unknown even to the literate Americans, was some such compensation. Implying that the Filipinos were still savages, President McKinley declared it his policy "to civilize" the Filipinos. It was only when the imperialist groups had gotten the upper hand in the American political scene that McKinley frankly admitted American intention in the Philippines. His pious avowal that he walked up and down the corridor of the White House and fell to his knees to pray the Almighty to give him light was a fiction that he foisted on the gullible sector of the American public in order to make him appear as a sort of Sir Galahad in the purity of his aims.

Lastly, it may be recalled that once in possession of the City of Manila (Intramuros), the American military authorities in the Philippines refused to truckle to Aguinaldo in so far as political questions were concerned, but nevertheless recognized him as the legitimate Filipino leader when they wanted concessions from him. There was in this attitude an ambivalence that can be explained by a lack of moral compunction in the American military. Had the Americans been disposed to let the Filipinos carve out their destiny they would have left the Philippines as soon as the surrender of Manila was consummated. That they did not but on the contrary assumed a hostile attitude toward Aguinaldo and his government proved that, once the Spaniards were conquered, they were ready to junk the Filipino allies and conquer them, if need be, to bring American goods safely to this side of the Pacific. Nobody but the extremely naive would believe the official American rationalization that McKinley and his host of advisers did not know at the outset what to do with the Philippines. The rationalization is now understood to be a piece of propaganda to calm down the fears of the American anti-imperialists and, especially, the bulk of the American public, whose national experience had been to look askance at any trace of imperialistic pretensions. If the final decision to take the Philippines was put off to a later date, it was not because McKinley and the men around him had no intention to subjugate the American ally, but because the American public had not been sufficiently prepared to accept the idea of American imperialism. Only when this seemed certain did McKinley and his propagandists—the military, the businessmen, and the Protestant missionaries—make known his final decision to the American peace Commissioners in Paris.

Such was the ruthlessness with which Aguinaldo and the Filipino Government were treated by the American authorities that even the American Consul in Manila, O. F. Williams, said in a dispatch to the State Department:

> Aguinaldo was aided to return here—helped to rifles—permitted to take cannon from warships sunk by us—and cannon, ammunition and stores from an arsenal surrendered to our forces,—allowed to land arms from China,—given arms taken at Subig [*sic*],—entrusted with prisoners there taken, and so, by the world's fair understanding was and is our ally—a Congress even, to the contrary notwithstanding and under the law of Nations and by the common law of Agency we, the Principal become responsible for reimbursement and proper indemnification. This is law! It is right! And better than all it is policy and wise economy.
>
> If as an ally or agent Aguinaldo and his forces be fairly dealt with our flag will be hailed forever here, and so meager has been his pay to soldiers, and so meager his war commissary that his total war expense, which I claim is our debt, is not one-tenth if indeed one-one-hundredth

part of what it would have cost our forces to accomplish the same
results for our good.

Obviously, Consul Williams had a conscience and openly admitted to
his superior in the State Department that the American policy in the
Philippines was unjust, particularly because the Filipinos, as allies of
the Americans, deserved a better treatment than was shown to them.
But the military, represented by Merritt and, later, by Otis, viewed
Aguinaldo's government as a doormat to be trampled upon when the
proper occasion arose. Not were Merritt and Otis honest enough to
acknowledge Aguinaldo's important role in restoring a semblance of
order in places where there was near-anarchy. Said Williams:

> Small garrisons of Spanish here and there have been captured by
> Aguinaldo—have been uniformly well treated—but this finally broke
> Spanish power—we Americans did this only at Cavite and Manila.
> Aguinaldo did the rest over nearly all this Insular Empire. It is like one
> belligerent holding New York and Brooklyn with the rest of their state
> and all New England beyond its reach and control.
>
> We may laugh at the quasi government of Aguinaldo since May 1,
> but his is the only government this great island, and others also, have
> had—and but for him and his subordinates anarchy, riot and murder
> would have terrorized several millions of people. . . .

But Williams' was a lone voice in the wilderness. The military, con-
temptuously disdaining Aguinaldo and what he represented, stuck to
their guns and thus prepared the way for the Filipino-American hostilities. Had Aguinaldo listened to his military advisers who believed
that the Americans should be attacked while they were still numerically
weak, perhaps the history of the Philippines would have taken a different course.

Robert L. Beisner

THE ANTI-IMPERIALISTS' CASE AND FAILURE

The McKinley administration's rejection of the Filipino plea for independence provoked sharp debate in the United States. In this essay, Robert L.
Beisner of American University focuses on the independent-minded,
reform-conscious "mugwumps" who organized the Anti-Imperialist League.
In his book *Twelve Against Empire*, Beisner probes the failure of these dissenters to stem the imperial surge. His balance sheet on their performance
helps us to compare the anti-imperialists with the imperialists with regard
to motive, ideas, political acumen, influence, and results. Professor Beisner
has also written *From the Old Diplomacy to the New, 1865 1900* (2d
edition, 1986).

A few days after the United States Senate ratified the Treaty of Paris,
the old abolitionist Thomas Wentworth Higginson attended a local
meeting of the Anti-Imperialist League and returned home to note in
his diary that it had "seemed like an old Mugwump gathering."
Higginson's observation was both accurate and obvious, for a striking
parallel did exist between mugwumpery and anti-imperialism. In June,
1884, for instance, when Boston newspapers had printed a "Call"
publicizing the unwillingness of a number of local Brahmins to support James G. Blaine, the Republican candidate for President, the
signers included Higginson, Charles R. Codman, William Endicott,
Jr., Moorfield Storey, Edward Atkinson, Charles W. Eliot, Charles
Francis Adams, Jr., Winslow Warren, William Lloyd Garrison, Jr.,
Erving Winslow, Gamaliel Bradford, and Thomas Bailey Aldrich—all
known as "mugwumps" in 1884 and later to be among the anti-imperialists of the 1890s. In fact, a large proportion of the most active anti-
imperialists were political independents, "mugwumps" in the strictest
sense. They had spent a good part of their mature lives bolting from
one party to another or systematically proclaiming their independence
of any party. They were political mavericks who saw no value in party

From *Twelve Against Empire: The Anti-Imperialists, 1898–1900*, pp. 5, 7–10, 17, 216–20,
226–28, 230–39, by Robert L. Beisner. Footnotes omitted. Copyright © 1968.
Reprinted by permission of the author.

loyalty as such. Regardless of its origins or onetime virtues, they believed a party was no more than what its current principles, policies, and leaders made it. . . .

Mugwumps also looked upon themselves as heralds of reform, at liberty to use their uncommitted votes to force reform upon the existing political parties or, if reforms were resisted, to threaten the parties with destruction. If need be, the mugwumps stood ready to create a new political grouping of high moral commitment, just as they had done when they helped found the Republican Party in the 1850s. As Thomas Wentworth Higginson explained to a Boston audience in 1873, party organizations "are truly prosperous only in advancing that idea which gave them birth," and, just as the Democrats had long outlived their Jeffersonian beginnings, so now the Republicans were losing sight of their founding principles, thus proving once again that "reform must be accomplished first by the free lances. . . ." The mugwump was seldom deflected from his purpose by the knowledge that as a "free lance" reformer he would often be in the minority or by the certainty that at times he would be derided and persecuted in the pursuit of his vision. Political virtue was its own reward, and, in any case, the truth would ultimately prevail and he would be vindicated. The mugwumps of 1898 knew they were right. . . .

Above all, the mugwump thought that his first duty in politics was to be true to himself. He did not look to successful results for justification of his position. He believed that as long as he pursued the right as he saw it, no other defense of his conduct was necessary. Neither party nor country could hope to receive his loyalty if it afforded him no moral justification for extending it. "A man's first duty," wrote Mark Twain to William Dean Howells in 1884, "is to his own conscience & honor—the party & the country come second to that, & never first . . . the only necessary thing to do, as I understand it, is that a man shall keep *himself* clean, (by withholding his vote for an improper man), even though the party & the country go to destruction in consequence."

Being a mugwump involved more than voting according to certain moral principles. It also involved belonging to what Richard Hofstadter has called a "mugwump culture." In their own eyes mugwumps were the representatives of the "highest intelligence and the best culture of the country," the people who possessed "moral weight" or "solid character." More often than not, the mugwump saw himself as a person with an indisputable right to lead his country. This complacence reflected the fact that most leading mugwumps were men of substantial backgrounds, comfortable circumstances, and long-established Anglo-Saxon stock, in many cases the direct descendants of seventeenth-century New Englanders. They had received excellent educations, often at Harvard. Some of them lived on independent and inherited incomes. A recent study of the mugwumps in the state of New York who led the campaign for Cleveland in 1884 shows that out of a sample list of 396 mugwump names, 100 (or 25 per cent) could be found in the *Social Register*. Included in the sample were 101 lawyers, 97 businessmen, 57 financiers, 27 journalists, 25 physicians, 25 teachers, 22 white-collar workers, and 13 clergymen. It comes as no surprise to find that "only one labor leader and one farmer were found in the sample."

Although many of the New York mugwumps of 1884 were young men in their twenties and thirties, the leading mugwump anti-imperialists of the late 1890s, most of them New Englanders, were a much older group. Among them were Thomas Wentworth Higginson, who turned seventy-five in 1898; William Endicott, seventy-two; Charles Eliot Norton and Edward Atkinson, both seventy-one; James Burrill Angell, Charles Codman, and Carl Schurz, all sixty-nine; E. L. Godkin and Gamaliel Bradford, sixty-seven; Horace White and Charles W. Eliot, sixty-four; Charles Francis Adams, Jr., Mark Twain, and William Croffut, sixty-three; Thomas Bailey Aldrich, sixty-two; William Dean Howells, sixty-one; William Lloyd Garrison, Jr., sixty; Wendell Phillips Garrison and William Graham Sumner, fifty-eight; William James, fifty-six; Richard Watson Gilder, fifty-four; and Moorfield Storey, fifty-three. . . .

It took the issue of American imperialism in 1898–1900 to arouse the fears of the mugwumps and bring them back to the center of political controversy. They held that the price of expansion abroad would be the repudiation of America's past and the abandonment of her special place in the world—a coin too valuable to pay. In their campaign against imperialism, the mugwumps made their last great fight and returned to the heart of national affairs for the last time. . . .

The anti-imperialists offered a wide range of objections to the acquisition of new territories. They may be summarized as constitutional, economic, diplomatic, moral, racial, political, and historical.

A large number of anti-imperialists believed that imperialism violated the United States Constitution. Some simply contended that the spirit of the Constitution had been contradicted, that it was not right for a government based upon principles of representative rule and the protection of individual liberties to govern other peoples without regard for these principles. Assurances that American colonial rule would be humane did not mollify them, since they believed that benevolence arbitrarily offered could be just as arbitrarily withdrawn. Those who were convinced that imperialism violated not only the spirit but the letter of the Constitution averred that neither Congress nor the President possessed the legal authority to pass laws or set rules for the governing of colonial peoples which were not in strict accord with those established for the people of the United States themselves. Thus Benjamin Harrison, protesting that there could not be one law for the citizen and another for the subject, held that it was unconstitutional for Congress to impose a tariff on goods entering the continental United States from the territory of Puerto Rico; his position was summarized in the popular phrase, "the Constitution follows the flag." The Supreme Court, however, somewhat ambiguously affirmed Congress' extra-constitutional powers in the colonies in the "Insular Cases" of 1901, a verdict that reportedly prompted Elihu Root, the urbane Secretary of War, to comment: "Ye-es, as near as I can make out the Constitution follows the flag—but doesn't quite catch up with it."

In making an economic case against imperialism, critics denied the truth of another contemporary aphorism, to wit, that "trade follows the flag." Men like Carl Schurz and Andrew Carnegie felt that it was unnecessary to plant the flag in the spongy soil of the tropics in order to capture the area's trade. The laws of commerce would determine how successful the Americans were in selling their surplus abroad. If they found profitable markets it would be because the products of their mills, mines, factories, and farms were cheap and attractive enough to compete with those of other nations and not because they had seized and roped off markets for their exclusive use. Occasionally an anti-imperialist would add that a reduced tariff schedule which allowed foreigners a better opportunity to sell their wares in the United States would enhance their ability to purchase American goods in return and thus promote a greater increase in American exports than McKinley's policy of imperialism.

Businessmen Andrew Carnegie and Edward Atkinson suggested additional economic reasons for rejecting an annexationist policy. According to the former, any effort to regularize commercial relations within an American empire would be accompanied by hopeless economic and political difficulties. Free trade between the United States and the Philippines would bankrupt American farmers and certain groups of raw material producers, yet a tariff on the colony's goods would violate the Constitution and destroy the islands' economy. To open the market of the Philippines on equal terms to the United States and other nations would fulfill the principle of the open door but would ruin American exporters who had to pay heavier transportation charges than those incurred by their German, British, and Australian competitors. If, on the other hand, the Philippines market were kept exclusively for the United States the resulting anger of European powers interested in Far Eastern trade would produce a dangerous diplomatic crisis.

Edward Atkinson took another tack. For years he had been an eager advocate of increased economic activity in Latin America and the Far East, but in 1899 he concluded that the prize of Oriental trade (and, to a certain extent, of Latin American trade) was not worth the cost of acquiring it. There would be time enough to bid for those markets when China and other undeveloped nations had industrialized and generated enough purchasing power to buy in quantity the kind of sophisticated goods that the United States produced. In the meantime more significant profits could be made from trade with America's traditional partners, the industrial nations of Europe and Canada.

Anti-imperialists also objected to a policy of colonialism because it threatened to involve America more deeply in international politics, especially in Asia. They abhorred this prospect on three counts. First, it was a contradiction of their conception of American diplomatic traditions, a departure from the path of non-entanglement laid down by the founders of the nation and a negation of the Monroe Doctrine, which they interpreted as meaning "Europe for the Europeans" and "Asia for the Asians" as well as "America for the Americans." Secondly, involvement in Asian imperial politics would endanger the security of the United States. Anti-imperialists charged that by extending American responsibility to Hawaii and the Philippines, the McKinley administration had broken the nation's ocean belt of security and placed the flag in outlying regions where it was vulnerable to intimidation or attack by other powers. With its security no longer ensured by geography, the United States would have to build an enormous navy and an army of respectable strength to protect its new possessions against any action that seemed to threaten them, however remotely. Thirdly, the domestic repercussions of a leading role in world politics would prove costly. Future wars and the permanent maintenance of forces strong enough to wage them would require a vast amount of money, discourage industry, impose heavy tax burdens on the American people, and distract attention from the solution of domestic problems that had a far greater bearing on the future than any foreign policy issues could have—problems of race and radicalism, currency and the cities, trusts and the tariff.

The moral critique of the anti-imperialists requires few words to summarize although it was just as important as their constitutional, economic, or strategic objections to imperialism. They believed— simply, genuinely, and emphatically—that it was *wrong* for the United States forcibly to impose its will on other peoples. No economic or diplomatic reasoning could justify slaughtering Filipinos who wanted their independence. No standard of justice or morality would sustain the transformation of a war that had begun as a crusade to liberate Cuba from Spanish tyranny into a campaign of imperialist conquest.

As genuine if not as high-minded were the racial attitudes that contributed to the anti-imperialist stand. With a few rare exceptions like George Hoar, the opponents of imperialism shared entirely the expansionists' belief in the inferiority and incapacity of the world's col- ored races (and of some that were not colored). But while those in the imperialist camp usually proceeded from these racist assumptions to a belief in the duty of Americans to uplift and care for the backward and benighted savages of Puerto Rico and the Philippines, the anti-imperi- alists appealed to these same assumptions to justify excluding such peoples from a place in the American political system. They believed that the United States should belong to its own kind, the Anglo-Sax- ons (or "Germanic" races as Carl Schurz would have it). The blood of tropical peoples would taint the stream of American political and social life and further complicate the nation's already festering racial prob- lems. As the *New York World* asked on June 19, 1898, did the United States, which already had a "black elephant" in the South, "really need a white elephant in the Philippines, a leper elephant in Hawaii, a brown elephant in Porto Rico and perhaps a yellow elephant in Cuba?"

In their political objections to expansionism the anti-imperialists were guided by abstract principles. For the most part they were politi- cal fundamentalists—they believed in the literal truth and universal applicability of the ideas of liberty and republican government. Free of the skepticism and self-consciousness of later generations, they asserted that a republican government could not also be an imperial government; that the rule of self-government did not permit exceptions of faraway territories; that freedom was a value of universal appeal, in the Philippines and Puerto Rico as well as in the United States; and that all men, whatever their attainments and wherever they lived, possessed the right to enjoy the blessings of freedom. The United States could not preserve its own democracy if it denied the right of self-rule to others.

Finally, anti-imperialists had what might be called historical motives for opposing imperialism. Most of them were traditionalists who believed imperialism to be in sharp conflict with established ideals and practices. Acquiring overseas colonies and joining the worldwide struggle for power and empire were inconsistent with American diplomatic traditions, with America's historic identification with the ideal of liberty, and with the lofty notion that America should serve the world not through force but through the force of her example. Imperialism destroyed the unquestioned belief in American innocence and uniqueness.

The anti-imperialists were primarily and overwhelmingly concerned with their own country—its security, prosperity, constitutional integrity, and moral and political health—and not with the fate of Filipinos, Cubans, Hawaiians, or Puerto Ricans. Although they could and did defend the rights of these peoples, their fundamental purpose was to defend the interests of the United States. . . .

The failure of the anti-imperialists to prevent the expansionists' victory of 1898–1900 had several causes. The most obvious was simply their inability to persuade their countrymen of the truth of their dire forecasts.

Hitches, flaws, inconsistencies, and compromises in their own activities and arguments weakened the anti-imperialist position. Those who listened to Carl Schurz must have been confused by the fact that he alternated between an insistence upon immediate and full independence for the new possessions and schemes for setting up protectorates until the inhabitants were "ready" for independence. No matter how honest his motives or practical his objectives, Charles Francis Adams' attack on his fellow anti-imperialists in the spring of 1899 certainly did the movement no good in the eyes of the general public. Nor did the strained logic revealed by Andrew Carnegie and many others when they declared imperialism wrong as a matter of principle but stood firm only against the annexation of the Philippines. Or George Hoar's willingness to accept an expansionist victory by default in Hawaii prior to putting up a real fight against the annexation of the Philippines and Puerto Rico. How impressive could the anti-imperialists be when Benjamin Harrison waited until the dust had settled from the 1900 campaign before entraining for Ann Arbor to make his tardy declaration against imperialism? Or when [Speaker of the House Thomas] "Czar" Reed, at the very moment when his voice and influence were badly needed by other anti-imperialists, quit Congress for money-making and the scribbling of ironical anti-imperialist memos that never left the privacy of his study?

President McKinley's own actions made it difficult for the anti-imperialists to translate their moral and idealistic fervor into a political force strong enough to block his program. Understanding a President's tremendous power to take the political initiative, McKinley committed the United States to a series of *faits accomplis* before any effective protest could be made: ordering [Commodore George] Dewey to Manila Bay, sending American troops to the Philippines to secure the results of the Commodore's triumph, and dispatching a compliant peace commission to Paris to negotiate the treaty. These events occurred within the space of a few months, and it would have taken an extraordinarily strong, united, and determined lot of anti-imperialists to check the President during this period.

But anti-imperialists were in no such position of strength and unity. The Democrats were at a disadvantage because they had bellowed for war in 1898 as loudly as anyone, because Bryan had intervened in behalf of the peace treaty, and because their party had no other leader of national importance who could take charge of a bi-partisan anti-imperialist coalition aimed at defeating the treaty. The impact of the mugwumps was limited by their disunity on objectives and their position as independent critics standing completely aloof from the national party system. Suspicious of the wiles of professional politicians and hostile to compromise, they spent valuable time reciting the past errors of both Republicans and Democrats, thus courting trouble in broadening the base of their support. The Republican anti-imperialists, on the other hand, were hamstrung by partisanship. It prevented either Hoar or Harrison from making full-fledged commitments to the movement. Hoar, who refused to consider taking the lead of any but a pure Republican protest, spent an inordinate amount of time fending off and quarreling with mugwumps and justifying McKinley to other anti-imperialists. Harrison, though full of venom against the President, delayed attacking his administration until December, 1900, precisely because he wished to do nothing that would cause it political damage.

Another handicap facing the anti-imperialists in their attempts to influence public opinion was the matter of age—their average age was over sixty-nine years. Men born in the 1820s and 1830s were unlikely to have great powers of persuasion over a nation just entering a brave new century.

Finally, the anti-imperialists labored under the disadvantage of having the negative side of the debate. They had to say no, to ask a people aroused by American armed triumphs to surrender the fruits of victory. They had "to blow cold upon the hot excitement," as William James put it. Failure came in part because it was not possible to make Americans ashamed of themselves and afraid of the future at a time when they were enjoying fresh breezes of prosperity, glory, and optimism after more than a decade of depression and social strife. The anti-imperialists had run headlong into the fact that nothing succeeds like success. . . .

The historian has the duty to judge as well as analyze and describe. Besides appraising their impact on America it is necessary to appraise the anti-imperialists themselves and weigh both their errors and their achievements.

As political tacticians they are vulnerable to criticism, not only because they failed to maintain a united front (the result of honest disagreements) but also because they took a perverse delight in airing their differences in public. This open squabbling spoke well for their irrepressible individualism and their faith in free debate but not so well for their political judgment. They made another tactical error by reacting to all their opponents as if they were headstrong and romantic belligerents like Theodore Roosevelt and Albert Beveridge. The more cautious and influential, like McKinley and Hay, saw no way to escape from the Philippines, and perhaps did not even want to, but they had no interest in studying the map for new lands to conquer. In fact, when McKinley sent civilian commissions to the Philippines to study the problems of governing the islands, he twice appointed as chairmen men who had originally opposed annexing them, Jacob G. Schurman and William Howard Taft. Anti-imperialists certainly had grounds for disagreement with the administration, but few of them understood how narrow the grounds of opposition were on certain issues.

The anti-imperialists may be criticized as diplomatic strategists and as advocates of alternative policies that were notably impracticable. It is the virtually unanimous judgment of diplomatic historians that there was no politic way to get out of the Philippines after Dewey's naval victory of May 1, 1898. The American people would have rejected returning the islands to Spain as a perfidious betrayal of those Filipinos who had cooperated in the American victory at Manila. A protectorate, a favorite scheme of some of the more prominent anti-imperialists, would have committed the United States to involvement in the Far East without providing it with the power necessary to exercise its responsibilities. Ceding the Philippines to a foreign power other than Spain would have sparked fierce resentment among other nations and endangered the peace of the area. It is highly unlikely that it would have been possible to create any kind of international consortium to guarantee the neutrality and protect the security of the Philippines, or to make it work if it could have been created. Giving the Philippines immediate independence and then leaving them to their own devices might have touched off a general Asian war among the great powers with interests in the Far East, a war into which the United States would almost surely have been drawn. One can only speculate on these matters, of course, but there is little assurance that Aguinaldo and his followers could have united the Filipinos behind them and established a workable system of self-government and even less that they could have resisted falling prey to the aggression of another country. . . .

As prophets the anti-imperialists also fell into error. Three of their most important prophecies were proved wrong by the passage of time. Undemocratic modes of colonial rule did not produce a tyrannical backlash in the United States. The annexation of the Philippines, Hawaii, and Puerto Rico, although foreshadowing a long-term extension of American interests in Asia and three decades of interventionist diplomacy in Central America and the Caribbean, did not lead to a continuing orgy of territorial expansion. And American colonial rule, however imperfect, was not characterized by incompetence, corruption, brutality, or injustice. Perhaps because the United States had no vital need to exploit the resources of its colonies it made a record as imperial master which, compared with traditional European examples, was notably intelligent, restrained, and humane.

There is also the question of whether the anti-imperialists failed

"Hurrah for Imperialism!" 1898. An anti-imperialist cartoonist doubted that the United States could foresee the consequences of empire building. (*Life, 1898*)

as moralists. Christopher Lasch, noting that many anti-imperialists believed the Filipinos unfit for self-government by American standards, charges that they were "un-Christian" in wanting to abandon the natives to their own fate. This criticism fails to reckon with what most anti-imperialists thought the consequences of independence would be. Despite their prevailing assumption that Filipinos were not as competent in political matters as their American masters, the anti-imperialists did not believe that independence would be followed by anarchy, misery, and resumed foreign domination. Impressed by Aguinaldo's talent in setting up his own insurrectionary "republic" and leading the fight against American forces, the advocates of independence were convinced that their policy would lead, not to disaster, but to the founding of an independent Philippine republic. Had the Filipinos tried and failed in their attempt to govern themselves and fend off foreign pressures, the anti-imperialists would have been proved wrong as prophets, not as moralists.

They can be condemned as racists. Whether they used words like "superior" and "inferior" or "civilized" and "uncivilized," they thought of peoples in the categories of racism. George Hoar was generally an exception, but even he gave himself over to this kind of thinking on occasion. The unhappy fact is that few Americans were immune to the prevailing racism of the late nineteenth century. The anti-imperialists were no better or worse than their countrymen.

The anti-imperialists also left much to be desired in their role as guardians of and spokesmen for the nation's ideals. Their idealism and selflessness were too often offset by a narrow conservatism and mean-ness of spirit. Their motives were both noble and ignoble, their decla-rations both grand and picayune. At times they seemed to be men with little faith in the resiliency of their own nation. Although they claimed to regard it as the most wonderful on earth, they made it sound like one of the most fragile. How much faith could Carl Schurz have had in the strength and viability of America's vaunted democratic princi-ples and institutions if he believed that colonial rule in the Philippines would rapidly erode the principles or that Puerto Rican statehood would inexorably poison the institutions?

Finally, the anti-imperialists failed to offer an alternative vision of the nation's future. Criticizing the new expansionist conception of America's place in international affairs, they prescribed nothing more enticing than a return to the past. They knew that the annexation of faraway territories and alien peoples was inconsistent with America's past traditions, but it did not occur to them to question the continued worth and relevance of the traditions themselves. Making no effort to remold the American heritage. in new patterns and adapt it to the twentieth century, they served notice that an imperial career would signal the end of the America that had been. They did not offer a vision of what America could become.

There is also much to praise in the anti-imperialist record. Later events vindicated their prediction that the possession of Pacific colonies would weaken rather than strengthen the diplomatic and military position of the United States. As early as 1907 President Theodore Roosevelt acknowledged that the distant and poorly defended Philippines were the "heel of Achilles" of American policy in the Far East and considered announcing to the world that they would soon be given their independence. Nothing of the sort was done, however, and for forty years the islands remained a hostage to American strategy in Asia, complicating and inhibiting policy *vis- -vis* Japan from the time of Theodore Roosevelt to Franklin Roosevelt. When Japanese-American relations finally degenerated into open hostility, war commenced with a Japanese strike at the two exposed flanks of American power—Hawaii and the Philippines, the gains of 1898.

A judgment on the anti-imperialists' contention that colonies would not add important strength to the American economy depends upon one's definition of the word "important." Individual firms and industries obviously profited from the colonies while many others were quite unaffected by the new order. What is clear, however, is that Edward Atkinson and others were correct in their belief that imperial possessions would not measurably enhance the health and vigor of the American economy. Exports to Latin America and the Far East have increased significantly in the course of the twentieth century, as have capital investments, but the increase has been a general one, not restricted to or explainable by America's presence in her new colonies.

Although the anti-imperialists were wrong in their dark predictions of what would happen in the United States as a direct result of colonialism abroad, their political logic on this point was irrefutable. There *is* no answer to their charge that a nation that believes in representative government has no business ruling other peoples against their consent, no matter how gentle the rule or how little it impinges on the lives of the people in the mother country. . . .

There was a great need in 1899 and 1900 for someone to challenge the self-congratulatory paternalism of expansionists in the

Philippines, who explained that the bloody spanking they were administering to the childish but devious natives was for the latter's own good. The anti-imperialists provided the moral challenge to this arrogant and expedient explanation. William James, remarking the ease with which imperialists justified killing in the name of political abstractions, launched devastating attacks against the amorality and pointlessness of Theodore Roosevelt's love of violence and struggle. Even earlier Charles Eliot Norton had warned that the United States could not escape guilt by punishing Spanish murder in Cuba with still more death. The moral dilemmas and ironies of imperialism were perhaps never dissected more expertly than by Finley Peter Dunne's "Mr. Dooley," who declaimed:

> We say to thim: "Naygurs," we say, "poor, dissolute, uncovered wretches," says we, "whin th' crool hand iv Spain forged man'cles fr ye'er limbs, as Hogan says, who was it crossed th' say an' sthruck off th' comealongs? We did,—by dad, we did. An' now, ye mis'rable, childish-minded apes, we propose fr to larn ye th' uses iv liberty. In ivry city in this unfair land we will erect schoolhouses an' packin' houses an' houses iv correction; an' we'll larn ye our language, because 'tis aisier to larn ye ours than to larn oursilves yours. An' we'll give ye clothes, if ye pay fr thim; an', if ye don't, ye can go without."

The anti-imperialists displayed admirable spirit in making their protest in the face of hostile public opinion. They constantly encountered bitter criticism, including the accusation that they were encouraging the Filipino rebels in their resistance to American authority and thus indirectly causing the deaths of American soldiers. The *New York Times* declared: "The Anti-Imperialist League might go one step further. It might send rifles, Maxim guns, and stores of ammunition to the Filipinos . . . it would be more openly and frankly treasonable." The commander of the New York chapter of the Grand Army of the Republic proclaimed in 1899 that anti-imperialists were unworthy of "the protection of the flag they dishonor and . . . the name of American citizens." After his June 7, 1898, address on "True Patriotism," Charles Eliot Norton was the target of abusive letters and public scoldings, even from George Hoar, a fellow anti-imperialist. One correspondent informed him that "there are stray bullets somewhere that are liable to hit our country's enemies," and another simply warned: "You had better pull out[.] Yours with contempt—A white man." The *Chicago Tribune*, not passing up a chance to criticize an eastern professor, accused Norton of trying "to kill the generous impulses of patriotism and to besmirch the noble cause of humanity upon which the war against Spain is based." Vice-President Roosevelt in 1901 described the anti-imperialists in a letter as "simply unhung traitors, and . . . liars, slanderers and scandalmongers to boot." Dissent in the face of such condemnation was an act of considerable moral courage.

Above all the anti-imperialists served their countrymen well by reminding them of their own identity and purpose in the world. Knowing that it was a departure from traditional American practice to acquire distant, heavily populated colonies for which statehood was not intended, they also understood the deeper significance of this change—that it denoted America's intention to take a place among the great powers of the world in active international politics. The anti-imperialists deserve credit for drawing attention to the magnitude of this new departure, for pointing out the political and moral problems that would follow in its wake and for refusing to concede that America's new status must necessarily mean the abandonment of her traditional practices. Great powers are not expected to conduct themselves like YMCA counselors. This the anti-imperialists did not fully appreciate, but they did hold out the hope that great power could yield, not greed and amorality, but a sense of national security and a record of justice and magnanimity.

The anti-imperialists' concern was always more with the morality and justice of American policy than with the diplomatic decisions and judgments that influenced it. It was partly for this reason that they were unable to propose feasible alternative policies. But this is not a fatal shortcoming in movements of this sort. Their primary accomplishment was to lodge a protest, to demand answers to moral questions that were hard and perhaps impossible to answer, to reassert traditional American ideals. The anti-imperialists are still a reminder of the value of conservative dissent; with their concern for America's traditional values and their own ideological heritage, they were better able than the less historically minded to compare present performance with past principle and then ask: Do they match? Can they be reconciled?

Their answers did not always satisfy a people nurtured on optimism and faith in progress. Their conservatism often prevented them from appreciating the beneficial effects change could have on their nation. Even so, they did comprehend the need for a changing society to remain aware of its founding principles. They understood that a nation that violated its own declared purposes could be wrenched from its moral and spiritual moorings. The anti-imperialists knew that a democratic people were ill-suited to a career as colonialists. They knew that war and imperialism could have unfortunate and unpredictable effects on their own nation and that a preoccupation with problems halfway around the world might divert important national resources to unworthy ends, lower standards of government and political conduct, cause the neglect of pressing domestic problems, and even alter the moral foundations of society itself.

When Charles Francis Adams expressed his misgivings during the Spanish-American War, he was told, "Oh, no!—such ideas are 'pessimistic'; you should have more faith in the American people!" These reassurances came from a people who believed they were beyond the reach of history—that they could live forever and that nothing could ever happen to their liberties and privileges. The anti-imperialists found it difficult to see far into the future, but at least they knew that it could bring decay, deterioration, and the perversion of principle just as easily as endless progress. It was their office, their purpose, and their achievement to warn a nation of optimists that America could not escape the consequences of its own conduct.

Allen F. Davis

JANE ADDAMS'S DISSENT FROM MILITARISTIC PATRIOTISM

Opposition to the imperial course of U.S. foreign policy was not limited to the prominent men who led the Anti-Imperialist League. In this selection from *American Heroine*, his biography of Jane Addams, Allen F. Davis discusses how the social reformer, famous for founding the Chicago settlement house Hull House, came to link her neighborhood reforms with global politics. Addams challenged Theodore Roosevelt and other leaders who tied patriotism to imperialism and the martial spirit. She later became an active member of the international peace movement and an opponent of U.S. entry into the First World War. Professor Davis, who teaches at Tem-

From *American Heroine: The Life and Legend of Jane Addams* by Allen F. Davis, pp. 135–36, 139–44. Copyright © 1973 by Allen F. Davis. Reprinted by permission of Oxford University Press, Inc. Footnotes omitted.

ple University, specializes in the history of social-reform movements in the United States. He has also written *Spearheads for Reform* (1967) and *Generations: Your Family in Modern American History* (1983).

Jane Addams became a pacifist gradually over a period of years. Her peace activities and her search for a moral equivalent for war were closely related to her experience in an immigrant neighborhood in Chicago. Her attitude was also influenced by her reading of [Leo] Tolstoy and by the problems raised by the Spanish-American War. Her opposition to war had nothing to do with her Quaker heritage, a convenient explanation cited in many popular accounts of her life. In fact, her father's Quakerism was so vague that he was not even a pacifist, and helped recruit a regiment during the Civil War. There is no indication that when Jane was a child or in college that she was troubled by the thought of war, and her letters written during her two European adventures reveal a lively interest in the military displays and marching soldiers she saw all across Europe. She was especially fascinated as were many Americans, by exploring the battlefields, monuments, and other artifacts relating to Napoleon. Certainly when she moved to Hull House in 1889 she was in no sense a pacifist, but on the other hand war and peace were not especially vital issues in the world of the 1880s.

She discovered the writings of Leo Tolstoy during the interlude between her two European trips, but it was not until after she had moved to Hull House that some of the implications of his theories began to take effect. In the beginning it was not so much his doctrine of non-resistance to force and violence, as his courage in acting out the logic of his ideas, that attracted her. Tolstoy's decision to give up the life of a celebrated writer and live like a peasant, to wear peasant garb, work in the fields, eat coarse and simple food, and to spend his spare time making boots with his own hands, had a particular attraction to many Americans in the late nineteenth century who were worried about their own idleness and luxury. Clarence Darrow, William Jennings Bryan, John P. Altgeld, Ernest Crosby, Brand Whitlock, Samuel Jones, William Dean Howells, Hamlin Garland, and many others felt the influence of Tolstoy. . . .

* * *

In 1897 Jane Addams was searching for an inner peace, and for the right relationship with the neighborhood and the world. She was not at this point, however, particularly interested in world peace, nor in international affairs. She belonged to no peace societies; she may have attended some of the sessions of the World Peace Congress held in connection with the World's Fair in Chicago in 1893, but she was not a participant. For her, Tolstoy's doctrine of non-resistance had little to do with international disagreements, but with forces at work in the neighborhood and the city.

Then in the spring of 1898 the Spanish-American War broke out. It was a lightning war, over within three months, but the issues raised by the war and the peace settlement were to be debated for years to come. They brought to a climax the controversy over American expansion abroad. There is no evidence that Addams had any interest in American foreign policy in the 1890s. She does not seem to have followed the Venezuelan Crisis of 1895–1896, or the events in Cuba that eventually precipitated the war, at least she mentioned none of these developments in her letters, or in her public addresses. After the war came, however, she became a participant in the controversy. Although she was not a prominent anti-imperialist, the debate over imperialism, and her own experiences, helped her bring together some of the ideas aroused by Tolstoy and made her a full-fledged advocate of peace.

Her first reaction to war was not so much shock and horror, as it would later be with the outbreak of World War I, but rather a realization that a far-off event was changing life in the Hull House neighborhood. Speaking at a meeting of the Academy of Political and Social Sciences in December, 1898, a few days after the signing of the peace treaty, in the middle of an address on the function of the social settlement, she noted that there had been in increase in murders in the neighborhood since the outbreak of war. Children were "playing war" in the streets. "In no instance . . . were they 'freeing Cubans,' but with the violence characteristic of their age, they were 'slaying Spaniards.' The predatory spirit is so near the surface in human nature," she added, "that the spectacle of war has been a great setback to the development and growth of the higher impulse of civilization."

In citing the "predatory spirit," the primitive instincts that lay close to the surface, especially in young people, she was borrowing from the thinking of psychologists G. Stanley Hall and William James. She was also taking the first halting steps toward formulating a theory for a substitute for the war spirit, for a "moral equivalent for war." She was not alone in this search; William James, always ambivalent about war, hating it yet appreciating its attraction, had also been searching for a way to sublimate the predatory spirit of man. As early as 1888, James, in trying out ideas for the prevention of war and the settling of international disputes, had written cryptically in notes for a lecture in one of his classes. "But how decide conflicts? . . . Follow the common traditions, Sacrifice all wills which are not organizable and which avowedly go against the whole. . . . Find some innocent way out, Examples: savage virtues preserved by athletics; warlike by organized warfare. . . ."

Jane Addams, however, did not have the benefit of hearing James' college lectures. She worked out her ideas about a moral equivalent for war from her own experience, though later she was to profit from hearing him speak, and he in turn learned from her. She agonized over the war and the problem of keeping the peace. "I sat in Mrs. Porter Palmer's box at the Peace Jubilee and otherwise exposed myself to its fascinations," she reported to a friend in October 1898, "but can do nothing but feel a lump in my throat over the whole thing. I have been really quite blue, not play blue but real depths and will have to be more of a Tolstoyan or less of one right off." She and

Jane Addams, 1860–1935. The renowned social reformer also became an anti-imperialist who decried the detrimental shift of U.S. resources from domestic priorities to foreign ventures. (*Sophia Smith Collection, Smith College*)

James both appeared on the same platform in Chicago for a discussion of Tolstoy's ideas, but both rejected his doctrine of non-resistance, and instead took a milder path of protest by joining the anti-imperialists.

Addams was not among those who organized the Anti-Imperialist League in Boston in June 1898, but she did support its action and later she joined the Chicago branch. She was always a minor figure in the anti-imperialist movement which was led by such mugwumps as Andrew Carnegie, George Hoar, Edward Atkinson, E. L. Godkin, Charles Eliot Norton, and Carl Schurz. She could agree with their opposition to President McKinley's policy of annexing the Philippines and forcibly destroying the nationals led by Aguinaldo. She could agree with their rejection of American expansion and imperialism, but she must have had some difficulty with their racist rhetoric, which depicted the Filipinos and other Orientals as inferior people not equipped for self-government.

She was in the audience in Chicago on October 17, 1899, when Carl Schurz delivered his stinging address attacking the McKinley administration for its actions in the Philippines. He denounced "the slaughter by American arms of a once friendly and confiding people." "I confidently trust," he announced, "that the American people will prove themselves . . . too wise not to detect the false pride or the dangerous ambitions or the selfish schemes which so often hide themselves under that deceptive cry of mock patriotism: 'Our country, right or wrong!' They will not fail to recognize that our dignity, our free institutions and the peace and welfare of this and coming generations of Americans will be secure only as we cling to the watchword of *true* patriotism: 'Our country—when right to be kept right; when wrong to be put right.' "

"Carl Schurz was so fine last night that I feel uplifted in spirit," she wrote Mary Smith, "that straight intellectual clearness that inevitably leads to uprightness appeals to me as nothing else does. He was fair and reasonable."

In her own speaking, she avoided direct attacks on the administration and instead took a broader view. She decried the narrow interpretation of patriotism in time of war; "patriotism as taught in our schools is fast becoming an abstraction," she argued, "to be patriotic is to salute a flag or to sing 'America,' rather than to feel responsible for the condition of the public school and its grounds, which may later lead to the same sense of responsibility in regard to the public streets and community duties." Peace as well as patriotism must be made meaningful, she argued; it must be more than the absence of war. "Peace is not merely something to hold congresses about and to discuss as an abstract dogma," she told an anti-expansion meeting at the Central Music Hall in Chicago on April 30, 1899. "It has come to be a rising tide of moral feeling which is slowly engulfing all pride of conquest and [is] making war impossible." She cited the Russian peasants who were refusing to drill and fight and the opposition of organized labor to imperialism. She did not, however, underestimate the appeal and fascination and horror of war. "The appeal to the fighting instinct does not end in mere warfare, but arouses these brutal instincts latent in every human being." "Let us not make the mistake of confusing moral issues sometimes involved in warfare itself," she warned. "Let us not glorify the brutality. The same strenuous endeavor, the same heroic self-sacrifice, the same fine courage and readiness to meet death may be displayed without the accompaniment of killing our fellow-men," she argued, in anticipating the thesis later made famous by William James.

The next year, speaking in St. Louis, she continued to explore some of the implications of peace and war, of "patriotism and duty." "The great pity of it all is that war tends to fix our minds on the picturesque," she announced, "that it seems so much more magnificent to do battle for the right than patiently to correct the wrong. A war throws back the ideals which the young are nourishing into the mold of those which the old should be outgrowing. We allure our young men not to develop but to exploit. We turn their imagination from the courage and toil of industry to the bravery and endurance of war. We incite their ambitions not to irrigate, to make fertile and sanitary the barren plains of the savage, but to fill it with military posts and to collect taxes and tariffs." But she also realized how difficult it was to find a substitute for the military virtues. She recalled how, some years before, she had tried to convince some of the boys from a Hull House gymnasium class that it was just as exciting to use long, narrow, sewer spades instead of rifles and bayonets in the military drill they so eagerly organized, but they soon pretended that the spades were guns and went back to their military tactics. "I honestly doubt," she decided, "if now I could even get them to touch a spade, so besotted have we all become with the notion of military glory."

She appeared at an anti-war, pro-Boer rally in Chicago and appealed for contributions to the Red Cross to help the wounded, as one positive action those who opposed war could take. "War in all its horror is a terrible thing," she announced. "It is the law of the jungle elaborated. It is the old story of the rulers of Persia and Rome, when they conquered other peoples and forced them into slavery to work for them and no longer for themselves alone. We are taken in once more . . . and go back again to where the Romans were a thousand years ago." She gave a series of lectures in the summer of 1902 at Chautauqua, New York, on Leo Tolstoy, and in an address before the Ethical Culture Society of Chicago in the spring of 1903 she talked on "A Moral Substitute for War."

William James and Jane Addams appeared on the same platform in Boston in the fall of 1904 at the thirteenth Universal Peace Conference. "The meetings are pretty courteous and some of them filled with platitudes, but on the whole it is a fine group of people trying to do a real thing and I rise up from time to time," she reported. In fact she gave three formal addresses and in one she spoke of the need for "a moral substitute for war." William James also spoke. "Our permanent enemy is the rooted bellicosity of human nature. Man, biologically considered and whatever else he may be into the bargain, is the most formidable of all beasts of prey and indeed, the only one that preys systematically on his own species. We are once for all adapted to the military status. A millennium of peace would not breed the fighting disposition out of our bone and marrow, and a function so ingrained and vital will never consent to die without resistance, and will always find impassioned apologists and idealizers." Therefore he argued, in much the same terms that Jane Addams had been stressing, we must find a way to absorb and sublimate the natural bellicosity of human nature.

William James formulated his ideas in their final form in his famous essay, "The Moral Equivalent for War," first written as a pamphlet for the American Association for International Conciliation in 1910 and then published as an article in *McClure's* and *Popular Science Monthly*. Jane Addams put her ideas in more permanent form in a book, published in 1907, which she called *Newer Ideals of Peace*. James' essay was more dramatic, with its plans for conscription into a peacetime army designed to preserve "the military ideals of hardihood and discipline." He appreciated, more than Jane Addams did, the appeal of the manly virtues and was convinced that warlike tendencies were deeply imbedded in human nature. On the other hand, she maintained that only the longing for adventure, for group approval, and the desire to do useful work were deeply ingrained, primitive instincts.

Richard E. Welch, Jr.

AMERICAN WRITERS AS ANTI-IMPERIALISTS

Many American writers and scholars became critics of the U.S. conquest and acquisition of the Philippine Islands. In this essay from his book *Response to Imperialism*, the late Richard Welch, Jr. (1924–89) quotes extensively from the anti-imperial essays and poems of such writers as Mark Twain and Edgar Lee Masters. Although the anti-imperialists failed to prevent the insular imperialism they decried, Welch suggests that their impact was not insignificant, because they educated the American public. Professor Welch, who taught history at Lafayette College, was a prolific scholar who also wrote *George Frisbie Hoar and the Half-Breed Republicans* (1971), *Response to Revolution* (1985), and *The Presidencies of Grover Cleveland* (1988).

If not unanimous in its response to the acquisition and subjugation of the Philippine Islands, the literary community divided into the few and the many. Among the supporters of American policy there were only a half-dozen poets and authors of note: Julia Ward Howe, Bliss Carman, Richard Hovey, Gertrude Atherton, Brooks Adams, Julian Hawthorne. These six writers offered little poetry and prose in behalf of the nation's Philippine policy or its military instruments, and what they offered was justifiably soon forgotten. The anti-imperialists, on the other hand, were numerous and prolific. At least twenty were men of letters of national reputation: George Ade, Thomas Bailey Aldrich, Ambrose Bierce, Gamaliel Bradford, George W. Cable, John Jay Chapman, Ernest Crosby, Finley Peter Dunne, Henry Blake Fuller, Hamlin Garland, Thomas Wentworth Higginson, William Dean Howells, Edgar Lee Masters, Joaquin Miller, William Vaughn Moody, Bliss Perry, Edwin Arlington Robinson, Lincoln Steffens, Mark Twain, Charles Dudley Warner.

Of the prose writers, probably the most effective were the satirists, Bierce, Dunne, and Twain. Even Theodore Roosevelt admitted to enjoying the observations of "Mr. Dooley," Finley Peter

From *Response to Imperialism: The United States and the Philippine-American War, 1899–1902,* © by Richard E. Welch, Jr. Footnotes omitted. The University of North Carolina Press. Used by permission.

Dunne's philosophical Irish-American saloon keeper, who defined the policy of "benevolent assimilation" as a belief that "twud be a disgrace f'r to lave befure we've pounded these frindless an' ongrateful people into insinsibility." And Samuel Clemens had created in Mark Twain a national institution almost immune to successful attack.

Twain was slow to join the ranks of the dissenters; indeed he did not enlist until the war in the Philippines was in its twentieth month. By the autumn of 1900, however, influenced in some measure by his anti-imperialist friend William Dean Howells and more decisively by the determination of the Filipino insurgents, Twain was prepared to declare American policy a mistake and a disgrace. When interviewed by reporters from the New York dailies upon his return from Europe, Twain informed them that he had become convinced that the aim of American policy was not redemption but conquest. He was opposed "to having the American eagle put its talons on any other land." After McKinley's reelection, Twain sought to compensate for his delayed conversion with a flurry of well-publicized labor. Between December 1900 and April 1902 there was seldom a month that did not see an interview, essay, or public letter from Mark Twain, wherein he mocked the hypocrisy of American policy and decried the brutality and destruction that marked the war in the Philippines. By the summer of 1901 he had in effect joined the Anti-Imperialist League and subsequently would sign various of its memorial protests; by February 1902 he was one of some twenty Americans petitioning Congress to arrange an armistice in the Philippines and to investigate charges of misconduct by the American army.

Twain's single most famous literary effort in denunciation of American policy in the Philippines was his article in the *North American Review* of February 1901 entitled "To the Person Sitting in Darkness." Read today, its irony seems rather labored and heavy-handed, but at points it flashes into angry eloquence. "The Person" is, of course, the benighted heathen who is being whipped into the march of progress by the "Blessings-of-Civilization Trust." While ostensibly seeking to reconcile the victim, Twain reviews the tangle of broken promises and acts of deceit that had characterized the relations of the American government with the people of the Philippines:

> There have been lies; yes, but they were told in a good cause. We have been treacherous; but that was only in order that real good might come out of apparent evil. True, we have crushed a deceived and confiding people; we have turned against the weak and the friendless who trusted

us; we have stamped out a just and intelligent and well-ordered republic; we have stabbed an ally in the back and slapped the face of a guest; we have bought a Shadow from an enemy that hadn't it to sell; we have robbed a trusting friend of his land and liberty; we have invited our clean young men to shoulder a discredited musket and do a bandit's work under a flag which bandits have been accustomed to fear, not to follow; we have debauched America's honor and blackened her face before the world; but each detail was for the best.

Reprinted in pamphlet form by the New York branch of the Anti-Imperialist League, Twain's essay brought him many compliments from the "antis" and charges of senility and dyspepsia from the more ardent supporters of the war and imperial expansion. *The Nation* praised Twain for endangering his popularity and sales, but Twain probably realized that in America a humorist was allowed considerable leeway. It was only when he attacked the new national hero, General Frederick Funston [the captor of Aguinaldo], that he risked more than rhetorical obloquy, and this attack came only with the spring of 1902 as the war limped to a conclusion. Twain's satirical essay, "A Defense of General Funston," was not, in any case, one of his more effective antiwar efforts. He had some mordant fun with the disguises and false tricks that made possible the capture of Aguinaldo, but Twain appeared uncertain whether Funston was the perpetrator or simply the willing instrument of an evil policy.

A far more effective parody of Funston's career was that published by Ernest Crosby in his novel, *Captain Jinks, Hero*. Though neither widely reviewed nor widely read, it was an ambitious effort to combine the techniques of a farcical *roman à clef* with the purposes of the propaganda novel. In Crosby's hands Funston-Jinks becomes a character both contemptible and funny. The victim of insatiable ambition and greed and the perpetrator of countless self-serving hypo-pr crisies, he threatens to become at points almost engaging in self-serving exploits. Crosby was known in literary and anti-imperialist circles primarily as a poet, and his most famous work for the cause was his parody of Kipling's "The White Man's Burden." One of many such parodies, it was possibly the most bitter.

Take up the White Man's burden;
  Send forth your sturdy sons,
And load they down with whiskey
  And Testaments and guns.
Throw in a few diseases

To spread in tropic climes
For there the healthy niggers
    Are quite behind the times.
            . . .

Take up the White Man's burden,
    And if you write in verse,
Flatter your Nation's vices
    And strive to make them worse.
Then learn that if with pious words
    You ornament each phrase,
In a world of canting hypocrites
    This kind of business pays.

It was the duplicity of McKinley's Philippine policy that angered
many of the anti-imperialist poets as much as its evil consequences.
Imperialism in their eyes was made doubly wrong by being wrapped
in the humbuggery of benevolent assimilation, Christian duty, and the
expansion of liberty. American policy in the Philippines was identified
with hypocrisy as well as sin, and the corruptions of the present day
contrasted with the presumed purity of the past. The statesmen of old
had not designed their policies for the satisfaction of the greedy; they
had not abandoned American ideals in a covetous search for land,
markets, and political boodle. The poets of protest would reveal the
evil consequences of "the new departure," and bring America home
again.

The call to repentance characterized the verses not only of such
major poets as Joaquin Miller and William Vaughn Moody but of such
lesser talents as Hezekiah Butterworth, favorite poet of *Youth's Companion*, and John White Chadwick, W. C. Gannett, William Lloyd
Garrison, Jr., and James J. Dooling. Many of their poems were more
effective as propaganda than poetry, but several demonstrated an ap-
titude for imagery as well as anger, and two works of William Vaughn
Moody are among the finest narrative poems in American literature.

In "An Ode in Time of Hesitation," published in the *Atlantic
Monthly* in May 1900, Moody contrasted the Civil War with the
Philippine-American War, the one fought to redeem the ideals of the
Declaration of Independence, the other to deny them. The soldiers
who had fought to free the slave had fought to enlarge liberty and had
brought glory to the republic; those who fought to subjugate the Filipino were the enemies of liberty and the unwitting instruments of the
nation's shame. America had fallen victim to "fluent men of place and

consequence," reciting "their dull commercial liturgies." For the moment, they had persuaded their countrymen to forget their traditions, but the evil consequences of our Philippine policy would soon be made clear and its authors castigated:

> For manifest in that disastrous light
> We shall discern the right
> And do it, tardily.—O ye who lead
> Take heed!
> Blindness we may forgive, but baseness we will smite.

Less than a year later Moody published what was the most elegiac of all anti-imperialist poems. Many anti-imperialists had sought to distinguish between the authors of our Philippine policy and its soldier instruments; to curse the deed while granting redemption to the doer. Not an easy task, it was never performed more effectively than in the last verse of the poem "On a Soldier Fallen in the Philippines." A soldier has been killed in Luzon while acting under orders to shoot down the Filipino guerrillas and destroy their hopes of self-government:

> Toll! let him never guess
> What work we set him to.
> Laurel, laurel, yes;
> He did what we bade him to.
>
> Praise, and never a whispered hint but the
>   fight he fought was good;
> Never a word that the blood on his sword
>   was his country's own heart's blood.

Whether as a result of their medium or their temperament, the poets of anti-imperialism were usually more emotional than the essayists, more prepared to personify as well as to denounce American aggression in the Philippines. Henry Blake Fuller was more vituperative than most when he compared McKinley to Nero and pictured Mark Hanna, "coarsely fleshed and gross," following the cross of imperialism:

> Nailed upon whose either side
> Hangs a Malay crucified.

But for many of the anti-imperialist poets McKinley was seized upon as the very symbol of the war and the greed and jingoism that had inspired it. Expressions of disgust with McKinley were indeed more frequent than expressions of sympathy for the Filipino. Poetic apologies were often extended to the Filipino and references made to "the slaughter of the brave," but the poets of anti-imperialism were addressing an American audience and the victim they would emphasize was the American Dream. They would set the Filipino free because America must be redeemed. When William Lloyd Garrison, Jr., wrote a poem addressed to Aguinaldo, praising his "heroic stand" and comparing him to such patriot liberators of the past as Kosciusko and Toussaint L'Ouverture, the poem ended on a note of mourning for the countrymen of Garrison, not those of Aguinaldo.

The same emphasis is to be found in the poems and essays of the feminist Abbie Morton Diaz and the Boston pacifist Robert Treat Paine. It furnished mood and theme for the "chapter" in *Spoon River Anthology* in which Edgar Lee Masters struck out against the false patriotism and twisted ideals responsible for the war and its American victims.

The best poet of his generation and an anti-imperialist, Masters contributed little to the literature of dissent during the years of the Philippine-American War. It was not until the publication of *Spoon River Anthology* in 1915 that Masters made public his despair and disgust. He spoke through the voice of "Harry Wilmans" in the burial ground of Spoon River:

> I was just turned twenty-one,
> And Henry Phipps, the Sunday-school superintendent,
> Made a speech in Bindle's Opera House.
> "The honor of the flag must be upheld," he said,
> "Whether it be assailed by a barbarous tribe of
>   Tagalogs
> Or the greatest power in Europe."
> And we cheered and cheered the speech and the flag
>   he waved
> As he spoke.
> And I went to the war in spite of my father,
> And followed the flag till I saw it raised
> By our camp in a rice field near Manila,
> And all of us cheered and cheered it.
> But there were flies and poisonous things;
> And there was the deadly water,
> And the cruel heat,
> And the sickening, putrid food;
> And the smell of the trench just back of the tents
> Where the soldiers went to empty themselves;

And there were the whores who followed us, full of
   syphilis;
And beastly acts between ourselves or alone,
With bullying, hatred, degradation among us,
And days of loathing and nights of fear
To the hour of the charge through the steaming
   swamp.
Following the flag,
Till I fell with a scream, shot through the guts.
Now there's a flag over me in Spoon River!
A flag! A flag! . . .

To count the pamphlets and columns of newsprint authored by members of the academic and literary communities during the years of the Philippine-American War would be an endless and a fruitless exercise, but it is not difficult to reach some rough quantitative judgments. A majority of professional commentators denounced our Philippine policy, whereas college presidents were more circumspect; a large majority of the more distinguished poets, novelists, and belle lettrists were in opposition, but literary magazines and journals of opinion divided more evenly. The difficult questions remain unanswered, however. Did the spokesmen of these communities, on either side of the issue, influence other segments of public opinion? Did they influence public policy or the prosecution and conduct of the war? The easiest and likeliest answer to these questions is No. Policy makers and their political supporters appear to have received little inspiration from the writings of the expansionist minority in the academic and literary communities and to have viewed the anti-imperialist writers and academics as an irritation rather than an obstacle. Certainly the mood of pessimism that characterized so much of the writing of anti-imperialist intellectuals in the years 1901–2 would support the belief that they had little immediate impact on American policy in the Philippines.

To admit this, however, is not to prove that they left no imprint on public policy or the education of American public opinion. It is possible that they were of some influence in publicizing and so limiting instances of torture and military misconduct in the Philippines; it is probable that they influenced the shifting ideological rationale of the imperialists; and it is conceivable that the imprecations of the anti-imperialist Jeremiahs as well as the unexpected length of the Philippine-American War lessened the enthusiasm of policy makers and public alike for further adventures in insular imperialism.

The Impact of U.S. Imperialism

Arturo Morales Carrión

PUERTO RICO: COLONIAL TUTELAGE

In late July 1898, near the end of the Spanish-American-Cuban-Filipino War, U.S. troops occupied the Caribbean island of Puerto Rico. The U.S. military commander proclaimed that his forces had come to free Puerto Ricans from Spanish oppression and to bestow the "blessings of an enlightened civilization." Although Puerto Rican leaders had just secured autonomy and home rule from Madrid, they nonetheless welcomed the Americans, because they believed that the United States would either protect their autonomy or perhaps confer citizenship and statehood upon the people of the island. In this selection from his book *Puerto Rico*, Arturo Morales Carrión of the University of Puerto Rico explores the U.S. denial of the right of self-government to Puerto Ricans and the impact of colonial tutelage on them. He has also written *On Puerto Rican Cultural Values* (1975) and numerous studies in Spanish on Puerto Rican history and culture.

Even before the island's [Puerto Rico's] territorial status had been determined by Congress, a peculiar set of colonial interrelationships came into being; an institutional structure was established; a form of political behavior developed; and power was centralized in such fields as justice, education and security. In this sense, the old tradition of the Spanish centralized government based on the authority to govern the island as a place under siege, was replaced by an emerging tradition of centralized power, which contradicted many American principles and values. The *mentorado* [tutelage] was, indeed, on its way, but over a rather bumpy road.

[George W.] Davis, the fourth military governor in less than a year, was not a West Pointer; as professor Henry Wells has pointed out, Davis and his civil and military officers represented a cross section of American middle class values at the turn of the century. He was more scholarly and tactful than [Guy V.] Henry, but his very strong prejudices marred his good intentions. The different race and high illiteracy rate of Puerto Ricans were to him very strong arguments

Reprinted from *Puerto Rico: A Political and Cultural History*, pp. 147–57, by Arturo Morales Carrión, by permission of W. W. Norton & Company, Inc. Footnotes omitted. Copyright © 1983 by American Association for State and Local History.

against home rule. He could well understand the economic crisis and became a champion of free trade with the mainland. . . .

In fact, Davis was one of the two primary shapers of the McKinley administration's colonial policies towards Puerto Rico. The other was Elihu Root, secretary of war since July, 1899. A prominent New York lawyer with close ties to the eastern Republican establishment, Root was known as a man of keen intellect and as a flexible negotiator. A friend of [Theodore] Roosevelt, Root was a political conservative, who admired the British imperial system; hence, much suited to the tutorial role expected of him. On most matters he agreed with Davis and was influenced by his reports.

Davis continued the centralization of power with the executive. But in order to conform to American practices, somehow he had to take into account the people's wishes. Having considered the Puerto Ricans unfit for self-government, Davis relied on hand-picked advisory boards of what he called "distinguished citizens of Puerto Rico." The aim, he insisted in an August 15, 1900, circular, was to prepare for territorial government. To the actions undertaken by [John R.] Brooke and Henry [the first military governors], he added significant legal measures: the institution of the writ of *habeas corpus* and the appointment of a United States provisional court, with trial by jury and reorganization of the judiciary on recommendation of the judicial board. In the August circular he outlined a colonial administration by a governor working with a cabinet which with little modification was to continue in Puerto Rico after civil government was established in 1900. He left the practice of self-government to the municipal area which he considered chaotic. To Davis, cooperation from the political parties was the first step of the learning process. Only when this lesson was mastered would the people be ready for an insular legislature. The political education of Puerto Rico was thus to proceed gradually under the watchful eyes of a hopeful tutor.

With his August circulars and other acts, Davis had boldly entered into the area of legislative fiat. Root, too, was searching for an administrative diagram of what he called "The Principles of Colonial Policy." In his 1899 Report as Secretary of War he outlined his views: Since the United States was a nation endowed with the powers essential to national life, it had all the powers with respect to the territory which it had thus acquired. The people of the territories had no legal right whatsoever to assert against the United States, but had "a moral right to be treated by the United States in accordance with the underlying principles of justice and freedom which we have declared in our Constitution." The people of Puerto Rico, for instance, were entitled to demand not to be deprived of life, liberty, or property without due process of law, but when it came to the form of government, it was a different matter. Here, the most important fact to be considered was that the people had not been educated in the art of self-government or any really honest government. Since only 10 percent could read or write (the proportion was, indeed, higher), they did not have any real understanding of the way to conduct a popular government. In Root's view, Puerto Ricans were in the same rudimentary stage of political development as the rest of the West Indies and Central America. They had to learn the principles of self-control and respect for constitutional government. Root wrote:

> This lesson will necessarily be slowly learned, because it is a matter not of intellectual apprehension, but of character and of acquired habits of thought and feeling. . . . They would inevitably fail without a course of tuition under a strong and guiding hand. With that tuition for a time their natural capacity will, it is hoped, make them a self-governing people.

This passage clearly presents the American theory of colonial tutelage in the first half of the twentieth century. Together with the doctrine of congressional supremacy as provided by the Treaty of Paris, this stance denied the people of Puerto Rico any natural rights to self-government. They would have only the rights that their tutors and Congress chose to give them. The Jeffersonian philosophy of government by consent, based on inalienable rights, as set forth in the Declaration of Independence, was conveniently shelved.

While the new colonial policies were being shaped in Washington and Puerto Rico, the economic realities were adding unexpected new pressures. With the coffee market in sharp decline, the tobacco market closed, and the American sugar market still subject to a high tariff, Puerto Rican agriculture was plummeting. Furthermore, money exchange was working to the disadvantage of the Spanish *peso*. The economy, like the political structure, was also going through a traumatic period. Then a natural disaster struck. On August 8, 1899, *San Ciriaco*, the worst hurricane within memory, cut through the island. More than 3,000 lives were lost; the coffee crop valued at more than $7 million was totally destroyed. Plantain trees were washed away and whole coffee *haciendas* were abandoned.

American officials, new to the tropics, were appalled at the havoc wrought by the fierce storm. Davis' wires and dispatches told of the absolute helplessness of the population, the deaths, and the vast numbers of destitute. Davis asked for food, for a loan to help meet the financial losses, and especially recommended free trade with the United States, "a measure which I could not fully endorse until this calamity came upon the island."

San Ciriaco was, then, a disaster that touched the nerve of moral duty. Root was already reaching the conclusion that the island had been bottled up by Cuban, Spanish, and American tariffs on tobacco, coffee, and sugar. He now viewed opening the U.S. market as "the only essential thing." *San Ciriaco* was a call to action: "The terrible destruction and impoverishment of the people by the recent hurricane," he wrote the president, "brings matters to a climax." He asked that imports of Puerto Rican products to the United States be declared free by executive decree, or by a special session of Congress. "The great burst of public beneficence," he concluded, "will not last long, and we will have a starving people in our hands very soon—starving, because this great, rich country, after inviting the Puerto Ricans to place themselves in our hands, refuses to permit them to send their products in our markets without the payment of a practically prohibitory duty." While he mobilized with great effectiveness a nationwide humanitarian effort, Root viewed free trade as a moral duty. He was also receptive to the requests from planters and businessmen for help to keep the economy going, provide work for their *peones* (field hands) and restore agricultural production. The economy had to be put on its feet if the colonial diagram was to work.

Basic questions arose from the first two crowded years of contacts and crisis. How were the Puerto Ricans to be governed? What types of economic relationships were to be established? What values were to preside over this change from a Spanish to an American system? The issues were debated in Congress in 1900. But before then, Davis and Root, following Brooke and Henry, had already established the theory, provided the administrative system, and set the tone for the American tutelage over the island. And they prepared themselves with key recommendations so that the transition to civil government would confirm the usefulness and propriety of what Root called "The Principles of Colonial Policy.". . .

Between October, 1898, when the American flag was raised at *La Fortaleza* and November, 1948, when the Puerto Ricans chose their first elective governor, a full half century was to elapse. During this period, colonial tutelage was put to the test. The system called for the executive power to be controlled by Washington, especially in such key areas as justice, education, and security. Washington also controlled the legal system through presidential appointments to the Puerto Rican Supreme Court and the role of the U.S. District Court. Only in the legislative branch was the Puerto Rican voice fully heard. Obviously a clash between the legislative and the executive branches was inevitable. But power remained in Washington and in the hands of the presidential appointees, the key interpreters of U.S. tutelage.

The substance of colonialism was preserved, although the semantics changed. Puerto Rico was not called a "colony," but a "dependency" or "possession," juridically defined as an "unincorporated Territory." This era was . . . the era when sugar was king. It saw a profound economic transformation as American corporate capitalism, with huge investments, expanded and controlled the sugar industry. Modernized production turned Puerto Rico into a plantation economy, with emphasis on monoculture and deepening social and economic cleavages. When the burgeoning population and the 1929 depression combined, the situation became grave and explosive, a far cry from the hopes of the early tutors. Puerto Rico was not to be a happy, prosperous island, well-taught and well-behaved, but a poorhouse, and in the words of Rexford G. Tugwell, the last and brightest of the tutors, "a stricken land," foundering in despair. . . .

When President McKinley gave Root responsibility for colonial policies as secretary of war, he wanted Puerto Rico to have "the best possible form of government." Root and Davis did their homework, but the Philippines, Cuba, and Puerto Rico posed different problems. As a result, their recommendations to Congress were a hybrid of American experience of territorial government and British imperial touches.

When in 1900 Davis drafted his recommendations on Puerto Rico's future civil government, he admitted that there were no U.S. precedents to help him and that it was necessary to turn to the experience of other nations. In searching "points of resemblance," he turned to the island of Trinidad, captured by the British in 1797. At that time, Trinidad had had Spanish laws and institutions, some slaves, no Indians, the Catholic religion, and sugar. Davis praised Trinidad's stability under the British: the rise in population, revenues, and production; the expansion of education; the presence of religious freedom;

and the emphasis on road-building. Davis believed that the native population of Spanish, Negroes, and "maroons" would have reduced Trinidad to chaos. "Home rule," he pointed out, "was fortunately not accorded to this island, but instead it was governed at first by military officers directly. It is now a crown colony, having an executive council of five officials and three native appointed members, the governor presiding." Trinidad also had an elective council of twelve members. According to Davis, the island's population was content. This was, then, the model that influenced Davis. In Puerto Rico, he thought, there were men of learning and ability who would abuse power and take advantage of the profound illiteracy of the people. Since he considered both the people and the elite incompetent, he recommended withholding self-government unless there was "a plain demonstration of their competence to exercise it." In his view, only a few wanted it, the masses were stolid and the business class opposed it.

Davis also recommended that Puerto Rico be called a "dependency," with a governor, an executive council and later on a legislative assembly. The resemblance to a British crown colony model was obvious. The executive council would consist of a governor and seven chiefs of administrative offices plus four other members chosen from the legislative assembly. The legislative assembly would be composed of thirty-five assemblymen, with a town council for each municipality. All members of the Supreme Court and the United States Federal Court would be appointed by the president, who would also have the authority to disallow, repeal, alter, or annul any action of the governor or the assembly. Power was, therefore, firmly to remain in Washington.

But even this scheme, Davis insisted, should not be immediately enacted in its entirety. For the present, the governor and executive council should control legislation. "When experience shall have shown that the people comprehend the gravity of the duties and obligations of self-government will be soon enough to establish the lower house," he wrote. Only the tutor would judge when the time would come.

Root agreed with Davis. He too recommended a form of insular government, but with the United States in complete control of the rights, property, and obligations of the people. He accepted elections for mayors and municipal councils, but specified that if they failed to perform their duties, the governor could remove them and order free elections.

Invasion of Puerto Rico, 1898. Troops from Wisconsin marched into Ponce, Puerto Rico, to replace the Spanish flag with the Stars and Stripes. (*Library of Congress*)

Root considered the people too inexperienced to elect a legislature, and recommended that until they learned how to govern themselves at the municipal level, they should not have a legislature. He viewed elementary education as the key to success; if necessary, it should be defrayed by the United States. But the overriding consideration was economic: free trade should be established at the earliest possible moment.

The president and the Congress had other advisers who viewed Puerto Rican abilities with more respect and less ethnic prejudice. McKinley's special commissioner, Henry K. Carroll, was one such observer. Carroll's report, based on first hand information from all classes, was complete and up-to-date. While supporting American sovereignty over Puerto Rico, Carroll came to like the people, tried to understand the culture, and had some profound insights into the problems of governance and intercultural relations.

Carroll often relied on Puerto Rican opinion; and he admitted the liberality of the system of autonomy, and some positive features of Spanish administration. He was particularly impressed with the human values of the poor: their system of mutual helpfulness, kindness, and hospitality. He did not equate extreme poverty and squalor with vice and unhappiness. He saw the Puerto Ricans as peace-loving, law-abiding, and deeply desirous of a civil government. Above all, Carroll insisted that illiteracy should not bar the people from self-government. He observed:

> They may be poor but they are proud and sensitive, and could be bitterly disappointed if they found that they had been delivered from an oppressive yoke to be put under a tutelage which proclaimed their inferiority. . . .

"Education," he wrote, "is not the invariable line which separates good citizens from bad, but active moral sense." He argued that Puerto Ricans were better prepared to govern themselves than most Latin Americans, and reiterated that they could learn the art of government the only possible way: "by having its responsibilities laid upon them, by learning from their blunders."

Early in January, 1900, legislation was introduced in the House and Senate, providing for civil government for Puerto Rico. Senator Joseph P. Foraker of Ohio led the debate in the Senate. Republican Congressman Sereno Payne, chairman of the Ways and Means Committee, was in charge on the House side. The hearings brought out the clash between the gradualist tutors and the partisans of autonomy. But economic issues were also prominent, especially free trade, which was opposed by the U.S. sugar and tobacco lobbies. The long Republican tradition of protectionism which had helped elect McKinley was now challenged by Puerto Rico's claim to free access to the American market. To some, like the New England Tobacco Growers' Association, this meant nothing less than the destruction of the American system of political economy. Lobbyists for the beet sugar industry invoked old prejudices: free trade meant that "the Latin race, after years of the rule of despotism, if suddenly given power, is a troublesome if not a dangerous power with which to deal."

The two main questions in the debate were the extension of the constitution to the newly acquired territories and the question of free trade. Both issues were hotly debated.

The debate was held under the shadow of a larger issue: whether the people and products of the Philippines should have free entry into the United States. The fear that legislation for Puerto Rico would set a precedent for the Philippines influenced many positions and filled the debate with racist rhetoric. Senator [William B.] Bate of Tennessee, an anti-imperialist, described the Philippines as "Pandora's box, full of ills, some of which are upon us, and others are to come. That is the real question. Puerto Rico is but its front shadow." He talked disdainfully of the "mongrels of the East" and feared the omnipotence of Congress as asserted in the Puerto Rican bill. Here racism was an ally of anti-colonialism.

The question of citizenship further complicated these issues. Root, for instance, never wavered from his view that U.S. citizenship should not be extended to Puerto Rico. He did not favor the complete incorporation of the island into the United States. For strategic reasons, he wanted to keep Puerto Rico, but he thought Puerto Rico should eventually have self-government, increasing as the people grew more competent.

McKinley's Special Commission, on the other hand, recommended both free trade and citizenship. This was the line originally taken by Senator Foraker. But the urgent need to raise customs revenues until tax legislation was enacted, together with the fear that granting citizenship implied statehood, led Foraker to reverse himself. American citizenship was denied in the final version which was approved by the House and Senate in April 1900. In providing the congressional framework for tutelage, incorporation and citizenship were both discarded.

The result of this debate was an "Act temporarily to provide revenues and civil government" which was to last for seventeen years. It was based on compromise. Free trade was put off for two years and in the meantime a 15 percent tariff was imposed on all merchandise coming into the United States from Puerto Rico, and vice versa. These revenues would be used by the president to benefit Puerto Rico until the new civil government enacted and put into operation a local system of taxation. The President would then decree free trade.

The act created a body politic under the name of "The People of Puerto Rico," composed of citizens of Puerto Rico entitled to the protection of the United States, but with very limited rights—a real colonial anomaly.

In the political field the Root and Davis doctrines of a hybrid executive council and the omnipotence of Washington prevailed, but with a significant change. Puerto Rico was granted a House of Delegates, elected by the people. This was another compromise between believers in the American commitment to representative democracy and those who insisted on strict imperial tutelage. The act created a paternalistic government, dominated by Washington, and run primarily by an American bureaucracy with a smattering of Puerto Rican participation.

Many Democrats bitterly opposed the bill, but few were as sharp and direct as Congressman William H. Jones of Virginia. He objected to the Republican tactics of railroading the bill through the House; he considered the executive council's power to grant franchises as "offensive and repugnant." Jones' concern foreshadowed later events. In 1916–1917, he was to steer the question of political reform in Puerto Rico during the Wilson Administration.

Another aspect of this legislation was crucial for the future. A Joint Resolution (S.R. 116), introduced by Senator Foraker, passed the Senate after the passage of the act. It provided for the continuation of military government pending the establishment of the permanent civil government [established in May 1900]. In the House, Congressman Jones pressed for an amendment to protect Puerto Rico from corporate latifundia by prohibiting corporations from carrying the business of agriculture. Jones warned that unless the amendment was adopted, the condition of the population would be reduced "to one of absolute servitude." The Senate did not accept this drastic measure, but compromised by limiting corporate ownership not to exceed 500 acres of land. The joint resolution then passed the Senate; behind the limitation adopted were the interests of the American Beet Sugar Association, the tobacco interests, and some Congressional prejudice against the power of the trusts. For almost half a century, however, the 500-acre restriction was a dead letter in the agrarian history of Puerto Rico.

Louis A. Pérez, Jr.

CUBA: THE PLATT AMENDMENT

True to its Teller Amendment pledge, the United States did not annex Cuba. The United States did occupy the island nation until 1902, however, and forced Cubans to accept the Platt Amendment (1901–33), which gave the U.S. government the right to supervise Cuba's external affairs and internal policies. The amendment also required Cuba to cede a military base (Guantánamo Bay) to the United States. Thereafter, under the aegis of the Platt Amendment, American troops repeatedly intervened in Cuba. In this selection from his interpretative history *Cuba: Between Reform and Revolution*, Louis A. Pérez, Jr., a historian at the University of South Florida, discusses the long-term U.S. interest in controlling the Caribbean island. He offers the provocative interpretation that the United States joined the war against Spain, which the Cubans were already winning, in order to prevent Cuban independence. In his treatment of the impact of U.S. imperialism on Cuba, Pérez finds that American authorities manipulated politics and suppressed nationalistic appeals for full independence. And as North American investors rapidly gained control over the island's wealth, Cuba also lost its economic sovereignty. Among Professor Pérez's other books are *Army Politics in Cuba* (1976), *Cuba Between Empires* (1982), *Cuba Under the Platt Amendment* (1986), and *Cuba and the United States* (1990).

With the end of 1897 and the start of 1898, all signs pointed to the imminent and inevitable dénouement: the triumph of Cuban arms. Preparations for the last desperate battles of the war [against Spain] had begun. Holding undisputed control over the Cuban countryside, the insurgent army command prepared for the final phase of the insurrection: the assault on the cities. In late 1897, Cubans had completed the organization of artillery units and were preparing to carry the war to urban centers. In Oriente, General Calixto García laid siege on Bayamo, a city of some 21,000 residents. In August, García mounted a stunning and successful artillery attack on Victoria de Las Tunas, a city of 18,000 people. In the succeeding six months, town after town in eastern Cuba fell to Cubans, including Guisa, Guáimaro, Jiguaní, Loma de Hierro, and Bayamo. In early 1898, Manzanillo was threatened. In April, García was engaged in final preparations for an assault against Santiago de Cuba.

Across the island, the Spanish army had ceased to fight. *Peninsular* units abandoned smaller interior towns for larger provincial cities, and then abandoned these to concentrate their defenses in provincial capitals. "The enemy," Máximo Gémez reported from Las Villas in March 1898, "has departed, ceasing military operations and abandoning the garrisons and forts which constituted his base of operations. Days, weeks and months pass without a column of troops appearing within our radius of action." He now wrote confidently about preparation for the final assault against Spaniards in the cities. With "cannons and a great deal of dynamite," a self-assured Gémez predicted, "we can expel them by fire and steel from the towns."

January was customarily the month in which the Spanish army command launched vigorous field operations—every dry season, for the previous two years, January announced the beginning of the winter campaign. Cubans braced themselves for what many believed to be the last and, perhaps, the most desperate enemy offensive. But nothing happened. In January 1898, Máximo Gémez wrote of a "dead war." The collapse was all but complete. "The enemy is crushed," Gémez reported with some surprise from central Cuba, "and is in complete retreat from here, and the time which favored their operations passes without their doing anything." Spain's failure to mount a new winter offensive confirmed the Cuban belief that the enemy was exhausted and lacked the resources and resolve to continue the war. One more campaign, the insurgent chieftains predicted confidently, would suffice to deliver the coup de grace to the moribund Spanish army. A new optimism lifted insurgent morale to an all-time high. Never before had Cubans been as certain of victory as they were in early 1898. "This war cannot last more than a year," Gémez predicted euphorically in January 1898. "This is the first time I have ever put a limit to it.". . .

The success of Cuban arms threatened more than the propriety of colonial rule or traditional property relations in the colonial regime. If challenged, too, pretensions of colonial replacement. For the better part of the nineteenth century the United States had pursued the acquisition of Cuba with resolve, if without results. The United States had early pronounced its claim to imperial succession in the Caribbean, but this proclamation had failed to deliver the coveted island into the North American union. In attempting to end Spanish sovereignty, Cubans also endangered the United States aspiration to sovereignty. Acquisition of Cuba was envisioned by North Americans as an act of colonial continuity, formally transferred and legitimately ceded by Spain to the United States—a legal assumption of sovereignty over a territorial possession presumed incapable of a separate nationhood.

The Cuban rebellion changed all this. Cuba was lost to Spain, and if Washington did not act, it would also be lost to the United States. By early 1898, U.S. officials were acknowledging what was already evident in Cuba: the days of Spanish rule were numbered. "Spain herself has demonstrated she is powerless either to conciliate Cuba or conquer it," former U.S. minister to Spain Hannis Taylor concluded in late 1897; "her sovereignty over [Cuba] is . . . now extinct." "To-day the strength of the Cubans [is] nearly double . . . ," Assistant Secretary of State William R. Day wrote in a confidential memorandum in 1898, "and [they] occupy and control virtually all the territory outside the heavily garrisoned coast cities and a few interior towns. There are no active operations by the Spaniards. . . . The eastern provinces are admittedly 'Free Cuba.' In view of these statements alone, it is now evident that Spain's struggle in Cuba has become absolutely hopeless."

Set against the landscape created by the receding tide of Spanish sovereignty, the United States confronted what was anathema to all North American policymakers since Thomas Jefferson—Cuban independence. The implications of the "no transfer" principle were now carried to their logical conclusion. If the United States could not permit Spain to transfer sovereignty over Cuba to another power, neither could the United States permit Spain to cede sovereignty to Cubans.

So it was that in April 1898 President William McKinley requested of Congress authority to intervene militarily in Cuba. War ostensibly against Spain, but in fact against Cubans—war, in any case, as an alternative medium of political exchange, just as [Carl von] Clausewitz posited.

The president's war message provided the purpose of policy: no mention of Cuban independence, not a hint of sympathy with *Cuba Libre*, nowhere even an allusion to the renunciation of territorial aggrandizement—only a request for congressional authorization "to take measures to secure a full and final termination of hostilities between the Government of Spain and the people of Cuba, and to secure in the island the establishment of a stable government, capable of maintaining order and observing its international obligations." The United States presence in Cuba, McKinley explained, consisted of a "forcible intervention . . . as a neutral to stop the war." "Neutral intervention" offered a means through which to establish, by virtue of arms, United States claims of sovereignty over Cuba. "The forcible intervention of the United States . . . ," McKinley announced to Congress on April 11, "involves . . . hostile constraint upon both the parties to the contest." This meant war directed against both Spaniards and Cubans, the means to establish grounds upon which to neutralize the two competing claims of sovereignty and establish by superior force of arms a third.

McKinley's message did not pass entirely unchallenged. The Cuban cause had won a wide popular following in the United States, and congressional defenders of *Cuba Libre* made repeated attempts to secure the administration's recognition of Cuban independence. By mid-April, the president grudgingly accepted a compromise. Congress agreed to forgo recognition of independence in exchange for the president's acceptance of a disclaimer. Article IV of the congressional resolution, the Teller Amendment, specified that the United States "hereby disclaims any disposition of intention to exercise sovereignty, jurisdiction, or control over said island except for pacification thereof, and asserts its determination, when that is accomplished, to leave the government and control of the island to its people." And the United States proceeded to war. . . .

The intervention changed everything, as it was meant to. A Cuban war of liberation was transformed into a U.S. war of conquest. It was the victory to which the United States first laid claim, and from which so much else would flow. A set of developments, articulated in successive stages, would together provide the basis upon which the United States would proceed to establish its claim of sovereignty over Cuba. The Cubans seemed to have achieved little in their own behalf, the North Americans concluded. The lack of decisive battles in the war and the apparent absence of noteworthy insurgent military achievements were attributed immediately to the deficiency of Cuban operations, if not to Cuban character. These impressions served to encourage the belief that Cubans had accomplished nothing in more than three years of war and that North American arms alone determined the outcome of the war.

There was a dark side to these pronouncements. North Americans wanted more than credit. That Cubans appeared to have vanished from the campaign altogether served immediately to minimize Cuban participation in final operations against Spain, and ultimately justified excluding Cubans from the peace negotiations with Spain. In appropriating credit for the military triumph over Spain, the United States established claim to negotiate unilaterally peace terms with Spain; in appropriating responsibility for ending Spanish colonial government, the United States claimed the right to supervise Cuban national government.

So it was that the Cuban war for national liberation was transfigured into the "Spanish-American War," nomenclature that denied Cuban participation and presaged the next series of developments. This construct served to legitimize the United States claim over Cuba as a spoil of victory. The Cuban struggle was portrayed as an effort that by 1898 had stalled, if not altogether failed. The United States completed the task the Cubans had started but were incapable of completing alone. The proposition was established early and advanced vigorously. Cubans were apprised of their indebtedness to the United States, from whose expenditure of lives, treasury, and resources Cuba had achieved independence from Spain. The denial of the Cuban success over Spain denied them more than laurels of victory—it deprived them of their claim to sovereignty. . . .

Military occupation began on January 1, 1899, and after nearly a century of covetous preoccupation with the island, the United States assumed formal possession of Cuba. It was not an unqualified possession, however. Certainly the Teller Amendment obstructed direct fulfillment of the nineteenth-century design of annexation. But the main obstacle to permanent acquisition was not the congressional resolution. A far more formidable challenge appeared in the form of *independentismo*. Three decades of revolutionary activity—spanning the years between 1868 and 1898, involving two generations of Cubans, and consecrated in three major wars—had created a nationalist movement of enormous popular vitality and political vigor. It was not a sentiment to be trifled with. The principal challenge to pretensions of U.S. rule originated within the ranks of the wartime populist coalition, and it was this central political reality that determined the purpose of the U.S. military occupation.

The proponents of *independentismo* persisted through the early period of the occupation, and the ideal never lost its appeal. A great deal of U.S. effort was devoted to discrediting both. Cuban motives for independence were suspect, as if opposition to the presence of the United States was itself evidence that self-serving if not sinister motives lurked behind separatist aspirations. Cubans were not inspired by love of liberty but by the lure of looting. "From the highest officer to the lowliest 'soldier,'" one North American wrote, "they were there for personal gain." The Cuban desire for independence, U.S. officials concluded, was motivated by a desire to plunder and exact reprisals. Cubans were possessed, one observer reported, by the "sole active desire to murder and pillage." "If we are to save Cuba," one New York journalist exhorted, "we must hold it. If we leave it to the Cubans, we give it over to a reign of terror—to the machete and the torch, to insurrection and assassination."

This was a proposition from which North Americans drew a number of inferences: first, Cubans were not prepared for self-government. Again and again the same theme came up. The ideological imperative of empire took hold early, and deeply. The consensus was striking. Admiral William T. Sampson, a member of the United States evacuation commission, insisted that Cubans had no idea of self-government—and "it will take a long time to teach them." Some United States officials believed Cubans incapable of self-government at any time. "Self-government!" General William R. Shafter protested. "Why those people are no more fit for self-government than gunpowder is for hell." General Samuel B. M. Young concluded after the war that the "insurgents are a lot of degenerates, absolutely devoid of honor or gratitude. They are no more capable of self-government than the savages of Africa." For Major Alexander Brodie the necessity for a protectorate, or outright annexation, was as self-evident as it was self-explanatory. "The Cubans are utterly irresponsible," Brodie insisted, "partly savage, and have no idea of what good government means." A similar note was struck by Major George M. Barbour, the United States sanitary commissioner in Santiago de Cuba. The Cubans, he insisted, "are stupid, given to lying and doing all things in the wrong way. . . . Under our supervision, and with firm and honest care for the future, the people of Cuba may become a useful race and a credit to the world; but to attempt to set them afloat as a nation, during this generation, would be a great mistake." General William Ludlow, military governor of Havana, concurred: "The present generation will, in my judgment, have to pass away before the Cubans can form a stable government." In mid-1899, Governor General John R. Brooke agreed: "These people cannot *now*, or I believe in the immediate future, be entrusted with their own government." "We are going ahead as fast as we can." Governor General Leonard Wood informed the White House in 1900, "but we are dealing with a race that has steadily been going down for a hundred years and into which we have to infuse new life, new principles and new methods of doings things."

The attempt to discredit independence was surpassed only by the effort to deprecate its advocates. Independence was as unworthy an ideal as its proponents were unfit to govern. Only the "ignorant masses," the "unruly rabble," the "trouble makers"—"the element," in General Wood's words, "absolutely without any conception of its responsibilities or duties as citizens"—advocated independence. "The only people who are howling for [self-government]," he concluded with undisguised contempt, "are those whose antecedents and actions demonstrate the impossibility of self-government at present."

The ideal of independence, however, persisted as a powerful force during the early years of the occupation. The popular appeal of those Cubans who opposed Spanish rule or defended national sovereignty was irresistible. Most North Americans in Cuba conceded, if only in private, that a majority of Cubans were devoted to the ideal of independence. But numbers alone, they were quick to counter, could not be permitted to determine the fate of Cuba—particularly when the sentiment of the majority was identified with disruption, disorder, and chaos. That Cubans in large numbers opposed annexation was cause enough to distrust and reason sufficient to discredit independence sentiment. If there were people who opposed United States rule, they probably knew no better or were led by wicked men. In either case, Cuban incapacity for self-government was confirmed. Over time, North Americans insisted, under the protection and patronage of the United States, the call for annexation would rise above the clamor for independence. There existed in Cuba a yet unrevealed majority, U.S. officials thought, that was silent in its preference but steadfast in its desire for annexation. "The real voice of the people of Cuba," General Wood reassured the White House in late 1899, "has not been heard because they have not spoken and, unless I am entirely mistaken, when they do speak there will be many more voices for annexation than there is at present any idea of."

In the meantime, if the United States found no support in the anti-annexation majority, it derived some consolation in the quality of the pro-annexation minority. The "better classes," the propertied, the educated, the white—those sectors, in short, most deserving of North American solicitude—wanted close and permanent ties with the United States. This offered North Americans some hope, for the purpose of the intervention was to foreclose more than the rise of a new political force; it was also to forestall the fall of an old social system. Propertied elites greeted U.S. intervention as nothing less than the providential deliverance from expropriation and extinction. It was to this group that the United States looked for political leaders and local allies. North Americans early detected in the shattered ranks of the creole property owners natural allies in its pursuit of control over Cuba. Both opposed Cuban independence. Both opposed Cuban government. Policymakers needed supporters, property owners needed security. The United States searched for a substitute for independence; *peninsular* and creole elites sought a substitute for colonialism. The logic of collaboration was compelling. There was an inexorable choicelessness about this collaboration, wholly improvised but as pragmatic as it was politically opportune. The old colonial elites in need of protection and the new colonial rulers in need of allies arrived at an understanding. United States efforts during the occupation centered on enrolling the services of the propertied elites as political surrogates in opposition to the *independentista* polity. The ascendancy of a political coalition organized around colonial elites promised not only to obstruct the rise of *independentismo* but also to institutionalize United States influence at the point of maximum effectiveness—from within. It would matter slightly less, then, if Cuba were to become independent, if that independence were under the auspices of a client political elite whose own social salvation was a function of United States control.

One certain way to foreclose the rise of the unruly masses, North American authorities believed, was to deny the *independentista* leaders the opportunity to mobilize the vast political force of Cuban nationalism. And the surest way to promote the ascendancy of the "better classes" was to exclude the "rabble" from the electorate. Secretary of

War Elihu Root proposed limited suffrage, one that would exclude the "mass of ignorant and incompetent," and "avoid the kind of control which leads to perpetual revolutions of Central America and other West India islands." All voters were required to be Cuban males over the age of twenty and in possession of one of the following: real or personal property worth $250, or an ability to read and write, or honorable service in the Liberation Army. All Cuban women and two-thirds of all adult Cuban men were excluded from the franchise. Suffrage restrictions reduced the Cuban electorate to 105,000 males, approximately 5 percent of the total population.

But early elections revealed the power of the *independentistas'* appeal. They prevailed in the municipal elections of 1900, and again in the constituent assembly elections later that year. General Wood lamented: "The men whom I had hoped to see take leadership have been forced into the background by the absolutely irresponsible and unreliable element. . . . The only fear in Cuba to-day is not that we shall stay, but that we shall leave too soon. The elements desiring our immediate departure are the men whose only capacity will be demonstrated as a capacity for destroying all hopes for the future." And to the point: "I do not mean to say that the people are not capable of good government; but I do mean to say, and emphasize it, that the class to whom we must look for the stable government in Cuba are not as yet sufficiently well represented to give us that security and confidence which we desire."

Wood shared his despair with Elihu Root. "I am disappointed in the composition of the Convention," Wood wrote in March 1901. The responsibility of framing a new constitution had fallen to some of the "worst agitators and political radicals in Cuba." Wood questioned again the wisdom of proceeding with plans for evacuation. "None of the more intelligent men claim that the people are yet ready for self-government," Wood insisted. "In case we withdraw," he warned, the convention represented "the class to whom Cuba would have to be turned over . . . for the highly intelligent Cubans of the land owning, industrial and commercial classes are not in politics." Two-thirds of the convention delegates were "adventurers pure and simple," not "representatives of Cuba," and "not safe leaders." . . .

By late 1900 the United States faced the unsettling prospect of evacuation without having established the internal structures of hegemony. Time was running out. So were justifications for continued military occupation. An anomalous situation arose. In 1900, the

United States found itself in possession of an island that it could neither fully retain nor completely release. By 1900, too, the United
States confronted the imminent ascendancy of the very political coalition that the intervention had been designed to thwart.

The outcome of the 1900 elections served to underscore the perils attending independence. By failing to elect the candidates approved
by the United States, Cubans had demonstrated themselves ill-suited
to assume the responsibility of self-government. Cubans could simply
not be trusted, United States officials contended, to elect the "best
men." Some conclusions, hence, seemed in order. The elections
revealed Cubans to lack political maturity. They were swayed easily by
emotions and led readily by demagogues. All of which pointed to one
last moral: Cubans were still not ready for independence. And a
corollary: the United States could not release Cuba into the family of
nations so palpably ill-prepared to discharge the responsibilities of
sovereignty. One member of the McKinley cabinet asserted bluntly
that the United States did not intend to expel Spain only to turn the
island "over to the insurgents or to any other particular class or faction." The United States purpose in Cuba was not to be guided by the
political issue of independence but by the moral necessity to establish a
"stable government for and by all the people." "When the Spanish-
American war was declared," Wood argued, "the United States took a
step forward, and assumed a position as protector of the interests of
Cuba. It became responsible for the welfare of the people, politically,
mentally and morally." This was the position of the administration in
Washington. "This nation has assumed before the world a grave
responsibility for the future of good government in Cuba," President
McKinley proclaimed in his 1899 message to Congress. He continued:

> We have accepted a trust the fulfillment of which calls for the sternest
> integrity of purpose and the exercise of the highest wisdom. The new
> Cuba yet to arise from the ashes of the past must be bound to us by ties
> of singular intimacy and strength if its enduring welfare is to be assured.
> . . . Our mission, to accomplish when we took up the wager of battle, is
> not to be fulfilled by turning adrift any loosely framed commonwealth
> to face the vicissitudes which too often attend weaker states.

The McKinley administration faced a policy dilemma: how to
respect the congressional resolution without relenting to Cuban
demands—when both called for independence. If the principle of the

"If General Wood Is Unpopular with Cuba, We Can Guess the Reason,"
1901. This cartoon demonstrated U.S. domination of the Caribbean island
and also reflected the American attitude toward Latinos at the time.

Teller Amendment could not be repudiated, its premises would be refuted. It was first necessary to devise a substitute for immediate independence that did not foreclose ultimate annexation, an arrangement, too, that neither defied the purpose of the congressional commitment nor disregarded the policy of the president. Not that Washington abandoned century-old designs on Cuba. Indeed, many in the administration persisted in the belief that annexation remained Cuba's ultimate destiny, if not at the immediate conclusion of the intervention or as the consummation of the occupation, then as the inevitable culmination of a future if still yet unresolved policy design. Annexation was a probability that could be temporarily postponed as long as its possibility was not definitively precluded.

Certainly the Teller Amendment had the immediate effect of obstructing annexation either as a deliberate outcome of the war with Spain or as a direct outgrowth of the occupation of Cuba. But it is untenable to suppose that the United States would suddenly renounce nearly a century of national policy, one based on the inevitability of the annexation of Cuba, solely as the result of a self-denying clause adopted by, many felt, an over-zealous Congress in a moment of well-meaning but ill-placed fervor. The administration's position was clear: formal annexation was proscribed, but complete independence was preposterous. A way had to be found to reconcile presidential resolve with the congressional resolution—a way to exercise sovereignty, if not permanently then provisionally, a means through which to exercise the substance of sovereignty without the necessity for the structures of sovereignty. . . .

In early 1901 the United States moved to resolve the dilemma. The "better classes" had shown themselves to be of limited political value. They had not fared well at the polls, and no amount of United States backing, it seemed, was adequate for the task of elevating them into power. In Washington, the administration was coming under increasing political pressure to comply with the Joint Resolution. In January, Secretary of War Root outlined the administration's views to General Wood in Cuba. The occupation was entering its third year, and had become, Root explained, a "burden and annoyance," and was expensive, too—half a million dollars a month, Root estimated. The administration was prepared, and even anxious, to end the occupation, but not without first securing guarantees necessary to United States interests. Root sought to give United States hegemony legal form, something in the way of binding political relations based on the Monroe Doctrine.

In January 1901 Root proposed to Secretary of State John Hay four provisions he deemed essential to United States interests. First, that "in transferring the control of Cuba to the Government established under the new constitution the United States reserves and retains the right of intervention for the preservation of Cuban independence and the maintenance of a stable Government adequately protecting life, property and individual liberty." Second, that "no Government organized under the constitution shall be deemed to have authority to enter into any treaty or engagement with any foreign power which may tend to impair or interfere with the independence of Cuba." Root also insisted that to perform "such duties as may devolve upon her under the foregoing provisions and for her own defense," the United States "may acquire and hold the title to land, and maintain naval stations at certain specified points." Lastly, that "all the acts of the Military Government, and all rights acquired thereunder, shall be valid and be maintained and protected." Root entrusted a draft of the proposed relations to Senator Orville H. Platt. During a meeting of the Republican senators to prepare the final language of the proposed legislation, two additional clauses were attached. One prescribed continuation of sanitary improvements undertaken by the military government. The other prohibited the Cuban government from contracting a debt for which the ordinary public revenues were inadequate. Together, the provisions became known as the Platt Amendment, enacted by Congress in 1901.

In its essential features, the Platt Amendment addressed the central elements of United States objectives in Cuba as determined over the course of the nineteenth century, something of an adequate if imperfect substitute for annexation. It served to transform the substance of Cuban sovereignty into an extension of the United States national system. The restrictions imposed upon the conduct of foreign relations, specifically the denial of treaty authority and debt restrictions, as well as the prohibition against the cession of national territory, were designed to minimize the possibility of Cuban international entanglements.

But restraints on Cuban foreign relations did not satisfy all United States needs. North American authorities could not contemplate Cuban independence without a presentiment of disaster. Self-government promised mis-government, officials warned freely, and the mismanagement of domestic and foreign affairs could have potentially calamitous repercussions on United States interests. If the United States would not permit the sovereignty of government to be challenged from abroad, it could not allow the solvency of government to be threatened from within. Elections had underscored the uncertainty if not inefficacy of democratic process. If extenuating circumstances prohibited immediate annexation, political considerations precluded complete independence. The Platt Amendment rested on the central if not fully stated premise that the principal danger to United States interests in Cuba originated with Cubans themselves, or at least those Cubans with antecedents in the revolution. Whether in the direction of foreign affairs, or in the management of public funds, or in the conduct of national politics, government by Cubans remained always a dubious proposition, an enterprise as unsound in its premises as it was uncertain in its permanence. Root was blunt. The proposed relations represented "the extreme limit of this country's indulgence in the matter of the independence of Cuba." Simply stated, the political leadership emerging in Havana did not inspire confidence in the United States. "The character of the ruling class," Root acknowledged, "is such that their administration of the affairs of the island will require the restraining influence of the United States government for many years to come, even if it does not eventually become necessary for this government to take direct and absolute control of Cuban affairs." "The welfare of the Cuban people," Senator Albert Beveridge warned, "was still open to attack from another enemy and at their weakest point. That point was within and that enemy themselves. . . . If it is our business to see that the Cubans are not destroyed by any foreign power, is it not our duty to see that they are not destroyed by themselves?" Senator Platt agreed. U.S. policy required "a stable republican government which the United States will assist in maintaining against foreign aggression or domestic disorder." He added: "We cannot permit disturbances there which threaten the overthrow of the government. We cannot tolerate a condition in which life and property shall be insecure."

News of the proposed relations stunned Cubans and precipitated protests and anti-U.S. demonstrations across the island. On the evening of March 2, a torchlight demonstration converged on Wood's residence to protest the Platt Amendment. In Santiago, speakers at public rallies alluded to the necessity of returning to arms to redeem national honor. Across the island, municipalities, civic associations, and veterans' organizations cabled protests to Havana.

The administration in Washington stood firm. There would be neither compromise nor concession to Cuban independence, Washington warned, until Cubans ratified the proposed relations. Either the Cubans would accept the Platt Amendment or there would be no end to the military occupation. Root was adamant. "No constitution can be put into effect in Cuba," Root warned, "and no government can be elected under it, no electoral law by the Convention can be put into effect, and no election held under it until they have acted upon this question of relations in conformity with this act of Congress." Continued resistance to United States demands, Root threatened, would have dire consequences. "If they continue to exhibit ingratitude and entire lack of appreciation of the expenditure of blood and treasure of the United States to secure their freedom from Spain, the public sentiment of this country will be more unfavorable to them." In early June the Cuban constituent convention acquiesced and by a margin of one vote accepted the Platt Amendment as an appendix to the new 1901 constitution. Two years later, the Platt Amendment was incorporated into the Permanent Treaty of 1903. . . .

* * *

The beneficiaries of North American rule were North Americans. They descended upon the war-ravaged island by the shipload, a new generation of carpetbaggers: land-dealers and speculators of all types, agents for corporations and small homesteaders, all in search of opportunity.

During the occupation, and continuing through the early years of the republic, U.S. control over sugar production expanded. In 1899, the Cuban-American Sugar Company acquired possession of the seven-thousand-acre Tinguaro estate in Matanzas and the Merceditas mill in Pinar del Río. In that same year, Cuban-Americans organized the Chaparra sugar mill around 70,000 acres of land in northern Oriente. In 1899 a group of North American investors acquired the old Manuel Rionda estate of Tuinucá and purchased the 80,000-acre Francisco estate in southern Camagüey province. At about this time, too, the Constancia estate in Las Villas passed wholly under North American control. The American Sugar Company acquired several damaged estates in Matanzas. In 1901, the United Fruit Company purchased some 200,000 acres in Banes on the north Oriente coast, a vast tract of land that included scores of partially destroyed and defunct estates. That same year, the Nipe Bay Company, a United Fruit subsidiary, acquired title to 40,000 acres of sugar land near Puerto Padre. Between 1900 and 1901, the Cuba Company completed the construction of the Cuban Railway through the eastern end of the island, acquiring in the process some 50,000 acres of land for rail stations, construction sites, towns and depots, and a right-of-way 350 miles long. The Cuban Central Railway purchased the Caracas estate in Cienfuegos from Tomás Terry. During these years, the Cape Cruz Company acquired a total of 16,000 acres near Manzanillo. Joseph Rigney, an investment partner with United Fruit, acquired the estates San Juan, San Joaquín, and Teresa, all in the region around Manzanillo.

United States land speculators and real estate companies acquired title to vast tracts of land and ownership of countless estates. Most were similar to the Taco Bay Commercial Land Company. Incorporated in Boston, the syndicate bought vast expanses of land in Oriente. In 1904, the Taco Bay Company purchased the Juraguá plantation. Consisting of some 20,000 acres of banana, coconut, and sugar land west of Baracoa, the Juraguá estate had been one of the most successful plantations in Oriente. Juraguá had been devastated by the war and never returned to prewar production levels. Typical of other victims of the insurrection, the owners of Juraguá were heavily in debt and lacked the capital to restore the damaged estate to production.

Land companies from the United States multiplied during the early years of the republic and accounted for a large share of North American purchases. One New York company purchased 180,000 acres along the banks of the Cauto River in Oriente. Another syndicate acquired 50,000 acres on Nipe Bay for the purpose of establishing a winter resort. Illinois Cuban Land Company acquired Paso Estancia, a 10,000 acre estate in central Oriente. The Herradura Land Company acquired title to some 23,000 acres of land in Pinar del Río. The Cuban Land Company bought up defunct estates in Las Villas, Matanzas, Pinar del Río, and Camagüey. The Carlson Investment Company of Los Angeles acquired 150,000 acres in the region of Nuevitas Bay. The Cuba Colonial Company, incorporated in Chicago, acquired some 40,000 acres in Camagüey. The Canada Land and Fruit Company purchased some 23,000 acres of land in Las Villas and the Isle of Pines. The Cuban Land and Steamship Company, incorporated in New Jersey, purchased 55,000 acres in the vicinity of Nuevitas. The Cuban Development Company, based in Detroit, purchased the

12,500-acre Vista Alegre estate in the region of Las Tunas in Oriente. The Cuban Agricultural and Development Company of Pittsburgh purchased over 135,000 acres of land around the region of Guantánamo. The Cuban Realty Company from New Jersey purchased 25,000 acres in western Oriente.

By 1905, some 13,000 North Americans had acquired title to land in Cuba, and these purchases had passed over the $50 million mark. An estimated 60 percent of all rural property in Cuba was owned by individuals and corporations from the United States, with another 15 percent controlled by resident Spaniards. Cubans were reduced to ownership of 25 percent of the land. Irene Wright wrote from Cuba in 1910, "I have heard their [foreigners'] real estate holdings estimated, by an office whose official business it is to know conditions here, at 90 or 95 percent of the whole. Foreigners (Americans and Europeans of many nationalities) are the owners of the far-reaching sugar fields, of the tobacco *vegas* [plantations] of account, of the bristling ruby pineapple fields, of the scattered green citrus fruit orchards."

Cubans faced exclusion from more than the land. In a capital-starved and credit-hungry economy, they were all but overwhelmed by foreign capital in almost every sector. Foreigners expanded control over tobacco production and cigar manufacturing. In 1899, the newly organized Havana Commercial Company, under New York promoter H. B. Hollins, acquired twelve cigar factories, one cigarette factory, and scores of tobacco *vegas*. Even before the military occupation came to an end, the newly organized Tobacco Trust in the United States had established control of some 90 percent of the export trade of Havana cigars. By 1906, the Tobacco Trust acquired possession of some 225,000 acres of tobacco land in Pinar del Río.

Foreigners also controlled mining. The iron mines of Oriente were almost entirely owned by U.S. investors. During the occupation, the military government issued some 218 mining concessions, largely to North Americans. The Juraguá Iron Company controlled more than twenty separate claims around the region of Caney. The Spanish-American Iron Company, a subsidiary of Pennsylvania Steel, obtained claims to Oriente iron mines. Smaller enterprises included the Sigua Iron Company (Pennsylvania Steel and Bethlehem), Cuban Steel Ore Company (Pennsylvania Steel), and Ponupo Manganese Company (Bethlehem). Copper mines around Cobre were owned by British and United States investors.

The railroad system was dominated almost wholly by foreign capital. The United Railways Company, the Western Railway Company, the Matanzas Railway Company, and Marianao Railway were controlled by the British. The Cárdenas-Jâcaro and Matanzas-Sabanilla systems were owned by Spaniards. The Cuban Eastern Railway and the Guantánamo Railroad were controlled by U.S. investors. The Havana Electric Railway Company, a New Jersey Corporation, established control of the capital's electric transportation system during the occupation.

Foreign capital controlled utility concessions as well. The Spanish American Light and Power Company of New York provided gas service to major Cuban cities. Electricity was controlled by two American corporations, the Havana Central and Havana Electric. United States contracting companies established branch offices in Havana and competed for government projects. The Havana Subway Company had sole right to install underground cables and electrical wires. United States capital controlled telephone service, the Cardenas City Water Works, and the Cardenas Railway and Terminal Company.

Banking remained under the control of Spanish capital, with England, France, and the United States participating. The two principal Spanish banking institutions, the Banco Espaäol and the Banco de Comercio, dominated island finances. The Banco Nacional de Cuba and the Banco de La Habana were formed with United States capital. North American capital held some $2.5 million in mortgages.

Foreign capital dominated the Cuban economy. Total British investments reached some $60 million, largely in railways, port works, sugar, and communications. The French share accounted for an estimated $12 million, principally in railroads, banks, and sugar. German investments reached some $4.5 million, divided between factories and utilities. But it was United States capital that overwhelmed the local economy. By 1911, the total United States capital stake in Cuba passed over $200 million. . . .

The reciprocity treaty of 1903, whereby Cuba received lower tariff rates for select exports in return for reducing duties on certain U.S. imports, delivered still another setback to Cuban enterprise and local entrepreneurs. Preferential access to U.S. markets for Cuban agricultural products served at once to encourage Cuban dependency on sugar and increase foreign control over this vital sector of the economy. Reciprocity also discouraged economic diversification by promoting the consolidation of land and the concentration of ownership.

The effects of reciprocity were not, however, confined to agriculture. The reduction of Cuban duties, in some instances as high as 40 percent, opened the island to United States imports on highly favorable items. The privileged access granted to United States manufactures created a wholly inauspicious investment climate for Cuban capital. Even before 1903, the dearth of local capital and depressed economic conditions combined to prevent development of national industry. After the reciprocity treaty, prospects for local enterprise diminished further. Undercapitalized small-scale industry and local manufacture were simply too weak to compete on the basis of prices and quality. The few owners of capital in Cuba had little inducement to invest in industry in the absence of a strong and protected market. U.S. goods quickly saturated the Cuban market.

Walter LaFeber

PANAMA: THE CANAL TREATY

Having annexed Puerto Rico and established effective control over Cuba, the United States was strategically situated to construct and safeguard an isthmian canal—long an American objective. But Colombia, whose province of Panama was a proposed site for the man-made waterway, grew suspicious of U.S. motives and refused to grant canal rights to the United States. In 1903 Colombia rejected the Hay-Herrán Treaty. In this selection from his book *The Panama Canal*, Walter LaFeber recounts how, conniving with Philippe Bunau-Varilla (the French agent of a bankrupt French company that had begun digging the canal) and exploiting a Panamanian independence movement, President Theodore Roosevelt managed to detach Panama from Colombia. Although Panamanian nationalists thereby gained their independence, they, like the Cubans and Puerto Ricans, were not sovereign in their own country. The U.S. empire engulfed them.

With an isthmian canal virtually within his grasp, [Theodore] Roosevelt refused to allow those "contemptible little creatures" in Colombia to frustrate his grand plan. But TR could not decide how to deal

From *The Panama Canal: The Crisis in Historical Perspective*, Updated Edition, by Walter LaFeber, pp. 23–26, 28–31. Copyright © 1978, 1979, 1990 by Scott LaFeber. Reprinted by permission of Oxford University Press, Inc. Footnotes omitted.

with the Colombians. He apparently held little hope the deadlock would be broken by a successful Panamanian revolt. As the President searched desperately for alternatives, [Philippe] Bunau-Varilla and the Panamanian nationalists were devising a solution. That solution, together with a 1904 agreement negotiated between Washington and Panama City by Secretary of War William Howard Taft, created the framework for sixty years of relations between the two countries and shaped the crisis of the 1970s.

Bunau-Varilla, with considerable help from top State Department officials, took the lead in solving Roosevelt's dilemma. During September and October 1903, the Frenchman held a series of talks with [Secretary of State John] Hay, Assistant Secretary of State Francis B. Loomis (whom Bunau-Varilla had known since a meeting in Paris two years before), and John Bassett Moore, a former Assistant Secretary of State, renowned international lawyer, and confidant of TR. Out of the conversations grew Bunau-Varilla's conviction that if the Panamanians tried to declare their independence the United States would use force, ostensibly to uphold its 1846 commitment to maintain transit rights across the Isthmus, but in reality to prevent Colombia from quashing the revolution.

As early as August, Moore sent a memorandum to Roosevelt arguing that the 1846 pact gave the United States the right to construct a canal. Loomis, who spent many hours with Bunau-Varilla, apparently inspired the memorandum; in any case, it completely reversed Moore's previous opinion of the 1846 treaty. Later in the autumn Bunau-Varilla asked Loomis how the United States would respond to an outbreak on the Isthmus. The Assistant Secretary of State said he "could only venture to guess that this Government would probably do as it had done in the past under like circumstances." Bunau-Varilla agreed, hoping that the North Americans "might freely do more rather than less." The Frenchman received the same reply from Moore and on October 10, 1903, probably heard similar words from the ultimate authority, Roosevelt. As the President later remarked, Bunau-Varilla "would have been a very dull man had he been unable to make such a guess." The Frenchman was many things, including devious, scheming, ambitious, and money-hungry, but he was certainly not dull.

And if he had been, Bunau-Varilla needed no more hints after a candid talk with Hay in the privacy of the latter's home. "I expressed my sentiments on the subject some days ago to President Roosevelt," the Frenchman began, "the whole thing will end in a revolution. You must take your measures. . . ." Hay played the game perfectly: "Yes, that is unfortunately the most probable hypothesis. But we shall not be caught napping. Orders have been given to naval forces on the Pacific to sail towards the Isthmus." As Bunau-Varilla later editorialized, "It only remained for me to act."

He first contacted the head of the revolutionary junta, Dr. Manuel Amador Guerrero, a physician closely associated with the Panama Railroad, now owned by the New Panama Canal Company. Amador happened to be in New York City to obtain money and support for the plot. Bunau-Varilla contacted Amador none too soon, for the Panamanian had just discovered that [William Nelson] Cromwell, the New Panama Canal Company's lawyer, was growing fearful that the revolution would abort and his company's concessions seized by a vengeful Colombia. The story of Cromwell getting cold feet has been embroidered by Bunau-Varilla and so is highly suspect; in his memoirs the Frenchman, with spectacular condescension and malice, always calls him "the lawyer Cromwell." Much of the malice doubtlessly resulted from Bunau-Varilla's fear that Cromwell would someday receive as many lines in history texts as he. But it does seem that his report to Amador of the TR and Hay conversations revived sagging Panamanian hopes.

Plans again moved forward on the Isthmus. The revolutionaries comprised an odd but not illogical assortment, for a number of them had one association in common. Other than Amador (the Panama Railroad's physician), the group included José Agustín Arango (the railway's attorney), James R. Shaler (superintendent of the railway), and James R. Beers (the railway's freight agent). It might have been Beers who first assured Arango that a Panamanian revolt would be supported by the United States. Amador and Arango were joined by the oligarchy's leaders: C. C. Arosemena, Ricardo Arias, Federico Boyd, and Tomás Arias. Once free of Colombian control—once they could develop their already extensive economic and political power according to their own interests and without concern for Bogotá—these oligarchs, their sons, and grandsons dominated Panama for sixty years. The motives varied, but for good reasons the railway officials and the Panamanian nationalists remained closely allied. As Roosevelt understood, "You don't have to foment a revolution. All you have to do is take your foot off and one will occur."

As the zero hour approached, however, TR displayed more optimism than did people in Panama. In early October the commander of the *U.S.S. Nashville* visited Colon, then reported to Washington that although three-quarters of the people would support a leader who would build a canal, "such a leader is now lacking, and it isn't believed that in the near future these people will take any initiative steps." The junta was preparing to provide the leadership, but the timing would be crucial. Closely following ship movements in the newspapers, Bunau-Varilla learned on October 30 that the *Nashville* was leaving Jamaica for an unspecified port. He correctly guessed it was heading for Colon and would arrive in two or three days. Given the intimacy between the Frenchman and Loomis, this was perhaps a mere deduction, not a lucky guess. Bunau-Varilla wired this news to Amador, who had returned to the Isthmus to lead the revolt. Both men now believed the United States was moving into a position to support their revolution. Loomis, however, jumped the gun and the result was nearly farce. "Uprising on the Isthmus reported," the Assistant Secretary anxiously cabled the United States Consul in Panama on November 3. "Keep department promptly and fully informed." Maintaining his composure, the Consul replied, "No uprising yet. Reported will be in the night. Situation critical."

Late that day Panamanian rebels moved to seize control of the Isthmus. The governor appointed by Colombia to rule the province, José Domingo de Obaldía, had long been sympathetic to Panamanian autonomy and gladly joined the revolutionaries. For his understanding he became one of Panama's first Vice-Presidents. Colombian army detachments were apparently bought off by Cromwell and the New Panama Canal Company; the commander received $30,000, other officers $10,000, and rank-and-file $50 each in gold.

Commander Hubbard aboard the *Nashville* received no orders regarding the uprising until late on November 2. Roosevelt and Loomis apparently did not trust the navy with their plans. Thus when 2500 Colombian soldiers appeared off Colon on November 2 to prevent the rumored revolution, a confused Hubbard allowed them to land. Shaler, the superintendent of the railway, saved the situation. He first moved his cars to the Pacific side of the Isthmus, 48 miles from Colon, so the Colombians could not use the railway. Then he talked the Colombian officers into traveling to Panama City, assuring them

THE MAN BEHIND THE EGG.

"The Man Behind the Egg," 1903. This contemporary cartoon suggested that conspiracy lay behind the delivery of the Panama Canal Zone to the United States. (*New York Times, November 15, 1903*)

that their troops would soon follow. In reality, the soldiers next saw their commanders when all were packed aboard ships for the return trip to Bogotá. The next day U.S. sailors finally landed to ensure that the Colombian troops behaved. An independent Panama had already been proclaimed by Amador. A new nation the size of South Carolina was born, and the labor pains had been easy. None of the belligerents was killed. The only deaths were a Chinese citizen who had gotten trapped in some desultory shelling, a dog, and, according to some reports, a donkey. . . .

* * *

TR and Hay focused on arranging the canal treaty with the Panamanians, or, more precisely, the Frenchman who had taken the opportunity to represent Panama. Bunau-Varilla engaged in a mini-power struggle with Arango, Tomás Arias, and Federico Boyd for control over negotiations in Washington. Since the three Panamanians were not yet in the United States, and because Bunau-Varilla convinced them he knew the political situation and financial channels, the

Frenchman was empowered to initiate talks with Hay. Amador and Boyd left Panama on November 10 to join Bunau-Varilla.

The new government meanwhile instructed the Frenchman that the negotiations were to be guided by three principles. First, no deals could be made that affected "the sovereignty of Panama, which [was] free, independent, and sovereign." Second, the United States should pledge to uphold the new nation's "sovereignty, territorial integrity, and public order." That clause would place North American troops, if necessary, between Panama and a vengeful Colombia. Third, a canal treaty would be drafted, but only after consultation with Amador and Boyd. "You will proceed in everything strictly in agreement with them," the Frenchman was told.

The instructions did not reach Bunau-Varilla in time, nor did Amador and Boyd. The minister made certain of that. On Friday the 13th of November he began talks with Roosevelt and Hay. Bunau-Varilla emphasized that time was all-important. If the treaty was not rushed to completion, he argued, a number of events would occur, all of them bad: a restless United States Senate, under Morgan's lashing, might turn back to Nicaragua; Colombia might seduce Panama back into the fold (the suave Reyes was on his way to Panama City); and isthmian politics might turn chaotic, forcing delays in the talks. Implicitly, but obviously, Bunau-Varilla also wanted to pocket the $40 million for his New Panama Canal Company as quickly as possible. Nor would he mind going down in history as the lone negotiator on the Panamanian side who signed the epochal pact.

Heartily sharing the Frenchman's mistrust of the Senate, Hay quickly prepared a treaty draft. It was largely the Hay-Harrán agreement that Colombia had rejected. The draft explicitly recognized Panamanian sovereignty in a canal zone, and even went further than the Hay-Herrán agreement by increasing Panama's judicial authority in a zone. Panamanian troops would protect the canal, and United States forces would be used in the area only with Panama's consent. The proposed treaty would run 99 years, or until about 2002.

Then, in what proved to be one of the most momentous twenty-four-hour periods in American diplomatic history, Bunau-Varilla worked all night and all day on November 16 to rewrite Hay's paper. The minister was afraid that the draft would not sufficiently appease the Senate, at least not enough to have the body act quickly on the treaty. Bunau-Varilla also wanted to complete the treaty before Amador and Boyd arrived. They were in New York City, but

Cromwell, for purposes of his own, had detained them. On November 17, Bunau-Varilla told the two Panamanians to remain in New York for another day, then rushed to the State Department to consummate the deal.

Hay could hardly believe his eyes. Bunau-Varilla's treaty ensured the canal's neutrality, proposed payment to Panama of an amount equal to that which the United States would have paid Colombia, and guaranteed Washington's protection of Panama's independence. The United States was to assume a virtual protectorate over the new country. But in return, the treaty gave the United States extensive powers in the Canal Zone, for Washington would have "all the rights, power, and authority within the zone . . . which the United States would possess and exercise if it were the sovereign of the territory within which said lands and waters are located to the entire exclusion of the exercise by the Republic of Panama of any such sovereign rights, power, and authority."

That was the most radical change, a change that has caused continual crises in U.S.-Panamanian relations for the next three-quarters of a century. But there was more. Bunua-Varilla surrendered Panamanian judicial power in the Zone, widened the zone area from ten kilometers (or six miles) to ten miles, and lengthened Hay's 99-year lease to "perpetuity." The astonished Secretary of State made only one change (the United States "leases in perpetuity" phrase was transformed into the more direct wording that Panama "grants to the United States in perpetuity the use, occupation, and control" of a canal zone). At 6:40 P.M. on November 18, the treaty was signed by the two men. Amador and Boyd arrived in Washington three hours later. Bunau-Varilla met them at Union Station, showed them the pact, and Amador nearly fainted on the train platform.

The Panamanian government angrily protested "the manifest renunciation of sovereignty" in the treaty. That protest echoed down through the years, becoming ever more magnified. If the new government rejected the pact, however, it faced bitter alternatives: the United States might seize the canal area without either paying for it or undertaking to protect the new republic, or Roosevelt might build in Nicaragua and leave the Panama City revolutionaries to the tender mercies of the Colombian army. In truth, the Panamanians had no choice.

They had leaped across an abyss to gain their independence, were hanging on the other side by their fingertips, and the United States held the rescue rope. Having helped put them in that position, Bunau-Varilla dictated the terms under which they could be pulled up to safety. Hay and Bunau-Varilla were too powerful and sophisticated to allow Panama to claim it accepted the treaty under duress, a claim that if declared legally valid could void the acceptance. Panama, however, did accept under duress. Having a French citizen disobey the Panamanian government's instructions, and then having no choice but to accept the Frenchman's treaty, compounded the humiliation. In the 1970s a documentary film made in Panama about the 1903 affair was entitled, "The Treaty that No Panamanian Signed."

Stanley Karnow

THE PHILIPPINES: AMERICANIZATION THROUGH EDUCATION

Colonial bureaucrats, military officers, and foreign investors were not the only instruments of empire. Missionaries, philanthropists, teachers, and physicians also wielded power and influence, frequently transforming the culture and values of foreign peoples. In this selection from his book In Our Image, **Stanley Karnow analyzes the impact of idealistic American educators on Filipino society. Even while the Philippine Insurrection bloodied the archipelago, teachers journeyed to the islands to "Americanize" Filipinos. In discussing the issue of cultural conflict, Karnow raises the question of whether good intentions can be fulfilled when the goals of progress, modernization, and cultural uplift are defined as "Americanization." Karnow, a veteran journalist, is also the author of** Vietnam **(1983), a companion to the Public Broadcasting System television series on the Vietnam War. Karnow served as chief correspondent for that series.**

Under a slate sky on a sultry August morning in 1901, a converted cattle ship, the *Thomas*, steamed into Manila Bay. Crowding its decks were five hundred young Americans, most of them recent college graduates, the men wearing straw boaters and blazers, the women in long skirts and large flowery hats. Like vacationers, they carried base-

From *In Our Image: America's Empire in the Philippines*, pp. 196–97, 200–202, 204–6, 207–9, by Stanley Karnow. Copyright © 1989 by Stanley Karnow. Reprinted by permission of Random House, Inc.

ball bats, tennis rackets, musical instruments, cameras and binoculars. Few had ever been abroad, and they scanned the exotic landscape with a mixture of fascination and anticipation. Precursors of the Peace Corps volunteers of a later generation, they were arriving as teachers. They quickly fanned out across the archipelago to set up schools and soon became known as "Thomasites," after the vessel that had brought them. The label, pinned on all American teachers of the time, had the ring of a religious movement. But their vocation, though secular, did have an evangelical design. Education would Americanize the Filipinos and cement their loyalty to the United States. "We are not merely teachers," Philinda Rand later wrote to her family in Massachusetts from the islands of Negros. "We are social assets and emissaries of good will."

Not all Americans who landed in the Philippines during those early years were so dedicated. There were swindlers, hucksters and dubious adventurers among them. Many who began with noble motives became lonely and discouraged and vented their bitterness in racial slurs against the Filipinos. But many—doctors, engineers, agronomists, surveyors, sanitation specialists and teachers like Philinda Rand—were driven by an unflagging faith in the virtue of their commitment.

The U.S. conquest of the Philippines had been as cruel as any conflict in the annals of imperialism, but hardly had it ended before Americans began to atone for its brutality. Inspired by a sense of moral obligation, they believed it to be their responsibility to bestow the spiritual and material blessings of their exceptional society on the new possession—as though providence had anointed them to be its savior. So, during its half-century in the archipelago, the United States refused to be labeled a colonial power and even expunged the word *colonial* from its official vocabulary. Instead of establishing a colonial office, as the British did to govern their overseas territories, President McKinley consigned the Philippines to the Bureau of Insular Affairs, an agency of the War Department. Nor did Americans sent out to supervise the islands call themselves colonial civil servants, a term that evoked an image of white despots in topees, brandishing swagger sticks at cringing brown natives. In their own eyes, they were missionaries, not masters.

The venture had originally been infused with apostolic fervor when McKinley divulged his divine directive to "uplift and civilize" the Filipinos—a goal he had earlier advertised as "benevolent assimilation." Elihu Root, his secretary of war, codified the doctrine in his instructions to William Howard Taft to promote the "happiness, peace and prosperity" of the natives in conformity with "their customs, their habits and even their prejudices." Seconding that sentiment soon after becoming governor, Taft intoned: "We hold the Philippines for the benefit of the Filipinos, and we are not entitled to pass a single act or to approve a single measure that has not that as its chief purpose.". . .

The spread of schools has been applauded as America's single greatest achievement in the Philippines. Guided by American teachers, the Filipinos rapidly attained the highest literacy rate in Southeast Asia and, after Christianity, the English language became the centripetal force that brought at least a semblance of unity to the far-flung archipelago. But the U.S. educational effort failed in many ways to satisfy its American promoters—partly because their expectations were illusory and partly because they could not agree on a consistent policy.

American propaganda notwithstanding, Spain had not condemned the Filipinos to abysmal ignorance. On the contrary, during the latter half of the nineteenth century, they were the most Westernized, sophisticated, modern elite in Asia. Rich families sent their sons to private Manila secondary schools and European universities and, by the 1890s, some two hundred thousand pupils were in primary schools throughout the islands. But the system was stymied by a lack of money and teachers as well as by the friars, who resented intrusion onto their turf. Even so, the Filipinos had tasted education and wanted more, and the U.S. Army saw on its arrival that their appetite could be turned against Aguinaldo's forces. American troops were ordered to conduct classes, largely to pacify the natives by demonstrating the benison of the U.S. mission—a strategy that, in later wars, was to be called "winning hearts and minds." Education, an American official noted, would make the Filipinos "less liable to be led by political leaders into insurrectionary schemes."

Following the U.S. conquest, many Americans maintained that education would deter native agitation for independence. Taft's aide, Daniel Williams, reckoned that "the Filipino, with a wider range of knowledge, would better appreciate his natural limitations and hesitate before demanding that he be cut adrift." McKinley had earlier judged that schools would deepen the allegiance of the natives to the United States and thus induce them to accept America's permanent presence in the Philippines. In April 1900, he transferred control of education from the army to the Taft commission, then poised to depart for

Manila to create a civilian administration. He directed Taft to set up a system of free primary instruction to "fit the people for the duties of citizenship and for the ordinary activities of a civilized community."

The typically amorphous order left Taft to contrive a practical plan. On the recommendation of Charles W. Eliot, the president of Harvard, he hired Fred Atkinson, a high school principal of thirty-five from Massachusetts. Six feet four inches tall, Atkinson was a Harvard graduate with an advanced degree from Germany who knew nothing about primary instruction. But Taft named him director of education for the Philippines, explaining indulgently that the Americans were only experimenting. "Experience in the United States can hardly seem to furnish much of a guide for what must be done here. It will be largely original work."

Atkinson, once in Manila, swiftly confected a centralized school system, with himself at its head and Americans supervising local districts. Costs would be shared by the U.S. administration in Manila and municipal councils throughout the islands, but scarce funds precluded compulsory education for all children. Devout Filipinos, inflamed by Atkinson's plan to bar religion from the schools, threatened a boycott unless the curriculum included Catholic instruction. As a compromise, Taft agreed to allow priests to teach the faith after hours—a concession that annoyed some Americans. Still, Philippine education was to be free of church control for the first time in three centuries.

The Americans violated a cardinal rule of imperialism. The Europeans, to insulate their colonial subjects from supposedly subversive Western concepts like liberty and equality, confined them almost entirely to education in the local language—if they educated them at all. Spain had similarly limited instruction in Spanish to only a handful of the Filipino elite. But Atkinson concluded that to teach the Filipinos in their vast assortment of languages and dialects would entail "a large corps of translators [and] books of every sort." Thus, for strictly practical reasons, English was to become the lingua franca of the Philippines. Yet the decision, perhaps subliminally, also reflected a basic purpose of the Americans: They intended to Americanize the Filipinos, not Filipinize themselves. As usual, Finley Peter Dunne's perceptive Mr. Dooley detected the distinction. "We'll larn ye our language," he remarked, "because 'tis easier to larn ye ours thin to larn oursilves ye'ers."

Most Americans hailed the move as idealistic, and it also drew praise from some Filipinos. Trinidad Pardo de Tavera, whose *Federal-*

ista party favored statehood for the Philippines, warmly welcomed the initiative. English, he declaimed, would instill the "American spirit" in Filipinos, inspire them to "adopt its principles, its political customs and its peculiar civilization" and thus further "our complete and radical . . . redemption." But to other Filipino intellectuals, English was a threat to tradition. Teodoro Kalaw, a popular polemicist, deplored its potential impact on Filipino women, the symbol of continuity. He could already see their degradation, he wrote in a florid essay in 1904. There they were, reading books in English and "chattering in a strange language," having become "unconscious victims of modernity," bereft of their "native simplicity," insisting on being known as "girls" instead of *dalagas*, or maidens. Corrupted by "Anglo-Saxon influence," these emancipated females would soon be "walking out alone" without *duennas*, "a handbag under the arm, just like bold little American misses." Eventually, too, they would even be taking "nonchalant trips" abroad—and all this after "only six years of American occupation."

For better or worse, however, English quickly caught on. By 1910, U.S. officials estimated that more Filipinos could read, write and speak English than any other single language. Critics of America's educational program ridiculed the claim, contending that most spoke a brand of English that was barely comprehensible. But whatever they learned was due to the pioneer American teachers in the Philippines.

More than a thousand young Americans volunteered to teach Filipino children and to train native instructors. Recruited from nearly every part of the United States, most were college graduates with some classroom experience. Eight thousand had applied, either out of altruism or for adventure. Money was also an attraction: As an inducement, they were offered as much as $125 a month, substantially more than teachers earned at home. Two groups reached Manila during the early summer of 1901, before the *Thomas* landed on August 21 with the largest contingent. Many kept journals or wrote often to their families, and their accounts frequently reveal an innocent exuberance. But the solitude, strangeness and hardships of a faraway land also made many melancholy, depressed and disgruntled. . . .

Other American teachers were frustrated by the clash of cultures in a society whose values differed almost diametrically from their own. They had brought a puritanical devotion to diligence and hard work, virtues they intended to ingrain in their pupils—only to find them ambling to an insouciant drumbeat. Students chronically cut classes to attend weddings, baptisms and fiestas, regular features of Philippine

Filipinos as Colonials, 1900. In an example of American cultural expansion, young Filipinos, perhaps not altogether understanding this aspect of U.S. empire, celebrated the Fourth of July in Manila. (*Library of Congress*)

towns, or they simply went fishing. As apostles of democracy, the Americans were stymied as well by a stiff social structure that blocked their efforts to imbue the children with egalitarian principles. To promote the dignity of labor, for example, many encouraged gardening as a school activity—whereupon the sons and daughters of rich families showed up with servants to till their plots. Wealthy parents often protested, too, against the presence of poor youngsters in the same classroom as their children.

Compounding their problems, the Americans lacked books, paper, pencils, blackboards and chalk. Their schools, often barns or sheds, leaked during rainy weather or broiled in the hot season. Within the first three years, twenty teachers died of dysentery, cholera or smallpox, six were murdered by bandits and one blew his brains out. Isolation in a tiny town could be sheer tedium. Benjamin Neal, stationed in Pangasinan province, nostalgically awaited mail that brought him and a fellow teacher football scores, fraternity gossip and other news from Syracuse University, their alma mater. "After supper each night," he wrote in his diary, "we sit in the front window and whistle the good old college tunes while the tropical sun sets gradually, fades and twilight deepens. Memory helps us to bridge over many an hour that otherwise would be lonesome." Roy Matthews, in Tayabas province, confessed to a quaint moral quandary in a letter to a friend. Despite his "rigid observance of Methodist principles," he was tempted to accept the gift from the town council of a live-in "*signorita* [*sic*]." How he resolved the dilemma remains a mystery.

Several American teachers exulted in the notion that they were the progenitors of a mighty transformation. His hope, Paul Gilbert lyrically wrote, was to "stir the Filipino from his dream of the dark ages, and point the way to modern progress." Others were content to discern fainter signs of Americanization in the natives. They were delighted when their students serenaded them with such popular American classics as "Good Night, Ladies" and "There'll Be a Hot Time in the Old Town Tonight," and they took special pride in their school bands, which gustily played Sousa marches—as school bands in even the smallest Philippine towns do to this day. Nothing impassioned them more, however, than the promotion of baseball, the obvious antidote to the native addiction to cockfighting. Baseball, wrote a Chicago *Daily News* correspondent, was vital to America's "civilizing" effort.

Many teachers sank roots. Philinda Rand married a fellow American, gave birth to a daughter and remained in the Philippines for seven years. Maud Jarman, who went to Manila to teach in 1901, died there a half-century afterward. Some spawned families that made the islands their home. Frederic Marquardt, the son of a Thomasite who founded a school in an obscure town on Leyte, served as a magazine editor in Manila until the start of World War II. Early in 1987, he returned to the town to unveil a bust of his father erected by local citizens—who, eighty-five years later, still remembered an early American benefactor. But the legend of the selfless American teacher in the Philippines, like the subsequent legend of the "ugly American" elsewhere in Asia, was also largely mythical.

Harry Cole lost heart in November 1901, after only three months on Leyte. "I find this work very monotonous, trying to teach these monkeys to talk," he wrote home. "Most of these people are lazy and indolent, and I do not think they can stick to it to get an education. . . . And oh! they are so dirty. Of course they have not been taught any better, and so they can hardly be blamed, and yet I do not believe they would care to exert themselves to clean up. . . . Their habits are frightful." Four months later, he was ready to quit. "The more I see of this lazy, dirty, indolent people, the more I come to despise them. I came here to help them, to enter their homes and to try to uplift them. But it seems to me a useless task. I am becoming more and more convinced that for years and years to come, the only business Americans ought to have over here is to rule them with severity."

Cole's wife, Mary, shared his disenchantment. "Everything mildews" while "pigs run about the streets and around the house," she lamented in a letter to her folks. There was "no butter, no flour, no milk except condensed [and] you never know when the cook is going to wash his feet in the dish pan or wipe them on the tea towel." The heat sapped her morale, as did her pupils. "Sometimes I get disgusted with the whole race and think it useless to try to teach them anything. . . . Only eight months and three weeks more of this detestable work, and we shall leave. Oh, how happy I shall be." But she did not despair that America might one day convert the Filipinos. "I suppose with patience and perseverance they will progress little by little until within two or three hundred years they may be quite Americanistic."

Some teachers were less charitable. Blaine Free Moore, a vintage Thomasite, hated "being shut up with a lot of little brown kids," as he wrote home. They were "wriggling, squirming, talking barbarians," and the United States had adopted a "pernicious" policy by "teaching these people that they are as good as anybody, that this country is for them and the Americans are only here for their benefit." His formula was simple. "If these people don't improve, it will show the absolute uselessness of this 'benevolent' business, and prove that the only way to manage these people is the way they understand . . . to which they will respond much quicker, viz., a show of force." Paradoxically, he later became a top U.S. educational official in the Philippines.

Taft soon realized that Atkinson had been a bad choice. Atkinson deluged teachers with memos on their decorum, dress and haircuts, and paid their wages erratically. He had also imported a curriculum better suited to Massachusetts than to the Philippines. History included George Washington's cherry tree and Paul Revere's midnight ride as "patriotic" lessons. He introduced the *Baldwin Reader*, a popular American primer that taught "A is for apple," a fruit alien to Filipinos, and pictured John and Mary in the snow, an equally odd substance.

A racial bias also skewed his concepts. He had visited Tuskegee Institute, the Negro school in Alabama run by the celebrated Booker T. Washington, who believed that American blacks should strive to attain equality through the "dignity of common labor" rather than through political agitation. Somehow seeing a parallel, Atkinson decided that Filipinos, like Negroes, were unfit for academic studies and ought to acquire such "practical" skills as pig breeding, carpentry and handicrafts. Taft received similar advice from his brother Horace, headmaster of an exclusive Connecticut prep school, who maintained that vocational training ideally suited the "deficient races." Rich Filipinos, who regarded manual labor as demeaning, backed the idea for the lower classes. But it was rejected by the lower classes, who saw formal education as an opportunity for their children to climb the social ladder.

Taft dropped Atkinson late in 1902 and brought in David Barrows, who ran the program until Frank White succeeded him six years later. The turnover was normal enough. But each man approached the job differently, and educational policy seemed to lurch from one extreme to another.

Barrows, an anthropologist from California, had worked in the archipelago since 1900 as an expert on aborigines. Intelligent, dynamic and ambitious, he hoped to parlay the assignment into a political career at home. He diagnosed the fundamental flaw of the Philippines to be its static social structure, which condemned the ignorant and submissive masses "without protest to the blind leadership of the aristocracy." As long as that structure remained, the Filipinos could never attain real self-government, America's goal for them. He prescribed a Jeffersonian answer: the creation of a literate peasantry through "universal primary instruction for . . . all classes and every community." He opened more schools and hired additional native teachers. His curriculum accented reading, writing and arithmetic, and he prepared textbooks especially for Filipino children. The primers now showed Juan and María walking through rice fields instead of John and Mary in the snow, and avocados and coconuts replaced apples and pears. Barrows also ordered teachers to deliver civic homilies. Mayors "are elected by the people" and should not "act like little kings," one went. Advised another, "If you want to be a farmer, you ought to own your own farm. You will be richer and happier.". . .

Barrows left some four thousand elementary schools in the Philippines when he quit in 1909—a threefold increase during his seven-year tenure. He had doubled the number of pupils to more than four hundred thousand, and tripled the size of the native teacher corps to some eight thousand. But behind the impressive statistics, the system lacked quality. Most of the Filipino teachers had not gone past the sixth grade and merely served as monitors. Truancy was endemic, especially among farm children who had to help their parents in the fields during the planting and harvesting seasons. Of all the pupils who enrolled in school, only one sixth reached the fourth grade. The rest dropped out to work.

Senior U.S. officials finally decided that Barrows had been misguided. The Jeffersonian concept of an educated yeomanry could not be replanted in foreign soil simply by teaching students a few lofty notions for a few hours a day over a few years. The United States returned to Atkinson's aborted idea of vocational training in hopes of preparing the natives for productive labor. Barrows left to teach at the University of California, and never went into politics.

Frank White, who took over in 1909, had already worked at various jobs in the Philippine educational system. At thirty-four, he was a picture-book American: the tall, handsome, clean-cut young man in the Arrow collar ad. His ideas coincided with those of Cameron Forbes, then the U.S. governor, for whom economic development was primordial. Until his death from tuberculosis in 1913, White concentrated on such "useful occupations" as basketry, weaving, embroidery, pottery and raising poultry at the expense of "impractical" subjects like reading, writing and arithmetic. He reduced the number of primary schools, and instead stressed secondary instruction for fewer students—a measure that reassured the Filipino oligarchy, which had been uncomfortable with the political and social implications of mass education.

By the 1920s, however, U.S. experts had concluded that the educational effort was faltering. A group led by Paul Monroe of Columbia University's Teachers' College, which visited Manila in 1925, found after testing thirty-two thousand pupils that very few who had finished four years of school were equal to American second-graders. Teaching was "so deficient," Monroe reported, that young Filipinos had not learned enough English for "a functional control over the language in adult life." He criticized the vocational courses as well for training students either in unwanted skills or to manufacture unwanted products. The verdict was harsh and probably unjust, since it assessed the Filipinos by American standards. But the Americans had no other yardstick than their own. Besides, America's objective was to Americanize the Filipinos.

To give high marks to the U.S. school system, as most Americans and Filipinos do in retrospect, is a fair judgment—as far as it goes. But education in itself was not a miraculous remedy for all the country's ills. The instrument could only be as effective as those who used it.

English, still the most widely spoken language of the Philippines, brought a degree of cohesion to the sprawling archipelago, which the Spanish had deliberately kept divided as a device to perpetuate their control. But its popularity deterred the development of a national Philippine language. Education also transformed political behavior. As Filipinos became more and more literate, they increasingly compelled their leaders to respond to their demands. The traditional *ilustrados*, no longer able to wield power arbitrarily, now staged elections that, with their campaign hoopla, resembled U.S. elections. The similarity was deceptive. The oligarchy continued to exercise authority through money, patronage and a web of dynastic alliances—as it does to this day. Yet Americans, to justify the U.S. tutelary role, proclaimed the Philippines a "showcase of democracy"—when Filipinos, with their talent for imitation, had merely learned enough from their American mentors to make the charade seem real.

Not that Filipinos have been insincere in their fondness for the United States. A sense of obligation toward those who render them service was deeply imbedded in their society, and their expressions of gratitude, couched in flowery Latin style, could be sentimental, even mawkish. A distinguished jurist, Benvenido Tan, effusively recalled some years ago that "next to God and my parents, I owe all that is good in me to my former American teachers." Older Filipinos still retain fond if misty memories of "Mr. Parker," from whom they learned to read, or "Miss Johnson," who taught them algebra.

The U.S. system created an almost compulsive appetite among Filipinos for education—or at least the appearance of being educated. Since the beginning of the century, primary-school enrollment has vaulted from two hundred thousand to ten million, a climb of forty-five times compared to sevenfold growth in population. By the 1980s, more than a million students were attending universities and colleges. But, once again, the figures fail to convey the distortions in the Filipino obsession with education.

Young Filipinos shunned floundering American vocational programs, preferring instead academic courses that promised the nebulous respectability of white-collar jobs. They even spurned skills like engineering and agronomy, sorely needed by the society, and flocked to diploma mills that ground out graduates in law, advertising and public relations. Thus, along with other developing countries, the Philippines has suffered from a scarcity of qualified labor in its rural areas and a surplus of nominally educated urban youths either unemployed or working as shop clerks and taxicab drivers. Ambitious students meanwhile struggle for gilt-edged degrees from a few elite institutions, like the University of the Philippines or the Ateneo de Manila, a Jesuit school. But nothing surpasses the prestige of an Ivy League laureate as Filipinos persistently seek an American imprimatur despite their search for a distinctive national character.

The Filipinos became Americanized without becoming Americans. But whatever the alchemy that finally shapes their national identity, a process that could take generations, the ultimate amalgam is bound to bear traces of their U.S. education.

Jane Hunter

CHINA: WOMEN MISSIONARIES AND CULTURAL CONQUEST

As entrepreneurs and diplomats were looking to opportunities in populous China at the time of the Open Door Notes, American missionaries were seeking to penetrate Chinese society. Suspicious Chinese leaders judged Western efforts to Christianize the population as threats to their official authority. The imperial court thus supported the Boxer Rebellion of 1900, which left 250 foreigners and nearly 2,000 Chinese Christians dead. The Western powers, with the assistance of U.S. troops stationed in the Philippines, forcibly suppressed the uprising. Over the next two decades, Western missionaries operated freely in China. In this selection from her book *The Gospel of Gentility*, Professor Jane Hunter of Colby College analyzes the efforts of women missionaries, who constituted more than 60 percent of the American Protestant missionaries in China. Hunter poses a difficult question: In the weakened China at the turn of the century, was religious conversion distinguishable from cultural conquest?

From *The Gospel of Gentility: American Women Missionaries in Turn-of-the-Century China*, pp. 5–8, 177–83, 185–89, by Jane Hunter. Footnotes omitted. Copyright © 1984. Reprinted by permission of Yale University Press.

As China became more receptive to the lessons of the West, the American missionary force in China increased rapidly; it more than doubled between 1890 and 1905, and by 1919 had more than doubled again, to thirty-three hundred workers. This rapid growth in the American force reflected a resurgent interest in missions accompanying late-nineteenth-century American expansion, and a particular enthusiasm for the development of the "New China" rising from the ashes of the Boxer debacle. By the early twentieth century, American missionaries seeking a hearing from the Chinese had replaced their reliance on military force with a reliance on the broad appeals of their culture. American national leaders supported this shift in strategy, and with missionaries, sought cultural rather than political empire in China.

American missionaries who first arrived in South China in the 1830s were inspired by the emotional certitudes of the Second Great Awakening and welcomed the use of Western force to gain their ends. Imprisoned in the foreign factories of Canton, which served as the Chinese land base for the tea, silks, and opium trade, they construed the Anglo-Chinese Opium War as a providential measure, a gift of God. At the first sign of trouble, for instance, Henrietta Shuck, an American Baptist, wrote of her hopes from Macao: "How these difficulties do rejoice my heart because I think the English may be enraged, and God, in His power, may break down the barriers which prevent the gospel of Christ from entering China." To Shuck, Christian faith was its own justification; even military force was righteous when it was on the side of God.

The treaty accompanying the end of the Opium War granted missionaries and Chinese converts the right to practice Christianity in five coastal cities. But missionaries were largely unsuccessful in converting the heathen of the treaty ports. Their struggles to acquire land within the walls of such cities as Foochow excited antipathies, and popular association of them with the sailors and merchants of the opium trade did not enhance their stature. One Canton native described the Westerner as one who "loved to beat people and to rob and murder" and often "could be seen reeling drunk." Missionaries succeeded in winning their first convert in Foochow only after a decade of proselytizing in the crowded streets. By the end of 1860, four years later, the fifty missionaries from several denominations could still count only sixty-six converts.

The Treaty of Tientsin (1858) extended rights to proselytize to the countryside, and there missionaries discovered more fruitful territory. Using Chinese workers, hired and trained as they went, missionaries poured more energy into opening outstations, shifting their focus from the major ports. By 1880, for example, the Congregational missionaries at Foochow had opened ninety-six new outstations in the countryside with Chinese help, and claimed three thousand new adherents. Outstations were the scenes of some of the greatest victories; perhaps not surprisingly, they were also the scenes of frequent antiforeign disturbances. The less sophisticated peoples of the interior were both more susceptible to the heterodox appeals of Christian ritual and more suspicious of its magical powers.

When missionaries were threatened, they unambivalently called for protection. "Missionary incidents" of the 1860s, 1870s, and 1880s, in which outraged Chinese attacked foreign intruders, involved far more French Catholics and British than Americans, but property disputes and popular outbreaks occasionally sent American missionaries to their legation demanding that their rights be defended or avenged. At the time of the Boxer uprising in 1900, of course, voices from the field were particularly loud. They demanded full American participation in any allied European military solution and vigorously protested the early withdrawal of American troops. The retaliatory raids of American board missionaries William Ament and Gardner Tewksbury received immediate coverage, first by *The New York Sun* and then by Mark Twain, in his famous essay, "To the Person Sitting in Darkness."

Until the 1890s, however, the American State Department was reluctant to defend aggressively either missionary rights to hold property in the interior, never officially deeded by the Chinese, or the provocative actions of American evangelicals, who attacked Chinese folk religion and challenged gentry sovereignty. Forced to face Chinese protests over the American maltreatment of Chinese laborers in the United States, the State Department did not have the temerity to press demands for protection abroad that it could not honor at home.

By the time of the Boxer uprising, though, the gulf between the forces of church and state had narrowed. President Benjamin Harrison's 1893 order for the construction of gunboats for use in Chinese waters foreshadowed a newly aggressive China policy. From that point, his administration began to follow up missionary claims with threats and personnel. With the Spanish-American War and the occupation of the Philippines, Washington briefly considered whether its presence in China might be extended to limited empire.

But church and state found other common ground during the early decades of the twentieth century. Wary political leaders and missionary supporters of the social gospel converged in a campaign for American influence rather than empire in China. The attendance at a 1900 Conference on Missions in New York suggested what would be a new compromise coalition of American leaders supporting informal empire in China. In addition to noted imperialists Admiral George Dewey and Alfred Mahan, many opponents of empire also attended. Former President Benjamin Harrison, the honorary president of the conference, had refused to endorse McKinley that year because of his expansionist policies. And Grover Cleveland, also in attendance, like most Democrats opposed territorial aggrandizement. Supporters of American empire considered Christian religion a necessary accompaniment to American expansionism, and in some cases the very justification for it. (In fact, the patriotic and militarist enthusiasms of the Spanish-American War were responsible for a needed outpouring of contributions to the mission cause.) But when the costs of imperialism became apparent, American leaders withdrew their support for political expansion and used mission organizations as a partial strategy to retain the exhilaration of empire without paying its bills or taking on its corrupting responsibilities. . . .

The Protestant missionary effort was unsuccessful in achieving the wide-scale conversions in China hoped for by the American churches. In contrast to Africa, where entire tribes fell under Christian sway, Chinese conditions were not conducive to mass conversion. Official hostility and a strong state orthodoxy, combined with the thriving heterodox Taoist and Buddhist folk traditions, left little room for a demanding and exclusive Christian God. The precariousness of the Chinese economy, however, presented opportunities to missionaries which Christian ideology alone could not have done. The Taiping uprising and the colonial wars of the mid-nineteenth century added political unrest to the ongoing problems of population expansion, and the once stable Manchu court began to lose control. Family and clan organizations helped provide relief to those left helpless by the century's devastations, but many destitute remained for missionaries to approach with the possibilities they offered for employment, for schooling, and, many Chinese thought, for legal intercession. As one woman put it, "the unspeakable conditions of physical suffering constitute both our call and our opportunity to minister."

Women in China, as in most societies, suffered disproportionately in hard times. Considered economic liabilities, they were less valued at time of birth and more subject to abandonment or sale in times of famine. At marriage, women were cut off from friends and family and transferred as property to husbands and families they knew little of. Though a woman's family, particularly her brothers, retained some responsibility for her well-being, only the most visible and well-substantiated abuse could free her from a disastrous match. Missionaries gained their early converts from a disadvantaged class; the significant numbers of women converts could be explained in part by the disadvantages of their sex.

Tales of abandoned children, daughters rescued from sale or death, and women saved from cruel mothers-in-law and brutal husbands filled missionary letters and propaganda. In the retelling, they assumed the proportions of melodrama. Jessie Ankeny wrote of a woman who overtook her in the road and "told me about her daughter who was about to commit suicide because of the cruelty of the mother in law 'Ah let me give her to you and you can do with her as you like—let her study or be your *slave*'!" Emma Martin, too, wrote of a woman attempting suicide to escape a "wretch" of a husband; she had been adopted by a Bible woman "till she can find new courage to live." Ella Glover provided care for a sick woman whose mother-in-law, according to mission story, had instructed her to "never mind, let her die." Although the numbers and the circumstances of needy women were exploited and perhaps exaggerated, they were not fabricated. Women missionaries working in China used their abilities to offer economic and institutional support to the needy as perhaps their most powerful means of recruiting loyal converts and Christian workers.

The dynamics of support varied from outright purchase to the acceptance of abandoned children; support or hire was sometimes a lure for potential converts, sometimes a reward for already professing church members. Missionary women offered economic support without cynicism, and sometimes even reluctantly, in conjunction with personal interest and institutional advocacy. Nevertheless, the ability of missionaries "to provide" remained central to the missionary appeal.

Those who fled to missions did so because missions had first taken initiatives in recruiting, supporting, and sometimes purchasing Chinese. When missionaries first moved into the interior after 1860, they often could not secure students for their schools. Missionaries aiming to demonstrate their good intentions by example would accept unwanted children, sometimes in return for cash favors, to begin their mission schools. As late as 1922, the Methodist mission interceded to save a worker from unwanted marriage to a non-Christian and settled a cash payment of $300 on the prospective bridegroom. "Didn't know we were in the girl buying business, did you?" quipped Monona Cheney.

Missionaries who believed in the righteousness of their God were willing to compete for the souls of those they desired. Usually they competed with "cruel," non-Christian husbands or "tyrannical" mothers-in-law, but sometimes their adversaries were rival Catholic or Buddhist religious institutions. Louise Campbell wrote of a sixteen-year-old girl she had admitted to her school to "save her from the nunnery," and Martha Wiley described her daring "rescue" of a child from Buddhist priests: "I dashed out and there some Buddhist priests had bought one little chap and were bargaining for the brother and had their money out. I grabbed that boy and carried him into my gate and locked the gate. The Buddhist priests went off." Missionaries condemned the stealing of children by rival religious organizations and private citizens, and certainly Martha Wiley's tactics were not those of most missionaries. Nonetheless, mission organizations did convince Chinese villagers that they wanted bodies as well as souls, and it is perhaps no wonder that during the xenophobic mid-nineteenth century Chinese imagined that missionaries used the bodies they were so eager for in perverse and diabolic rituals.

Women's mission organizations commonly argued in behalf of women students reluctantly betrothed or married to non-Christian men. They supported the domestic state for women married to Christians, but encouraged Christian women who were fighting the certain spiritual death of marriage into a pagan home. Missionaries' stress on the importance of maintaining Christian homes also reflected concerns that the Christian community perpetuate itself. The Swatow Baptists not only fought marriages of church-trained girls to heathens but to Christians of other denominations as well. Generally, missionary women supported a woman's right to choose a husband or to remain single altogether when marriage meant that she would be pressured to leave the church.

This position drew women missionaries further into the Chinese struggle for women's rights than would have been their temperamental

inclination. In a letter to Hu Shih, a prominent liberal Chinese educa-
tor, Sarah Goodrich justified her position:

> Is there anyway to force a girl to marry against her will—any law to
> force her. . . . Perhaps you may deem me very one-sided but when a
> young man marries the young woman to whom his parents have
> betrothed him, even if she has not had his advantages intellectually, I
> feel he is doing right. The husband has it in his power to mold the life
> of his wife. He can have interests outside the home. I have seen wives
> wonderfully improve becoming real help meets under the loving patient
> guidance of a thoughtful husband. But a wife if wedded to an unlettered
> husband is often treated as if her education was a curse, a reason for
> making the husband seem inferior. . . .

She concluded, "personality grows through self-sacrifice, but there is a
kind of self-sacrifice that kills every power of soul and body. It is from
this we would save Miss Chang." Goodrich's pleas for help for a
teacher in a mission school demonstrated the cautiousness of the missionary argument. She did not mean to challenge parental authority,
arranged marriages, or the virtue of feminine self-sacrifice. Only the
combination of these factors, exacerbated by the proper and inevitable
subordination of wife to husband, convinced her that Christian
women could not marry heathen men.

   This position frequently led missionaries to aid and protect the
youthful rebellions of schoolgirls against their parents. Lydia Wilkin-
son and Evelyn Sites persuaded a student's father to allow her to
remain single for church work rather than betroth her to a heathen,
and Lucy Mead wrote home that the entire women's residence was
encouraging another student's rebellion: "What do you think of missionaries trying to give all kinds of opportunities to a pupil to disobey
her parents?! That is what a number have done, and just this minute
I'm praying hard that the girl may have courage and strength to hold
out and refuse to go home, altho her mother has now come for her."
The divinity of woman's higher sphere depended on male acknowl-
edgment of its existence. In pagan homes, Christian women would be
denied the moral and cultural ambience in which they could transform
their subordination into elevation. The fragile flower of domestic
refinement could not blossom in truly heathen soil.

   When missionary women encouraged Chinese women's independence, they incurred responsibilities to provide them with support
and protection. Missions offered a variety of occupations to uprooted
Chinese women, including training as teachers and nurses for young

women, training as Bible women to assist in the preaching of the gospel for older women, and assorted menial jobs as cooks, seamstresses, and amahs for women of all ages. These occupations were frequently temporary and did not guarantee security, but they did offer short-term relief. Christian women, as well as many Christian men, found that their religion cut them off from old sources of support. The gradually narrowing restriction of support of the mission community inevitably increased the personal dependence of Chinese Christians on foreign missionaries.

Missionaries liked to exaggerate the extent to which unattached Chinese women depended on them for protection from angry fathers or husbands. Emily Hartwell, for instance, within three pages of her mission history wrote of three women whom she had saved from dangerous relatives. She had kept one from being sold as a child; another "ran away" to her "for protection" from a cruel mother-in-law; to rescue a third "lovely girl from the opium fiend father," she kept her virtually a prisoner until after his death. The physical protection provided by missionary women was occasionally overdramatized, but the protection of female reputation was always a real and serious responsibility. Lida Ashmore expressed "just a bit of fear" for the woman she had saved from marrying a pig butcher when she journeyed to Swatow "in with so many men and boys," and though Luella Miner swore she was not cut out to be a Female Seminary teacher, she did not mind supervising young girls in the streets in China because "there seems so much more reason for guarding Chinese girls." When Jessie Ankeny's Chinese teacher and friend Ding Miduang broke her engagement, she experienced ridicule from the local boys' school. Ankeny and her coworker Mamie Glassburner decided "not to let Miduang go outside the yard and not even downstairs only to teach her classes." Having encouraged the breaking of sacred Chinese custom, missionary women had to be prepared to provide a moral haven as well as a physical one for Christian women. Beginning conservatively, they found themselves offering a radical social alternative to Chinese women. This alternative sometimes included a professional career, a single life, a rupture with family—and virtually complete economic dependency on the mission institution.

Women missionaries who bargained for the freedom of their converts frequently seemed surprised at their own audacity. American women did not customarily rely on their economic resources as their means to social authority, and they almost inadvertently discovered the

American Missionary in China, 1903. A missionary teacher studies the Bible with her Asian converts beneath the American flag in Manchuria. (*Houghton Library, Harvard University*)

power which their mission organizations possessed as employers and advocates. Their China circumstances had led them to adopt a new institutional strategy. But missionaries brought with them a more traditional female tactic in the struggle for souls. Economic support may have won a woman's body for Christ, but missionary women aimed to win her heart through personal influence and intimate evangelism.

The women's missionary enterprise had never departed far in theory from the domestic ideology which sanctioned it. Woman's extended responsibility for nurture allowed her to teach school and care for the sick, but the home remained her central province and sentiment her central strategy of conversion. Missionary women carried on a personal evangelism which aimed to gain access to women's houses and their hearts. Anna Kauffman explained her belief that the "greatest sphere for any woman is the sphere of the home," which influenced her plan to bring her "deepest and best vision of home and womanhood" to the homes that most needed it. "I have found no greater opportunity than to place my life in the rising homes of China," she wrote. Gaining access to those "rising homes" presented missionaries with major challenges. The missionary women of Peking, Luella Miner wrote in 1893, had had no success at all in securing admission to family courtyards. Nellie Russell of T'ungchow, however, with her more winning style, had succeeded in gaining access to over thirty homes "and is making the work boom."

Even for those who taught Chinese girls in schools, entry to the Chinese home remained symbolically important. Miss R. J. Miller, who ran a Presbyterian girls' school in T'ungchow, frequently went on three-week trips through the countryside visiting the homes of her schoolgirls. Her reason for these trips, she explained, was that "it brings these girls nearer to me." Entry to the home represented an important physical analogue for the entry to the heart which was the ultimate missionary goal.

Justifying their service on the basis of the uniqueness of their gifts, missionary women emphasized the power of Christian love to stimulate individual conversion. Of course, the evangelical tradition which spawned the mission movement had always placed a strong emphasis on the power of love and a faith founded on feeling. Whether the large female church memberships of the nineteenth century encouraged this emotional strategy or were recruited by it is unclear. But, as Ann Douglas has argued, as the century progressed, Protestant religion and female culture became sentimentalized in tandem. Distinctions between the evangelism of men and women were reinforced by the ordination requirements of the majority of the Protestant churches. Male preachers assembled congregations to hear the Word, while women were more likely to "look love."

Evelyn Worthley Sites's description of an evangelizing meeting in a mountain village demonstrated the peculiarly personal nature of women's work. Clement Sites was conducting a service in the local church while Evelyn and a fellow woman missionary, a "live-wire California girl," were working the crowd outside. Sites's fellow worker encouraged a Taoist priest to enter the church by taking him gently by the coat and coaxing him inside. Once there, Sites wrote, "we divided the work, he prayed, with head bowed, and I watched! Watched to see if he really mastered the words! I slipped along beside him and quietly repeated them over and over two or three times until he knew the prayer." Such personal work had been the province of women all along. In revivals in Rochester, New York, in 1831, for instance, women engaged in house-to-house visitation to complement the preaching of such male spellbinders as Charles Grandison Finney. Personal work continued to be a woman's responsibility. In 1917 Ruth White could recollect with another YWCA worker "how our mothers used their opportunities for doing personal work" in talks with grocers and tradespeople; White identified her YWCA work in China in that tradition.

Ideally, the missionary encounter consisted of an effusion of encouragement and love on the part of the missionary, manifested in soulful eye contact and frequently a held hand, to be met with an outpouring of guilt and remorse, leading to conversion, on the part of the potential covert. The intensity of the individual attention was the key. When YWCA evangelist Ruth Paxson came to China in 1918, she emphasized that souls could be conquered only one at a time. Missionaries customarily targeted particularly promising souls in advance. Congregationalist Sarah Goodrich hoped to "get hold of the heart of young Mrs. Wei," and added, "I covet her womanhood for Christ." When a Baptist woman's "special one" had become a believer, she selected another, a friend wrote. Anna Hartwell wanted every Christian to be a "soul-winner" and seemed to advocate totting up souls as if they were scalps, when she described a dying Chinese woman as "one of the trophies our Tommie [Jane Thompson] will lay at the Savior's feet."

The love and encouragement the missionary poured out was sentimental rather than truly personal—what Sarah Goodrich referred to as the "releasing of power through personality through prayer." The successful evangelist aimed to inspire an outpouring on the part of the target soul rather than to give herself away. Irwin Hyatt's study of Julia Mateer noted that her strategy for "getting a hold" on her students entailed first an effort to learn personal information about each student, followed by a home visit, which showed results only when they started to talk more than she did. Ida Pruitt's Southern Baptist mother spent long hours doing handwork and conversing with Chinese women. Though she could not recall whether her mother herself told stories, Pruitt noted "she could get more out of people."

The Christian conversion involved more than a surrender of secrets, however; it involved a surrender of will itself. With such high stakes missionaries ardently entered the fray. Luella Huelster described one conversion battle:

> Gwei Lan's whole body was in a tremor. Her teacher, sitting beside her, took her hands and held them firmly in her own as she prayed that the soul-struggle, so evidently going on, might cease. She hastily penned an informal little pledge and placed it in Gwei Lan's hands; but she, reading it, smiled and shook her head in negation; she was not ready to sign it. But the Father coveted her, and less than ten minutes had passed before the little pledge, which no other eyes were to see, was quietly signed and slipped into the teacher's hand, and Gwei Lan was on her feet.

Gwei Lan's surrender was a victory not only for the Lord but also for His insistent aide, who in His name had presumed an awesome intimacy.

Not all missionary women in China endorsed the extreme intimacy of much of women's evangelical work. Particularly women associated with schools and higher education were dismayed at the emotionalism of women's evangelism. Luella Miner, president of Peking's North China Union Women's College, feared the "strong emotional element" which characterized revivals, and Matilda Thurston, patrician president of Ginling College in Nanking, wrote disapprovingly of Methodist Laura White, who was "full of sentiment" and was a supporter of "mother-craft" rather than higher education for women. Religious emotion did sometimes seem to have substituted completely for content. An old sick Chinese woman relayed a story of one missionary woman who had stayed overnight with her: "She pressed my hand and said Ah Sham, Ah Sham and I knew she was loving me and I have loved her ever since, but have never seen her again. I knew she must have been one of your people who tell of Jesus, though she could not talk to me of Him. She could not speak Chinese." Given the less stringent language requirements for women, undoubtedly many women evangelists had marginal skills in speaking Chinese and relied on sentiment to make up for their inability to preach the Word. But intelligence or language competence by no means separated female evangelists from educators. Nor for that matter did a concern for personal influence. Evangelists and teachers simply differed on the goals for intimate communion between missionary and convert.

For just as female religious work had transformed nineteenth-century religion, so the feminization of the teaching profession brought with it a new emphasis on Christian nurture, on the personal relationship between student and teacher. Female missionary teachers, like female evangelists, sought a moment of emotional recognition in which Chinese students surrendered their reserve and their hearts. Lucy Mead hoped that she might be allowed to "get close to the hearts of the people" rather than study the thought of Confucius over one summer, and Ruth White wrote that those teaching English classes who teach "with the real aim of getting in close touch with the individual girls" were "in love with their job." Even Alice Reed, who was persuaded to enlist despite her religious skepticism, talked of the values of "making contacts" outside of the classroom. Alice Frame, later dean of Yenching's women's college, was also concerned with getting "in vital touch" with students.

Missionary teachers sometimes approached the problem of getting to know their students systematically. Lulu Golisch wrote to a friend of how much she loved the schoolgirls "and how they each have won a place in my heart." She was interested now, she wrote, "in writing up a little history of each girl and making a special study of each girl's disposition." Frederica Mead, who taught at Ginling College, wrote that she was getting "side lights on the girls characters" from their compositions and that she planned to keep a card catalogue of the girls in her classes to record individual difficulties. Female missionary teachers, like missionary evangelists, aimed to do more than communicate knowledge; they aimed to transform character itself, and for them the best catalyst to this transformation was the power of intimate, personal contact.

Missionaries did not find the Chinese easy to influence, and that perhaps helps to explain their particular preoccupation with this problem. Chinese propriety demanded polite toleration of a stranger's viewpoint. Missionaries railed with frustration at the impenetrable "face" which thwarted their efforts to get in "vital touch." They complained about problems ranging from the lack of student responsiveness in class to the formalism of the Chinese religious tradition, but their dissatisfactions stemmed from a fundamental difference in the etiquette of emotion.

American evangelical traditions demanded that outward demeanor reflect inner soul, and although consistence between inner and outer states was hard to ascertain, at least a display of sincerity remained a strong cultural expectation. American evangelical and feminine traditions reinforced each other on this point. Evangelical thinking required that a pure countenance manifest a pure heart, while feminine values required that both heart and countenance communicate feeling.

American women faulted the Chinese for lack of feeling in their personal relations and their religion. At first Chinese students seemed "very unresponsive, like talking to a wall," Alice Reed remembered. In 1914 Matilda Thurston described the girls at Ming Deh as "too repressed and the most unresponsive girls I ever had to do with." Monona Cheney's description of visiting hours emphasized the lack of enthusiasm among students greeting relatives: "Some of them never can seem to find anything to say to their relatives, and the visits are short; others of them seem as glad as we would be—but these are all too few." American teachers constantly remarked upon the absence of emotional display among students and associates.

Although missionaries admired Confucian ethics, they agreed that Chinese religion lacked feeling and "hasn't the life." They considered Chinese obeisance to Taoist and Buddhist deities to be empty ritual. "Keeping up appearances before the images seems to be the sole end of the religion, if one can judge from outward show," Elsie Clark wrote. Monona Cheney judged that she "had more comprehension of things spiritual at five years old" than most Chinese did at seventy-five, so "narrow and materialist" were their backgrounds. Even when Chinese did accept Christianity, missionaries worried that they did so in the wrong spirit. There is much evidence for Elsie Clark's impression that many times converts simply added Christian sacraments to Taoist and Buddhist practices. "Christian religion is made a fetish to many of these people. Prayer and the Holy Spirit are to them tools to be used, forces to have on one's side, magic to be evoked," Clark wrote. With probably less basis, Clara Foster saw Christian belief in China as a rational decision within a Confucian tradition and thought that such belief lacked "the sorrow for sin and the joy of knowing Christ as their Savior which are experienced in the homeland." She went on, "They are ready to talk glibly of all being great sinners and only by accepting Christ's righteousness can we be saved, but somehow it is difficult for them to make it a personal matter."

Helping Chinese to make it "a personal matter" was at the heart of the missionary's self-appointed task in China. Professional, religious, and feminine traditions would have directed women toward personal work in any case, but the stubbornness of Chinese cultural resistance seemed to intensify missionary efforts. Their instructions in character became also lessons in culture. Alice Reed lamented that the Chinese lack entirely "what we call pep," and Agnes Scott, who had taught music at Fukien Christian College, felt that music offered an important emotional outlet to students and gave the school "college spirit." In 1894 Luella Miner delighted that "our Chinese associates are learning better every year how to be informal and 'folksey,' " but Frederica Mead in 1915 still lamented that "our girls have lots to learn in being at ease in entertaining and losing themselves in the fun of it." When missionaries stressed the personal nature of their work, they were in part stressing the fundamental changes they were seeking. Their lessons in Christian "character" frequently also fostered Western personality.

Missionaries' highest triumphs came when they could participate in a moment of personal transformation. Usually the moment involved a debate within an individual between "right" and "face." Florence Manly remembered some private talks with a Christian "in which my view of what he ought to do meant losing face and was at first intolerable to him, but I held firm and he finally gave in." When the potential convert had been recalcitrant, the victory was most gratifying. Lucy Mead described the resistance of one girl in her school to the conversion efforts of a YWCA evangelist:

> She came to the first meeting and sat thru it with a straight back, arms folded, and scorn on her face, even all thru the prayer. The next meeting was about the same attitude, an occasional expression in the following meetings betrayed a struggle in her soul, still she would not admit it, the girls still worked and all prayed. As she started to the last meeting she

said with pride and scorn "She can't touch me, I'm not going to be effected by anything she says."

When by the end of the service she had confessed her sins and surrendered her pride, her missionary sponsors were euphoric. Clearly, delight in conquering such a proud resister exceeded the delight in a less challenging conquest, though both alike totted up a soul for God.

In theory, however, God and not man brought about conversion. "There is no human agency that can cause a Chinaman to 'lose face,' " Jessie Ankeny wrote in describing the divine presence which inspired a Haitang revival. Her denial of the missionary's role was correct and orthodox. A month later, however, she noted that "People have confessed things in meetings that no official could possible make them confess." Missionary tendencies to personalize religion meant that victories were often quite personal as well. Missionaries who wanted to feel the wonders of the Lord's work in bringing a chosen one into the fold could not help but feel a quite earthly gratification. When a Chinese disclosed confidences, or became "informal and folksey," furthermore, it was hard to know whether he had found Christ, was on the road to salvation, or more simply, as was often the case, was responding to human attention. When religion was so much more a matter of feeling rather than thinking, it was often difficult to tell religious transformation from cultural conquest.

SUGGESTIONS FOR ADDITIONAL READING

The study of American imperialism at the turn of the century has long attracted scholars, whose books and articles provide a wide array of interpretation and subjects. This bibliography emphasizes the most recent secondary literature. For other works, see the bibliographies of the books listed below and Richard Dean Burns, ed., *Guide to American Foreign Relations Since 1700* (1983). Guides to literature on U.S. policy in Asia and Latin America include Jessica S. Brown et al., eds., *The United States in East Asia* (1985); James M. McCutcheon, comp., *China and America* (1973); Michael P. Onorato, *Philippine Bibliography* (1968); David F. Trask et al., eds., *A Bibliography of United States–Latin American Relations Since 1810* (1968); Michael C. Meyer, ed., *Supplement to a Bibliography of United States–Latin American Relations Since 1810* (1979); and Thomas M. Leonard, ed., *Central America and United States Policies, 1820–1980s* (1985).

Major ideas and movements in U.S. foreign policy, such as the Monroe Doctrine, anti-imperialism, and economic expansion, are explained in Alexander DeConde, ed., *Encyclopedia of American Foreign Policy* (1978). Textbooks that provide broad context and contain comprehensive bibliographies are Thomas G. Paterson, J. Garry Clifford, and Kenneth J. Hagan, *American Foreign Policy: A History* (1988), and Walter LaFeber, *The American Age* (1989). Older edited collections of essays on U.S. imperialism are Richard H. Miller. ed., *American Imperialism in 1898* (1970), and Thomas G. Paterson, ed., *American Imperialism and Anti-Imperialism* (1973). Both collections contain bibliographic essays.

Works that attempt to define and characterize imperialism include Anthony Brewer, *Marxist Theories of Imperialism* (1980); Norman Etherington, *Theories of Imperialism* (1984); Johann Galtung, "A Structural Theory of Imperialism," *Journal of Peace Research* 8, no. 2 (1971): 81–117; David F. Healy, *Modern Imperialism: Changing Styles of Interpretation* (1967); Richard H. Koebner and Helmut D. Schmidt, *Imperialism: The Story and Significance of a Political Word, 1840–1960* (1964); William Roger Louis, ed., *Imperialism: The Robinson and Gallagher Controversy* (1974); Wolfgang J. Mommsen and Jürgen Osterhammel, eds., *Imperialism and After* (1986); and Tony Smith, *The Pattern of Imperialism* (1981).

Because U.S. imperialism was part of an international trend, comparative histories are helpful. Edited collections of essays, with useful bibliographies, are Ralph Austen, ed., *Modern Imperialism, Western Overseas Expansion, and Its Aftermath* (1969); William B. Cohen, ed., *European Empire Building* (1980); Robin W. Winks, ed., *British Imperialism: Gold, God, Glory* (1963); and Harrison M. Wright, ed., *The "New Imperialism"* (1974). Paul Kennedy, *The Rise and Fall of the Great Powers* (1987), is an important comparative overview that contains an excellent bibliography on Western imperialism. See also Philip Darby, *Three Faces of Imperialism: British and American Approaches to Asia and Africa, 1870–1970* (1987).

For studies that broaden traditional definitions of imperialism and measure the impact of powerful countries on vulnerable cultures, see David Arnold, ed., *Imperial Medicine and Indigenous Societies* (1988); Robert F. Arnove, ed., *Philanthropy and Cultural Imperialism* (1980); Alfred W. Crosby, *Ecological Imperialism: The Biological Expansion of Europe, 900–1900* (1986); Daniel F. Headrick, *The Tentacles of Progress: Technology Transfer in the Age of Imperialism* (1988) and *The Tools of Empire: Technology and European Imperialism in the Nineteenth Century* (1981); and Lewis Pyenson, *Cultural Imperialism and Exact Sciences* (1985).

The imperialism of the 1890s had a long preparatory period. For background on U.S. diplomacy, expansion, empire, and Manifest Destiny during the nineteenth century, see Charles H. Brown, *Agents of Manifest Destiny: The Lives and Times of the Filibusters* (1980); William H. Goetzmann, *When the Eagle Screamed* (1966); Thomas R. Hietala, *Manifest Design* (1985); Reginald Horsman, *Race and Manifest Destiny* (1981); Michael H. Hunt, *Ideology and U.S. Foreign Policy* (1987); Lester D. Langley, *Struggle for the American Mediterranean: United States–European Rivalry in the Gulf-Caribbean* (1976); Frederick Merk, *Manifest Destiny and Mission in American History* (1966); Richard W. Van Alstyne, *The Rising American Empire* (1960); Paul A. Varg, *United States Foreign Relations, 1820–1860* (1979); and Albert Weinberg, *Manifest Destiny* (Baltimore, 1935). For the removal of and wars against native Americans, see Robert F. Berkhofer, Jr., *The White Man's Indian* (1978); Francis P. Prucha, *The Great Father* (1984); Robert M. Utley, *The Indian Frontier of the American West, 1846–1890* (1984); and Mary E. Young, *Redskins, Ruffleshirts, and Rednecks* (1961).

Different interpretations of and approaches to U.S. foreign relations during the late nineteenth century are presented in Robert L. Beisner, *From the Old Diplomacy to the New* (1986); Charles S. Campbell, *The Transformation of American Foreign Relations* (1976); James A. Field, Jr., "American Imperialism," *American Historical Review* 83 (June 1978): 644–68; John A. S. Grenville and George B. Young, *Politics, Strategy, and American Diplomacy* (1966); Walter LaFeber, *The New Empire* (1963); Tennant S. McWilliams, *The New South Faces the World* (1988); Milton Plesur, *America's Outward Thrust* (1971); David Pletcher, *The Awkward Years: American Foreign Relations Under Garfield and Arthur* (1962); Emily S. Rosenberg, *Spreading the American Dream: American Economic and Cultural Expansion, 1890–1945* (1982); Homer E. Socolofsky and Allan B. Spetter, *The Presidency of Benjamin Harrison* (1987); Richard E. Welch, Jr., *The Presidencies of Grover Cleveland* (1988); and William Appleman Williams, *The Tragedy of American Diplomacy* (1972).

American economic expansion abroad in the late nineteenth century is examined in the works of Beisner, LaFeber, Plesur, Rosenberg, and Williams cited above. See also William H. Becker, *The Dynamics of Business-Government Relations: Industry and Exports, 1893–1921* (1982); Robert B. Davies, *Peacefully Working to Conquer the World: Singer Sewing Machines in Foreign Markets* (1976); David M. Pletcher, *Rails, Mines, and Progress: Seven American Promoters in Mexico, 1867–1911* (1958) and "Rhetoric and Results: A Pragmatic View of Economic Expansionism, 1865–98," *Diplomacy History* 5 (Spring 1981): 93–104; Robert W. Rydell, *All the World's a Fair: Visions of Empire at American International Expositions, 1876–1916* (1984); Howard B. Schonberger, *Transportation to the Seaboard: A Study in the "Communication Revolution" and American Foreign Policy, 1860–1900* (1971); Tom Terrill, *The Tariff, Politics, and American Foreign Policy, 1874–1911* (1973); and Mira Wilkins, *The Emergence of Multinational Enterprise* (1970).

The development of the U.S. Navy is explored in James C. Bradford, ed., *Captains of the Old Steam Navy: Makers of the American Naval Tradition, 1840–1880* (1986); B. Franklin Cooling, *Gray Steel and Blue Water Navy* (1979); Kenneth J. Hagan, *American Gunboat Diplomacy and the Old Navy, 1877–1889* (1973) and *This People's Navy: The Making of American Sea Power* (1991); Walter R. Herrick, *The American Naval Revolution* (1966); Peter Karsten, *The Naval Aristocracy* (1972); Harold Sprout and Margaret Sprout, with an introduction by Kenneth J. Hagan and Charles Conrad Campbell, *The Rise of American Naval Power, 1776–1918* (1990); and William N. Still, Jr., *American Sea Power in the Old World* (1980). Studies of key naval leaders include Frederick C. Drake, *The Empire of the Seas: A Biography of Rear Admiral Robert Wilson Shufeldt* (1984); Robert Seager II, *Alfred Thayer Mahan* (1977); and Ronald Spector, *Admiral of the New Empire: The Life and Career of George Dewey* (1974).

Most of the works cited in the preceding paragraph on U.S. foreign relations in the late nineteenth century analyze events and attitudes in the 1890s, America's path to empire, and the Spanish-American-Cuban-Filipino War. See also Richard D. Challener, *Admirals, Generals, and American Foreign Policy, 1898–1914* (1973); Lewis L. Gould, *The Spanish-American War and President McKinley* (1982); David F. Healy, *U.S. Expansionism: The Imperialist Urge in the 1890s* (1970); Richard Hofstadter, *The Paranoid Style in American Politics* (1962) and *Social Darwinism in American Thought* (1955); Ernest R. May, *Imperial Democracy* (1961); H. Wayne Morgan, *America's Road to Empire* (1965); John Offner, "President McKinley's Final Attempt to End War with Spain," *Ohio History* 94 (Summer–Autumn 1985): 125–38 and "The United States and France: Ending the Spanish-American War," *Diplomatic History* 7 (Winter 1983): 1–21; Göran Rystad, *Ambiguous Imperialism: American Foreign Policy and Domestic Politics at the Turn of the Century* (1975); Rubin F. Weston, *Racism in United States Imperialism* (1972); R. Hal Williams, *Years of Decision: American Politics in the 1890s* (1978); and William Appleman Williams, *The Roots of the Modern American Empire* (1969). See also Serge Ricard and James Bolner, eds., *La Republique imperialiste: L'Expansionnisme et la politique extérieure des États-Unis, 1885–1909* (1987), which contains several original essays in English by leading interpreters of U.S. imperialism. For a review of the scholarship, see Louis A. Pérez, Jr., "The Meaning of the *Maine*: Causation and the Historiography of the Spanish-American War," *Pacific Historical Review* 58 (August 1989): 293–322.

On military aspects of the Spanish-American-Cuban-Filipino War, see William R. Braisted, *The United States Navy in the Pacific, 1898–1907* (1958); Graham A. Cosmas, *An Army for Empire: The United States Army in the Spanish-American War* (1971); Hyman G. Rickover, *How the Battleship* Maine *Was Destroyed* (1976); and David F. Trask, *The War with Spain in 1898* (1981). The American home front is surveyed in Willard B. Gatewood, Jr., *Black Americans and the*

White Man's Burden, 1898–1903 (1975), and Gerald F. Linderman, *The Mirror of War: American Society and the Spanish-American War* (1974). Two studies of journalists and the war are Charles H. Brown, *The Correspondent's War* (1967) and Joyce Milton, *The Yellow Journalists: Hearst, Pulitzer & the Spanish-American War* (1989).

For U.S. leaders and their case for empire, begin with two historiograhic essays: Joseph Fry, "William McKinley and the Coming of the Spanish-American War," *Diplomatic History* 3 (Winter 1979): 77–98, and William Tilchin, "The Rising Star of Theodore Roosevelt's Diplomacy," *Theodore Roosevelt Association Journal* 15 (Summer 1989): 2–18. See also Howard K. Beale, *Theodore Roosevelt and the Rise of America to World Power* (1956); John Braeman, *Albert J. Beveridge* (1971); Richard H. Collin, *Theodore Roosevelt: Culture, Diplomacy, and Expansion* (1985); John Milton Cooper, Jr., *The Warrior and the Priest: Woodrow Wilson and Theodore Roosevelt* (1983); Kenton Clymer, *John Hay* (1975); John Dobson, *Reticent Expansionism: The Foreign Policy of William McKinley* (1988); Gerald Eggert, *Richard Olney* (1974); Lewis L. Gould, *The Presidency of William McKinley* (1980); Philip C. Jessup, *Elihu Root* (1938); Frederick Marks, *Velvet on Iron: The Diplomacy of Theodore Roosevelt* (1979); Richard W. Turk, *The Ambiguous Relationship: Theodore Roosevelt and Alfred Thayer Mahan* (1987); and William C. Widenor, *Henry Cabot Lodge and the Search for an American Foreign Policy* (1980). For a collective biography of the major U.S. foreign-service officers of the 1890s, see Henry Mattox, *The Twilight of Amateur Diplomacy* (1989).

For studies of the anti-imperialists and anti-imperialism, see Robert L. Beisner, *Twelve Against Empire* (1968, 1985); Kendrick A. Clements, *William Jennings Bryan, Missionary Isolationist* (1982); Allen F. Davis, *American Heroine: The Life and Legend of Jane Addams* (1973); Charles DeBenedetti, ed., *Peace Heroes in Twentieth-Century America* (1986); Thomas J. Osborne, *"Empire Can Wait": American Opposition to Hawaiian Annexation, 1893–1898* (1981); E. Berkeley Tompkins, *Anti-Imperialism in the United States: The Great Debate, 1890–1920* (1970); and Hans L. Trefousse, *Carl Schurz* (1982).

Toward the end of the nineteenth century, British-American relations became more cordial, and the British were not unfriendly toward the U.S. imperialist course in Latin America and Asia. For works on the Anglo-American flirtation and its impact on imperialism, see Stuart Anderson, *Race and Rapprochement: Anglo-Saxonism and Anglo-American Relations, 1895–1904* (1981); Alexander E. Campbell,

Great Britain and the United States, 1895–1903 (1960); Charles S. Campbell, *From Revolution to Rapprochement: The United States and Great Britain, 1783–1900* (1974); and Bradford Perkins, *The Great Rapprochement: England and the United States, 1895–1914* (1968).

An instructive introduction to the literature on U.S. policy in the Caribbean Basin is Louis A. Pérez, Jr., "Intervention, Hegemony, and Dependency: The United States in the Circum-Caribbean, 1898–1980," *Pacific Historical Review* 51 (May 1982): 165–94. See also Richard H. Collin, *Theodore Roosevelt's Caribbean* (1990); David F. Healy, *Drive to Hegemony: The United States in the Caribbean, 1898–1917* (1988); Walter LaFeber, *Inevitable Revolutions: The United States in Central America* (1984); and Lester D. Langley, *The United States and the Caribbean in the Twentieth Century* (1985) and *America and the Americas* (1989). For U.S. policy on individual countries, see Raymond Carr, *Puerto Rico* (1984); Arturo Morales Carrión, *Puerto Rico* (New York, 1983); Walter LaFeber, *The Panama Canal* (updated ed., 1989); Louis A. Pérez, Jr., *Cuba Between Empires* (1982), *Cuba Under the Platt Amendment, 1902–1934* (1986), and *Cuba and the United States* (1990); and Brenda Gail Plummer, *Haiti and the Great Powers, 1902–1915* (1988). All of these studies analyze the impact of U.S. imperialism.

For U.S. policy in the Pacific and Asia, see Roger W. Gale, *The Americanization of Micronesia* (1979); Paul M. Kennedy, *The Samoan Tangle* (1974); Barry Rigby, "The Origins of American Expansion in Hawaii and Samoa, 1865–1900," *International History Review* 10 (May 1988): 221–37; and Merze Tate, *The United States and the Hawaiian Kingdom* (1965). The literature on the United States in the Philippines is vast. A general work is Stanley Karnow, *In Our Image: America's Empire in the Philippines* (1989). Studies on the Philippine Insurrection and American colonialism include Teodore A. Agoncillo, *Malolos: The Crisis of the Republic* (1960); Kenton J. Clymer, *Protestant Missionaries in the Philippines* (1986); John M. Gates, *Schoolbooks and Krags: The United States Army in the Philippines* (1973); Brian M. Linn, *The U.S. Army and Counterinsurgency in the Philippine War* (1989); Glenn A. May, *Social Engineering in the Philippines* (1980) and "Why the United States Won the Philippine-American War, 1899–1902," *Pacific Historical Review* 52 (November 1983): 353–77; Stuart C. Miller, *Benevolent Assimilation: The American Conquest of the Philippines* (1982); Peter W. Stanley, *A Nation in the Making* (1974); and Richard E. Welch, Jr., *Response to Imperialism* (1979).

Two interpretative histories of U.S. policy toward China, including the Open Door Notes, are Warren I. Cohen, *America's Response to China* (1990), and Michael Schaller, *The United States and China in the Twentieth Century* (1990). For studies that explore the dreams and realities of American economic expansion in China, see David L. Anderson, *Imperialism and Idealism: American Diplomats in China, 1861–1898* (1985); Michael H. Hunt, *Frontier Defense and the Open Door: Manchuria in Chinese-American Relations, 1895–1911* (1973) and *The Making of a Special Relationship: The United States and China to 1914* (1983); Thomas McCormick, *China Market* (1967); Paul A. Varg, *The Making of a Myth: The United States and China, 1897–1912* (1968); and Marilyn Blatt Young, *The Rhetoric of Empire: American China Policy, 1895–1901* (1968).

Studies that explore the activities of educators, missionaries, and philanthropists, especially in Asia, include Nancy Boyd, *Emissaries: The Overseas Work of the American YWCA, 1895–1970* (1986); Peter Buck, *American Science and Modern China, 1876–1936* (1980); Shirley Garrett, *Social Reforms in Urban China: The Chinese YMCA, 1895–1926* (1970); Patricia R. Hill, *The World Their Household: The American Woman's Foreign Mission Movement and Cultural Transformation, 1870–1920* (1985); Jane Hunter, *The Gospel of Gentility: American Women Missionaries in Turn-of-the-Century China* (1984); and Valentin H. Rabe, *The Home Base of American China Missions, 1880–1920* (1978).